Freedom of Expression and Hate Speech in Europe

In recent years, the Danish cartoons affair, the Charlie Hebdo murders and the terrorist attacks in Brussels and Paris have resulted in increasingly strident anti-Islamic speeches by politicians. This raises questions about the limits to freedom of expression and whether this freedom can and should be restricted to protect the religious feelings of believers. This book uses the case law of the European Court of Human Rights to provide a comprehensive analysis of the questions: whether legal prohibitions of religious hate speech violate the right to freedom of expression; and, whether such laws should be used to prosecute politicians and others who contribute to current debates when they use anti-Islam rhetoric. A well-known politician who uses such rhetoric is Dutch politician Geert Wilders. He has been prosecuted twice for hate speech, and was acquitted in the first case and recently convicted in the second. These prosecutions are used to illustrate the issues involved in drawing the line between freedom of expression and religious hate speech. The author argues that freedom of expression of politicians and those contributing to the public debate should not be restricted except in two very limited circumstances: when they incite to hatred or violence and there is an imminent danger that violence will follow or where it stops people from holding or manifesting their religion. Based on this, the author concludes that the European Court of Human Rights should decide, if it is asked to do so, that Wilders conviction for hate speech violates his freedom of expression.

Erica Howard is Associate Professor in Law at Middlesex University, UK.

Routledge Research in Human Rights Law

Freedom of Expression and Religious Hate Speech in Europe

Erica Howard

Routledge
Taylor & Francis Group

LONDON AND NEW YORK

First published 2018 by Routledge

2 Park Square, Milton Park, Abingdon, Oxfordshire OX14 4RN
52 Vanderbilt Avenue, New York, NY 10017

Routledge is an imprint of the Taylor & Francis Group, an informa business

First issued in paperback 2019

British Library Cataloguing in Publication Data
A catalogue record for this book is available from the British Library

Library of Congress Cataloging in Publication Data
Names: Howard, Erica, author.
Title: Freedom of expression and religious hate speech / Erica Howard.
Description: New York : Routledge, 2017. | Series: Routledge research in
    human rights law | Includes bibliographical references and index.
Identifiers: LCCN 2017017462| ISBN 9781138243811 (hbk) |
    ISBN 9781315277257 (ebk)
Subjects: LCSH: Freedom of expression—Europe. | Freedom of
    religion—Europe. | Hate speech—Europe. | Convention for the
    Protection of Human Rights and Fundamental Freedoms
    (1950 November 5)
Classification: LCC KJC5154 .H69 2017 | DDC 342.408/53—dc23
LC record available at https://lccn.loc.gov/2017017462

ISBN: 978-1-138-24381-1 (hbk)
ISBN: 978-0-367-31307-4 (pbk)

Typeset in ITC Galliard Std
by Swales & Willis Ltd, Exeter, Devon, UK

Printed in the United Kingdom
by Henry Ling Limited

Contents

Table of cases

Other jurisdictions

EU

Human Rights Committee

Hungary

Netherlands

Acknowledgements

The topic of this book has been an area of personal interest for quite a few years. As a Dutch national, I have been intrigued by the rise of the far right politician Geert Wilders in the Netherlands in the last ten years or so. Wilders has made a number of anti-Islam speeches over the years and has always used the language of human rights when challenged about his expressions. So, I wondered whether his speech is protected by human rights.

The idea for this book only really started to take shape during the research leave I was given by my employer, Middlesex University. A special thank you should go to Middlesex University for providing the opportunity and to my head of department and to my colleagues for their support and encouragement.

Thank you to everyone at Routledge for their help and support, both during the proposal stage and since then. Thank you also to the anonymous reviewers for their constructive and helpful comments and suggestions on the proposal for this book.

Last but not least, a very big and very special thank you to my husband Chris, without whom this book would not have been written. His never ceasing support and encouragement has kept me going and his patient proofreading, editing, formatting and general trouble-shooting has made it possible to get the book finished within the time limit.

Introduction

Main question and argument

'Free speech for everyone except bigots is not free speech at all' and, 'it is meaningless to defend the right to freedom of expression for people with whose views we agree. The right to free speech only has political bite when we are forced to defend the rights of people with whose views we profoundly disagree'.[1] This quote is undoubtedly true in that free speech or the right to freedom of expression[2] is a fundamental and universal human right of every human being. It can be found in global and regional human rights instruments, for example, in article 19 of the United Nations Universal Declaration of Human Rights, article 19 of the International Covenant on Civil and Political Rights and article 10 of the European Convention of Human Rights and Fundamental Freedoms (ECHR). It is also true that freedom of expression applies not only to expressions that are favourably received but also to those that offend, shock or disturb, as the European Court of Human Rights, the Court overseeing the ECHR, has held.[3] Therefore, along with everyone else, bigots also enjoy the right to free speech.

The right to freedom of expression, however, is not an absolute right, as all the human rights instruments mentioned allow for restrictions on this right under certain circumstances. One of the reasons this right can be restricted is when this is necessary for the protection of the rights of others. But where is the boundary between permissible speech and speech that should be restricted? When should restrictions be allowed and when should they be held to violate the freedom of expression of the speaker or author? The central question in this book is whether legal prohibitions of religious hate speech violate the speaker's or author's right to freedom of expression.

---

1 Molnar, P., 'Interview with Kenan Malik', in Herz, M. and Molnar, P. (eds) *The Content and Context of Hate Speech Rethinking Regulation and Responses* (Cambridge, Cambridge University Press, 2012) 84.
2 Throughout the book, the terms 'free speech', 'freedom of speech' and 'freedom of expression' will be used interchangeably.
3 *Handyside v the United Kingdom*, Application No. 5493/72 (1979–1980), 7 December 1976, para 49. This is the same for the other human rights guarantees of freedom of expression, see: Human Rights Committee, General Comment No. 34, Article 19: *Freedoms of Opinion and Expression*, CCPR/C/GC/34, 2011, para. 11.

There does not appear to be a generally accepted definition of hate speech, but the Committee of Ministers of the Council of Europe has defined the term as follows:

> All forms of expression which spread, incite, promote or justify racial hatred, xenophobia, anti-Semitism or other forms of hatred based on intolerance, including intolerance expressed by aggressive nationalism and ethnocentrism, discrimination and hostility against minorities, migrants and people of immigrant origin.[4]

The term 'incitement to hatred' is sometimes used instead of the term 'hate speech' and, in the following, these terms will be used as being interchangeable and as having the same meaning.

The focus of this book is on religious hate speech or incitement to hatred on the grounds of religion or belief and whether and how the law should deal with this. Religious hate speech will be understood here as speech that incites to hatred on the ground of the religion or belief of the targets of the hate speech, of the victims and, thus, laws against religious hate speech, as understood throughout the book, protect persons holding religious beliefs. Religious hate speech could also be understood as hate speech based on the religion of the speaker or author, where religion or belief acts as a source of hate speech, provides the motivation for the perpetrator for inciting hatred against people because of other characteristics, for example sex or sexual orientation. However, this book will not include these latter expressions.

Therefore, the focus throughout this book will be on hate speech targeted at religions and beliefs or at religious believers. It will be argued that the freedom of expression of politicians and others who contribute to the public debate should not be restricted by the state through laws against religious hate speech or against incitement to religious hatred unless such expressions either: incite to hatred and violence and violence is likely to follow imminently; or, if they prevent someone from exercising their right to freedom of religion, or, in other words, from holding, practising or manifesting their religion or belief. Outside these situations, restrictions should be held to violate the right to freedom of expression of the speaker or author.

General background

In the last 50 years or so, many European countries have seen a number of waves of migrants from all over the world with the majority, up to recently, coinciding with labour needs and economic growth. In some instances, and increasingly so, these migrants have been from different religions to the dominantly Christian population of Europe. Whereas most of the countries in Europe have become more secularised in terms of traditional religious practices, with many Christians

4 Committee of Ministers, Council of Europe, Recommendation No. R(97)20 on 'Hate Speech'.

seeing religion as a private rather than a public issue, the incoming migrants often practice and promote their religion in a much more public manner. Goldschmidt and Loenen write that a number of developments have taken place in Europe in the last few decades, one of which is secularisation. They continue:

> Almost in the same period, or immediately after the beginning of secularisation in the traditional societies of Europe, however, the entrance of large groups of immigrants with an overwhelming Muslim background implied a revival of religious awareness. These groups claim the same protection that has been awarded to the traditional religious blocs and demand the same public support.[5]

Because of this and because of the events of 9/11, the bombings in Madrid and London and the recent attacks in France and Belgium and other acts of terrorism linked to Islamic religious motives, many European states now perceive Muslims especially as a threat to their liberal, tolerant, secular societies.

As a reaction to this, all over Europe, anti-immigration and anti-Islam rhetoric has become part of political and public discourse and many politicians have, in more recent years, become more outspoken in their criticism of Islam and Muslims. The anti-Muslim rhetoric became even more vociferous after the events at the French magazine Charlie Hebdo and the recent terrorist attacks in Paris, Brussels and Nice. Marine Le Pen of the National Front in France, Frauke Petry of the Alternative for Germany Party in Germany and Geert Wilders of the Party for Freedom in the Netherlands are good examples of politicians and parties using such rhetoric. And, although this type of language was first used by far right politicians, the language appears to have become more generally acceptable and now even less far right, mainstream politicians are using the same or similar language. This type of speech, expressing hatred of immigrant Muslim groups, can be said not only to have created and heightened fears in the general population about the targeted groups, but also to have fostered some sort of wider consensus that these groups do not fit in, do not want to integrate, do not want to accept 'our' values and do not want to be part of 'us', of 'our' society. You could say that it has created an 'us' versus 'them' atmosphere, which not only prevents people from feeling solidarity or empathy with the targeted groups, but also makes people bolder in discriminating against or speaking in a derogatory way about these groups and less likely to protest about such treatment of these groups by others.[6]

When challenged, politicians using this kind of rhetoric are usually very quick in invoking their right to freedom of speech and in defending their expressions by saying that they highlight and raise concerns that exist among many people in

---

5 Goldschmidt, J. and Loenen, M., 'Religious Pluralism and Human Rights in Europe: Reflections for Future Research', in Loenen, M. and Goldschmidt, J. (eds) *Religious Pluralism and Human Rights in Europe: Where to Draw the Line?*, (Antwerp/Oxford, Intersentia, 2007) 311.

6 Rorke, B., 'Free to Hate? Anti-Gypsyism in 21-Century Europe', in Molnar, P. (ed) *Free Speech and Censorship around the Globe* (Budapest, Central European University Press, 2015) 236.

their country and, thus, that they contribute to the current public debate. As will become clear throughout this book, some European politicians have been prosecuted and convicted under national laws for hate speech or incitement to hatred on the grounds of race, ethnicity or religion. They have taken their cases to the European Court of Human Rights and claimed a violation of their freedom of expression under article 10 ECHR. The Court has held that national laws against (religious) hate speech can be compatible with the right to freedom of expression but that they have to pass the justification test laid down in article 10(2) ECHR. This test and the case law of the European Court of Human Rights on (religious) hate speech are analysed in Chapters 1 to 5.

But the question can be asked whether this anti-immigrant and anti-Muslim rhetoric constitutes (religious) hate speech, and, if it does, whether this should be legislated against? Tulkens sums up the dilemma in this area where she writes that, on the one hand, 'hate speech targeting ethnic, religious, sexual minorities, immigrants and other groups is a widespread phenomenon within Europe' including in (mainstream) political discourse and, there is a serious concern about 'the growing success of populist parties that widely use hate speech, as well as trivialising its use'. On the other hand, 'political effort to limit hate speech has its dangers not only because it may encroach on freedom of expression but also because it could be misused as a tool for intimidating and containing opposition'. So, Tulkens then asks: 'which ideas are too dangerous or too offensive to be included in the public discourse'?[7] A preliminary question to this is whether some ideas should be considered to be too dangerous or too offensive for the public discourse. These questions as they relate to expressions about religions or beliefs and religious believers, are the focus of this book. Lopez Guerra makes a very good point where he states that the question of admissible limits on freedom of expression in religious matters

> Is relevant with respect to two factors present in modern societies: on the one hand, the particular intensity (and sensitivity) of the religious sentiment of individuals and groups; on the other, the increasing pluralism of convictions and beliefs derived from cultural and demographic changes, a situation that often results in opposition and confrontation of ideas and faiths.[8]

This is a good description of many European societies at the present time and the analysis in this book takes place against the background of this type of society. One more point needs to be stressed: the importance of freedom of speech for

---

7 Tulkens, F., *The Hate Factor in Political Speech: Where Do Responsibilities Lie?* (2013), paras 14 and 15 https://rm.coe.int/CoERMPublicCommonSearchServices/DisplayDCTMCont ent?documentId=09000016800c170e

8 Lopez Guerra, L., 'Blasphemy and Religious Insult: Offenses to Religious Feelings or Attacks on Freedom?' in Casadevall, J., Myjer, E., O'Boyle, M. and Austin, A., (eds) *Freedom of Expression, Essays in Honour of Nicolas Bratza* (Oisterwijk, the Netherlands, Wolf Legal Publishers, 2012) 307.

politicians because of the role political speech plays in the open public debate in a modern democratic society. This point will come back again and again throughout this book.

The reason for focusing on religious hate speech is that, in this period of populist parties, politicians often target Islam and Muslims with their criticism, as already pointed out above. A very good example is Dutch far right politician Geert Wilders, who has made a number of anti-Islam speeches over the years, always defending himself with an appeal to his right to free speech and with the argument that he is only saying what a lot of people in the Netherlands are thinking and thus that he is contributing to the political and public debate about current issues. Another of his frequently used arguments is that he is criticising the religion of Islam and not Muslim believers. In this, Wilders is, thus, clearly using the language of human rights to defend his expressions. As a Dutch person, the author was intrigued by these arguments and by the popular appeal that Wilders seems to have gained in the Netherlands in the last 10 years or so. He appears to have normalised anti-immigrant and anti-Muslim speech in the Netherlands and has created this 'us, normal, law abiding, liberal Dutch people' versus 'them, Muslim immigrants who do not want to live according to "our" Dutch values', referred to above. The last chapter of this book, Chapter 6, contains a case study of Geert Wilders, which is used to illustrate the arguments made in the previous chapters. Wilders is a good example because he has been prosecuted twice under Dutch criminal law for incitement to hatred (or hate speech) and for insulting a group on the grounds of race, ethnicity or religion. In December 2016, the second prosecution led to Wilders' conviction for group insult and incitement to discrimination. At the time of the trial, Wilders party would have gained the most votes and thus would have become the largest party in the Netherlands, at least according to the polls. Wilders is also a good case study because, if his conviction is upheld on appeal and after all domestic remedies in the Netherlands have been exhausted, Wilders might well end up going to the European Court of Human Rights claiming that his conviction violates his right to freedom of expression under article 10(2) ECHR.

Because the focus of this book is on European politicians, the ECHR and the case law of the European Court of Human Rights will be central to the analysis. This book will examine religious hate speech or incitement to religious hatred and restrictions on such speech under article 10 ECHR, but article 9, which guarantees the freedom of religion and the right to freely manifest one's religion, will be examined as well because this right could be engaged in relation to the group targeted by religious hate speech. As mentioned above, one of the situations in which restrictions on religious hate speech should be held justified is when such speech interferes with a person's or group's article 9 right.

Chapter summaries

The above forms the background for the analysis of the central question in this book: whether legal prohibitions of religious hate speech violate the right to freedom of expression. Chapter 1 contains an overview of both the right to freedom of expression (article 10 ECHR) and the right to freedom of religion (article 9 ECHR) and of the circumstances under which these rights can be restricted, including the margin of appreciation given to states in deciding on this. The arguments for the existence of a right to freedom of expression are also examined. An important question addressed in Chapter 1 is whether article 9 ECHR includes a right not to be offended in one's religious feelings. Article 10(2) ECHR imposes 'duties and responsibilities' on those who exercise their freedom of expression, including the duty not to be 'gratuitously offensive' in the context of religious opinions and beliefs. The meaning of the term 'gratuitously offensive', especially in relation to expressions by politicians that contribute to the public debate, is examined. This is followed by an analysis of the question whether politicians have a duty not to foster intolerance when they exercise their right to free speech.

The possible conflict between freedom of expression and freedom of religion that can arise where a person criticises a religion or belief or offends religious believers is the subject of Chapter 2. However, there could also be a clash between either or both of these rights and the right to be free from (religious) discrimination under article 14 ECHR or article 1, Protocol 12 to the ECHR. The latter articles will be examined and the question when a conflict between rights occurs and how to deal with the situation where it does occur, will be addressed as well.

This is followed, in Chapter 3, by an investigation of a number of concepts, including hate speech and religious hate speech, the differences between hate speech and blasphemy and the difference in protection between expressions that criticise religions or beliefs and those that offend believers. The question of when an expression becomes hate speech will be part of Chapter 3 along with an evaluation of the arguments for and against enacting laws against hate speech, or against incitement to hatred, and of the question whether such laws are useful and necessary in a democratic society. The particular problems with criminal laws against hate speech are highlighted and the enactment of the provisions against religious hate speech in the Racial and Religious Hatred Act 2006 in the United Kingdom will be used to illustrate these problems.

Chapter 4 contains a scrutiny of restrictions on freedom of expression to spare religious feelings and analyses the two different ways the European Court of Human Rights has dealt with such restrictions: through the abuse of rights clause in article 17 ECHR, which means that a person cannot invoke their right to freedom of speech to defend expressions that are aimed at the destruction of any of the Convention rights and freedoms. If the Court uses article 17, it will not require any evidence from the state that such interference is justified. The latter is required if the Court examines a case under article 10(2) ECHR which prescribes a three part justification test that can be summed up as a test of legality, necessity and proportionality. It requires that the restriction must be prescribed by law (legality); is necessary in a democratic society (necessity); and, is subject to a proportionality test: the means used must be proportionate to the legitimate aim pursued (proportionality). The last part of Chapter 4 contains an overview of the factors the European Court of Human Rights takes into account when it has to decide whether an interference with a person's freedom of expression is justified.

Chapter 5 opens with an overview of the way freedom of speech is seen in the United States, as this appears to be different from how it is seen elsewhere in the world. This is followed by an analysis of the possible harm hate speech inflicts on the individual or group(s) it targets. Because hate speech can do harm to the targeted group, possible alternative ways to using criminal law to deal with hate speech are examined, including the use of discrimination measures under both the ECHR and under EU anti-discrimination law. Codes of conduct, especially the Charter of European Political Parties for a Non-Racist Society, which was adopted in 1998 and has been endorsed by both the EU and the Council of Europe, are scrutinised. The last part of Chapter 5 discusses other ways of dealing with hate speech.

Chapter 6 contains a case study of Dutch politician Geert Wilders, who has been prosecuted twice for his expressions against Islam and Muslims and against Moroccans in the Netherlands. His prosecutions are analysed using the arguments examined in the five previous chapters as a yardstick. Geert Wilders is the leader of the Dutch Party for Freedom (PVV) and has, over the years, made many comments against Islam and Muslims. The first prosecution of Wilders led to an acquittal but the second prosecution led, in December 2016, to a conviction without the imposition of any punishment. The expressions that have led to him being prosecuted on two occasions are examined as will be the question what the European Court of Human Rights should decide if the case ever reaches that Court.

In the conclusion to the book, the question whether and under what circumstances legal prohibitions of religious hate speech violate the right to freedom of expression will be answered based on the arguments from the previous chapters. It is advocated throughout the book that restrictions on religious hate speech should only be allowed in very limited circumstances and that such restrictions should be very strictly scrutinised by the European Court of Human Rights.

1 Freedom of expression and freedom of religion under the European Convention on Human Rights

Introduction

In this Chapter, the fundamental human right to freedom of expression will be examined and this is followed by an analysis of the right to freedom of religion because both rights may be involved in cases of religious hate speech. Both rights are guaranteed by the European Convention for the Protection of Human Rights and Fundamental Freedoms (ECHR), freedom of expression in article 10 and freedom of religion in article 9.

Article 10 ECHR guarantees freedom of expression, which includes the freedom to hold opinions and the freedom to receive and impart information. Article 10(2) determines that this right can be subject to 'formalities, conditions, restrictions or penalties' under certain prescribed circumstances as explained below. Article 9 ECHR can be said to guarantee two different rights: the right to freedom of thought, conscience and religion as well as the right to manifest one's religion. As explained below, the protection for these two rights is different and restrictions or limitations are only allowed in relation to the right to manifest one's religion. The circumstances under which limitations or restrictions are allowed are clearly prescribed by Article 9(2) ECHR and will be discussed in this chapter. Both the right to freedom of expression and the right to freely manifest one's religion can thus be restricted and the circumstances under which this can be done are similar, but there are some differences and these will be examined in this chapter. Article 10(2) ECHR, for example, refers to 'duties and responsibilities' on those who exercise their right to freedom of expression, but there is no reference to duties and responsibilities in article 9(2) ECHR.

Article 9 ECHR explicitly mentions that the right to freedom of religion includes the right to change one's religion. As the Research Division of the European Court of Human Rights expresses, 'with regards to the particular case of religion, freedom of choice is important'.[1] To make the right to choose a religion or to change religion meaningful, open debates about religions and beliefs are essential. In these debates, there must be room for criticism and even denial of

---

1 European Court of Human Rights Research Division, *Overview of the Court's Case-law on Freedom of Religion* (Strasbourg, Council of Europe, 2013) para 18, www.echr.coe.int/Documents/Research_report_religion_ENG.pdf

other people's religion or beliefs. As mentioned, the right to freedom of expression in article 10 ECHR includes the right to receive and impart information and this covers debates about religions and beliefs. The right to freedom of expression applies, as will be explained below, not only to expressions that are favourably received but also to those that offend, shock or disturb. But does this mean that any expression, even if it is offensive to religious believers, is protected? Or does the right to freedom of religion include a right to respect for one's religion or belief and a right not to be offended in one's religious feelings? These questions will all be examined in this chapter.

According to the European Court of Human Rights in *United Communist Party of Turkey and Others v Turkey*:

> Democracy is without doubt a fundamental feature of the European public order. . . . That is apparent, firstly, from the Preamble to the Convention, which establishes a very clear connection between the Convention and democracy. . . . In addition, Articles 8, 9, 10 and 11 of the Convention require that interference with the exercise of the rights they enshrine must be assessed by the yardstick of what is 'necessary in a democratic society'. The only type of necessity capable of justifying an interference with any of those rights is, therefore, one which may claim to spring from 'democratic society'. Democracy thus appears to be the only political model contemplated by the Convention and, accordingly, the only one compatible with it.[2]

The European Court of Human Rights has also pointed out that pluralism, tolerance and openness are hallmarks of a democratic society.[3] It has also stressed the importance of both the freedom of religion and the freedom of expression for a democratic society. In *Handyside v the United Kingdom*, the European Court of Human Rights mentioned the principles characterising a democratic society, and stated that 'freedom of expression constitutes one of the essential foundations of such a society, one of the basic conditions for its progress and for the development of every man'.[4] So, according to Tulkens, 'freedom of expression is the sine qua non for a genuine pluralist society. This affirmation of the social function of freedom of expression constitutes the basic philosophy of all the Court's case law relating to Article 10'.[5] In a democratic society, open public debate is essential and this requires that people should be free to express their views. As article 10 ECHR states, freedom of expression includes the freedom to impart and receive information and this is of vital importance for an open debate. Weber points out

---

2 *United Communist Party of Turkey and Others v Turkey*, Application No. 19392/92, 30 January 1998, para 45.
3 *Handyside v the United Kingdom*, Application No. 5493/72, 7 December 1976, para 49.
4 Ibid.
5 Tulkens, F., 'When to Say is to Do: Freedom of Expression and Hate Speech in the Case-law of the European Court of Human Rights', in: Casadevall, J., Myjer, E., O'Boyle, M. and Austin, A., (eds) *Freedom of Expression, Essays in Honour of Nicolas Bratza* (Oisterwijk, the Netherlands, Wolf Legal Publishers, 2012) 287.

that freedom of expression stands as one of the roots of democracy and continuously fosters it and that 'without free debates and the freedom to express one's convictions, a democracy cannot progress or would simply not exist'.[6] Barendt discusses the arguments for having a free speech principle. One of these is 'the argument from citizen participation in a democracy': freedom of expression plays a crucial role in the formation of public opinion.[7]

The European Court of Human Rights has also stressed the importance of freedom of religion for a democratic society. In *Kokkinakis v Greece*, the Court held:

> As enshrined in Article 9 . . ., freedom of thought, conscience and religion is one of the foundations of a 'democratic society' within the meaning of the Convention. It is, in its religious dimension, one of the most vital elements that go to make up the identity of believers and their conception of life, but it is also a precious asset for atheists, agnostics, sceptics and the unconcerned. The pluralism indissociable from a democratic society, which has been dearly won over the centuries, depends on it.[8]

In the same case, the Court also said that it may be necessary, in a democratic society, to place restrictions on this freedom.[9] And, in subsequent cases, it has pointed out that the state, when it exercises its regulatory power in this sphere, must remain neutral and impartial[10] and that 'what is at stake here is the preservation of pluralism and the proper functioning of democracy, one of the principle characteristics of which is the possibility it offers of resolving a country's problems through dialogue'.[11] The right to freedom of expression will be examined first, as this is the most important right for the subject of this book.

Freedom of expression

The right to freedom of expression, or freedom of speech, is laid down in article 10(1) ECHR, which states:

> Everyone has the right to freedom of expression. This right shall include freedom to hold opinions and to receive and impart information and ideas without interference by public authority and regardless of frontiers. This Article shall not prevent states from requiring the licensing of broadcasting, television or cinema enterprises.

---

6 Weber, A., *Manual on Hate Speech* (Strasbourg, Council of Europe, 2009) 19.
7 Barendt, E., *Freedom of Speech* (2nd ed., Oxford, Oxford University Press, 2005) 18.
8 *Kokkinakis v Greece*, Application No. 14307/88, 25 May 1993, para 31.
9 Ibid. para 33.
10 *Hasan and Chaush v Bulgaria*, Application No. 30985/96, 26 October 2000, para 78; *Metropolitan Church of Bessarabia v Moldova*, Application No. 45701/99, 13 December 2001, paras 115–116.
11 *Metropolitan Church of Bessarabia v Moldova*, supra note 10, para 116.

It will be clear that this right contains what Grimm calls, 'both the active and the passive side – freedom to express one's own opinions and freedom to learn about the opinions of others'.[12] Grimm also writes that only if the right has both these sides can it be said to 'constitute a comprehensive freedom of communication'.[13] The right to freedom of expression in both the active and the passive form, in other words, the right to freedom of communication is an important right for a number of different reasons. Barendt defines the free speech principle as 'a principle under which speech is entitled to special protection from regulation or suppression'.[14] He also writes that 'a free speech principle need not entail absolute protection for any exercise of freedom of expression. Most proponents of strong free speech guarantees concede that its exercise may properly be restricted in some circumstances', but that the free speech principle 'does mean that governments must show strong grounds for interference'.[15] These restrictions will be analysed further below.

Barendt discusses four arguments that have generally been put forward to justify guarantees of freedom of speech, all linked and interrelated. These arguments could also be referred to as values in which freedom of expression is grounded. The first argument for or value of freedom of expression is that free speech and open discussion are important for discovering truth. 'If restrictions on speech are tolerated, society prevents the ascertainment and publication of accurate facts and valuable opinion.'[16] Fenwick and Phillipson describe this argument's basic thesis as, 'truth is most likely to emerge from free uninhibited discussion and debate'.[17] It will be clear that both active and passive freedom of expression play a role here. The European Court of Human Rights has not explicitly mentioned this argument in justification of the right laid down in article 10(2) ECHR, but it has, in a number of cases, held that 'it is an integral part of freedom of expression to seek historical truth'.[18]

The second argument or value brought forward by Barendt is that free speech can be seen as an integral aspect of an individual's right to self-development and self-fulfilment: our personality and its growth are inhibited if we are restricted in what we are allowed to say and write or to hear and read. 'A right to express beliefs and political attitudes instantiates or reflects what it is to be human', as

---

12 Grimm, D., 'Freedom of Speech in a Globalized World', in Hare, I. and Weinstein, J. (eds) *Extreme Speech and Democracy* (Oxford, Oxford University Press, 2009) 11.

13 Ibid.

14 Barendt, supra note 7, 6.

15 Ibid. 7.

16 Ibid, 7; for a more intensive discussion of this argument and the following arguments and the problems associated with them, see: Barendt, supra note 7, 7–23; Fenwick, H. and Phillipson, G., *Media Freedom under the Human Rights Act* (Oxford, Oxford University Press, 2006) 12–20.

17 Fenwick and Phillipson, supra note 16, 14.

18 See: *Chauvy v France*, Application No. 64915/01, 29 June 2004, para 69; *Dink v Turkey*, Application Nos 2668/07, 6102/08, 30079/08, 7072/09 and 7124/09, 14 September 2010, para 135; *Giniewski v France*, Application No. 64016/00, 31 January 2006, para 51.

Barendt writes.[19] In other words, the freedom of expression means that every person has the right to find out things for themselves and then to develop their own ideas and views. This would include views about religion or beliefs and whether to adopt these and whether to change religion or belief. And, again, both active and passive forms of freedom of expression are important here. In relation to both this and the previous argument, the term 'marketplace of ideas' has been used, meaning that there should be a market place for the exchange of competing ideas and beliefs, including religious beliefs.[20] In *Handyside v the United Kingdom*, the European Court of Human Rights mentioned that 'freedom of expression constitutes . . . one of the basic conditions . . . for the development of every man'.[21] Fenwick and Phillipson mention as a separate argument or value 'the argument from moral autonomy', and explain that this centres around the liberal conviction that matters of moral choice must be left to the individual. And, again, this includes choice about whether to have a religion or belief and whether to change a religion or belief. The state offends against human dignity, or treats certain citizens with contempt, if the coercive power of the law is used to force the moral convictions of some upon others.[22] It is submitted that this can be seen as part of the argument or value on self-development and self-fulfilment.

Barendt's third argument for and value of freedom of expression has already been mentioned above, when the importance of the right to freedom of expression for a democratic society was pointed out: 'freedom of expression plays a crucial role in the formation of public opinion on political questions'.[23] Barendt defines 'political speech' as 'all speech relevant to the development of public opinion on the whole range of public issues which an intelligent citizen should think about'.[24] This suggests that the term 'political expressions' should be interpreted broadly and would include expressions on religion and beliefs that also contribute to the public debate. This is confirmed by Barendt where he writes that 'the public discourse argument for freedom of speech applies, of course, most clearly to political speech, but it also covers speech concerning religious matters'.[25] Cram also writes that 'comments about Islam . . . would appear to fall within Professor Eric Barendt's definition of political speech as expression' and then cites the definition.[26] Fenwick and Phillipson also mention this argument and write that it 'is actually concerned to further two values: maintenance of the democracy and effective participation in it'.[27]

---

19 Barendt, supra note 7, 13. See also: Fenwick and Phillipson, supra note 16, 18–19.
20 Barendt, supra note 7, 11–12.
21 *Handyside v the United Kingdom*, supra note 3, para 49.
22 Fenwick and Phillipson, supra note 16, 13–14.
23 Barendt, supra note 7, 18.
24 Ibid. 162.
25 Barendt, E., 'Religious Hatred Laws: Protecting Groups or Beliefs?, 17(1) *Res Publica* (2011) 44.
26 Cram, I., 'The Danish Cartoons, Offensive Expression and Democratic Legitimacy', in Hare and Weinstein supra note 26, 324.
27 Fenwick and Phillipson, supra note 16, 17.

According to Barendt, 'this is probably the most easily understandable, and certainly the most fashionable, free speech theory in modern Western democracies';[28] and, 'the argument from democracy has been much the most influential theory in the development of contemporary free speech law'.[29] This argument or value is based on the importance of free and open debate on matters of public interest, including on religion or beliefs, and is linked to the previous two arguments or values: free and open debate is essential for discovering truth and for the self-development and self-fulfilment of the individual.

Leigh suggests that this is the main and almost only argument used by the European Court of Human Rights as he writes:

> So far as the ECtHR can be said to have a free speech theory, it is a very narrow and impoverished one. The contribution of a free press to democratic practice is recognised but the notions of a marketplace of competing ideas and beliefs or the value of expression as an outworking of personal autonomy barely feature in the jurisprudence.[30]

The European Court of Human Rights has, indeed, referred to this argument or value in a number of cases. It has, for example, repeatedly stressed the importance of freedom of speech for the public and political debate. In *Lingens v Austria*, the Court pointed out that 'freedom of political debate is at the very core of the concept of a democratic society which prevails throughout the Convention'.[31] In a number of cases, the Court has also held that 'there is little scope under Article 10 § 2 of the Convention for restrictions on political speech or on debate on matters of public interest'.[32] Moreover, the Court takes into account that expressions are made as a contribution to a wide-ranging and ongoing debate[33] or were expressed 'in the course of a pluralistic debate'.[34] And, according to the Court, states are required to create a favourable environment for participation in public debate by all the persons concerned, enabling them to express their opinions and ideas without fear.[35] The European Commission for Democracy through Law (the Venice Commission) points out that 'ensuring and protecting open public debate should be the primary means of protecting inalienable fundamental values

---

28 Barendt, supra note 7, 18.
29 Ibid. 20.
30 Leigh, I., 'Damned if They Do, Damned if They Don't: the European Court of Human Rights and the Protection of Religion from Attack', 17 (1) *Res Publica* (2011) 70.
31 *Lingens v Austria*, Application No. 9815/82, 8 July 1986, para 42. See also: *Erbakan v Turkey*, Application No. 59405/00, 6 July 2006, para 55.
32 *Ceylan v Turkey*, Application No. 23556/94, 8 July 1999, para 34. See also, for example: *Balsytė-Lideikienė v Lithuania*, Application No. 72596/01, 4 November 2008, para 81; *Perinçek v Switzerland*, Application No. 27510/08, 15 October 2015, para 197; *Bédat v Switzerland*, Application No. 56925/08, 29 March 2016, para 49.
33 *Giniewski v France*, supra note 18, para 50.
34 *Gündüz v. Turkey*, Application No. 35071/97, 4 December 2003, para 51.
35 *Dink v Turkey*, supra note 18, para 137.

such as freedom of expression and religion'.[36] Therefore, freedom of religion and expression are important for free and open debates in a democratic society, but such debates are also important for the protection of these rights.

Barendt's last argument is, as he writes, a negative argument: suspicion of government; 'there are particularly strong reasons to be suspicious of government in this context; it is a negative argument in that it highlights the evils of regulation, rather than the good of free speech'.[37] Governments might use laws to restrict speech that contains 'radical or subversive ideas', as they 'have strong reasons to fear the impact of these ideas, so they are naturally tempted to repress them. A free speech principle is necessary to counteract this tendency'.[38] This refers to the fact that laws restricting freedom of speech can be misused or abused by the government to stop opposition against or criticism of its policies. Or, as Buyse points out, 'such laws [restricting freedom of expression] can and have been used merely to quash the right of opponents of those in power or have been applied arbitrarily'.[39] This is clearly linked to the previous argument or value and the importance of a free and open debate. Such a debate cannot take place if states stop some people from taking part and expressing their views. This is why freedom of speech is seen as especially important for the press, which, according to the European Court of Human Rights, acts as public watchdog,[40] and for (opposition) politicians.[41] The Court subjects laws that restrict speech or that impose sanctions, and especially those that impose criminal sanctions, to particularly close scrutiny because such laws might have a chilling effect on the freedom of expression; or, in other words, such laws 'may also deter useful forms of speech because individuals and the media may apply self-censorship in order to avoid State sanctions'.[42] So these laws might stop journalists, politicians and others from expressing themselves and this would be detrimental to the free and open public debate in a democratic society. For example, In *Lingens v Austria*, the European Court of Human Rights considered:

36 European Commission for Democracy through Law (Venice Commission), *Report on the Relationship between Freedom of Expression and Freedom of Religion: the Issue of Regulation and Prosecution of Blasphemy, Religious Insult and Incitement to Religious Hatred* (Council of Europe, 2008, Study No. 406/2006, CDL-AD(2008)026) para 46, www.venice.coe.int/webforms/documents/?pdf=CDL-AD%282008%29026-e
37 Barendt, supra note 7, 21.
38 Ibid.
39 Buyse, A., 'Dangerous Expressions: the ECHR, Violence and Free Speech', 63 (2) *International and Comparative Law Quarterly* (2014) 493.
40 See, for example, *Castells v Spain*, Application No. 11798/85, 23 April 1992, para 43; *Jersild v Denmark*, Application No. 15890/89, 23 September 1994, para 35; *Sürek v Turkey No. 2*, Application No. 24122/94, 8 July 1999, para 35; *Şener v Turkey*, Application No. 26680/95,18 July 2000, para 42.
41 See, for example, *Castells v Spain*, supra note 40, para 41; *Incal v Turkey*, Application No. 22678/93, 9 June 1998, paras 45 and 46, *Féret v Belgium*, Application No. 15615/07, 16 July 2009, para 76.
42 Buyse, supra note 39, 493.

In the context of political debate such a sentence [as the fine imposed on applicant] would be likely to deter journalists from contributing to public discussion of issues affecting the life of the community. By the same token, a sanction such as this is liable to hamper the press in performing its task as purveyor of information and public watchdog.[43]

And, in *Koç and Tambaş v. Turkey*, the Court observed that the prohibition imposed on the applicants 'had the effect of censoring the applicants' very profession and was unreasonable in scope since the measure compelled the applicants to refrain from publishing anything likely to be considered to be contrary to the interests of the State'.[44]

All four of these arguments have been used, often together, in academic literature but also by courts, to give value to and to justify granting or upholding a right to freedom of expression. This freedom is important in both its active side: to enable an individual to impart information, to communicate views and ideas, including about their religion and beliefs; and its passive side: to enable an individual to receive information, to hear about others' views and ideas in order to form their own views, again including views on religion or belief issues. Both sides are paramount in relation to the freedom to manifest one's religion and to change one's religion, which are included in freedom of religion as guaranteed in article 9 ECHR. Both active and passive sides of freedom of expression are essential for free and open debate in society and, as will have become clear, such debates are also important for the protection of both freedoms. After examining freedom of expression, the next part will analyse the right to freedom of religion, which could be engaged in cases of religious hate speech as will become clear in this book.

Freedom of religion

Article 9 ECHR guarantees the freedom of religion and states:

Everyone has the right to freedom of thought, conscience and religion; this right includes freedom to change his religion or belief and freedom, either alone or in community with others and in public or private, to manifest his religion or belief, in worship, teaching, practice and observance.

This article thus guarantees two different freedoms: first, the freedom of thought, conscience and religion and, second, the freedom to manifest one's religion. Article 9(2) ECHR then states:

---

43 *Lingens v Austria*, supra note 31, para 44.
44 *Koç and Tambaş v. Turkey*, Application No. 50934/99, 21 June 2006, para 39. See also: *Erdoğdu v Turkey*, Application No. 25723/94, 15 June 2000, para 72.

Freedom to manifest one's religion or beliefs shall be subject only to such limitations as are prescribed by law and are necessary in a democratic society in the interests of public safety, for the protection of public order, health or morals, or for the protection of the rights and freedoms of others.

Therefore, according to article 9(2) ECHR, only the right to manifest one's religion can be restricted, but the right to freedom of thought, conscience and religion cannot. So, a violation of the latter right can never be justified. This is because a state cannot interfere with a person's thoughts or individual conscience. Article 9 thus contains an absolute, inviolable right to freedom of thought, conscience and religion and a qualified right to manifest one's religion. In *Kokkinakis v Greece*, the European Court of Human Rights explained that article 9(2)

Recognises that in democratic societies, in which several religions coexist within one and the same population, it may be necessary to place restrictions on this freedom in order to reconcile the interests of the various groups and ensure that everyone's beliefs are respected.[45]

The freedom to manifest one's religion or beliefs can thus be restricted. But what is covered by 'religion or beliefs'? The European Court of Human Rights has given a wide interpretation to the meaning of religion and belief. All traditional religions and beliefs are covered, but also non-religious beliefs such as pacifism, veganism, atheism; and, beliefs such as the Church of Scientology, the Moon Sect, the Divine Light Zentrum and Druidism.[46] Further, according to the Court, religious or philosophical convictions or beliefs are protected if they attain a certain level of cogency, seriousness, cohesion and importance; are worthy of respect in a democratic society; are not incompatible with human dignity; do not conflict with fundamental rights; and, relate to a weighty and substantial aspect of human life and behaviour.[47] Knights[48] and Pitt[49] both suggest that the European

---

45 *Kokkinakis v Greece*, supra note 8, para 33.
46 Pacifism: *Arrowsmith v the United Kingdom*, Application No. 7050/75, 16 May 1977; Veganism: *W v the United Kingdom*, Application No. 18187/91, 10 February 1993; Atheism: *Angeleni v Sweden*, Application No. 10491/83, 3 December 1986; Scientology: *X and Church of Scientology v Sweden*, Application No. 7805/77, 5 May 1979; the Moon Sect: *X v Austria*, Application No. 8652/79, 15 October 1981; the Divine Light Zentrum: *Omkarananda and the Divine Light Zentrum v Switzerland*, Application No. 8118/77 19 March 1981; Druidism: *Chappell v the United Kingdom*, Application No. 12587/86, 14 July 1987.
47 *Campbell and Cosans v the United Kingdom*, Application Nos 7511/76 and 7743/76, 25 February 1982, para 36.
48 Knights, S., *Freedom of Religion, Minorities and the Law* (Oxford, Oxford University Press, 2007) 40–41.
49 Pitt, G., 'Religion and Belief: Aiming at the Right Target?', in Meenan. H. (ed.) *Equality Law in an Enlarged European Union: Understanding the Article 13 Directives* (Cambridge, Cambridge University Press, 2007) 211.

Commission of Human Rights[50] and the European Court of Human Rights have sometimes simply assumed that the particular belief is covered without making an express finding on this point and have moved straight on to the question whether the restriction was justified under article 9(2) ECHR.

Article 9(1) ECHR mentions four forms of manifestation: worship, teaching, practice and observance. According to Knights, this 'protects rituals, rites, acts of worship and attempting to convert others'.[51] In *Eweida and Others v the United Kingdom*, the European Court of Human Rights held that, in order to establish that an act is a manifestation of religion or belief for the purposes of article 9, the applicant does not have to establish that he or she acted in fulfilment of a duty mandated by the religion in question. It is sufficient to establish the existence of a sufficiently close and direct nexus between the act and the underlying belief.[52] On the other hand, as Knights observes, the case law of both the European Commission and the European Court of Human rights is not always consistent and in some cases 'the necessary link has simply been assumed once the claimant's religious beliefs are established without the need for the claimant to prove that the manifestation is a necessary aspect of their belief'.[53] Therefore, the Court might simply accept that there is a protected religion or belief and that the applicant is manifesting that religion or belief and then move straight on to examine whether the interference complained of is justified under article 9(2) ECHR. The conditions under which a restriction of the right to freely manifest one's religion is justified will be analysed below.

Article 9(1) ECHR mentions 'teaching' as a form of manifesting one's belief. The quote from Knights, cited above, shows that this includes 'attempting to convert others'.[54] In *Kokkinakis v Greece*, the European Court of Human Rights stated that without the right to try to convince one's neighbour, for example through teaching, the freedom to change one's religion or belief 'would be likely to remain a dead letter'.[55] Here, there is a link with the freedom of religion of others, their right to be free from interference with their religion or belief, but there is also a link with freedom of expression: the right to freely speak about one's religion or belief and, in doing so, to try and convert others. But neither of these freedoms is unlimited. The European Court of Human Rights distinguishes between bearing witness to a religion and improper proselytism and has

50 The ECHR established a European Commission of Human Rights as well as the European Court Human Rights. Protocol 11 to the Convention which came into force in 1998, abolished the Commission, enlarged the Court and allowed individuals to take cases directly to the Court. In this book, the case law from the Commission from before 1998 will be referred to where relevant.

51 Knights, supra note 48, 44.

52 *Eweida and Others v the United Kingdom*, Application Nos 48420/10, 59842/10, 51671/10 and 36516/10, 15 January 2013, para 82.

53 Knights, supra note 48, 44–45.

54 Ibid. 44.

55 *Kokkinakis v Greece*, supra note 8, para 31.

held that the latter is 'a corruption or deformation' of bearing witness and is 'not compatible with respect for the freedom of thought, conscience and religion of others'.[56] Improper proselytism may 'take the form of activities offering material or social advantages with a view to gaining new members for a Church or exerting improper pressure on people in distress or in need; it may even entail the use of violence or brainwashing'.[57]

A case that shows the difference between bearing witness and improper proselytising is *Larissis and Others v Greece*, where three Greek air force officers tried to convert airmen serving under their command as well as civilians outside the air force. The European Court of Human Rights held that trying to convert the civilians was not improper proselytising, but trying to convert subordinates could be because the hierarchical structures in the armed forces could make it difficult for a subordinate to rebuff the approaches of an individual of superior rank or to withdraw from the situation initiated by him.[58] So, the right to bear witness to one's religion or beliefs and the right to express oneself about one's religion or beliefs can be limited to avoid interference with the right of others to be free from interference with their own religion or beliefs.

On the other hand, the right to freedom of religion also includes the right to change one's religion, as article 9(1) ECHR makes clear. The European Court of Human Rights has also held, in *Buscarini and Others v San Marino*, that article 9 includes the 'freedom to hold or not to hold religious beliefs and to practise or not to practise a religion'.[59] Therefore, 'freedom of choice is important', as the Research Division of the European Court of Human Rights has said.[60] But the right to choose a religion or belief, to change religion or belief or to choose not to hold or practise a religion or belief can only become real if open debates about religions and beliefs can take place, with room for criticism and even denial of other people's religions or beliefs. This is where the right to freedom of expression in article 10 ECHR plays an important role. This right includes the freedom to receive and impart information and this covers debates about religions and beliefs. After examining the rights to freedom of religion and expression, the following part will analyse when these rights can be restricted.

Restrictions on the freedom of religion and freedom of expression

Articles 9 and 10 ECHR both allow, in their second paragraph, for restrictions on the rights to freely manifest one's religion and to freedom of expression under certain circumstances. Although the two articles have a number of points in common, article 10(2) appears wider than article 9(2).

56 Ibid. para 48.
57 Ibid.
58 *Larissis and Others v Greece*, Application Nos 23372/94, 26377/94 and 26378/94, 24 February 1998, paras 51 and 57.
59 *Buscarini and Others v San Marino*, Application No. 24645/94, 18 February 1999, para 34.
60 European Court of Human Rights Research Division, supra note 1, para 18.

Article 10(2) ECHR reads:

> The exercise of these freedoms, since it carries with it duties and responsibilities, may be subject to such formalities, conditions, restrictions or penalties as are prescribed by law and are necessary in a democratic society, in the interests of national security, territorial integrity or public safety, for the prevention of disorder or crime, for the protection of health or morals, for the protection of the reputation or rights of others, for preventing the disclosure of information received in confidence, or for maintaining the authority and impartiality of the judiciary.

As mentioned, article 9(2) states:

> Freedom to manifest one's religion or beliefs shall be subject only to such limitations as are prescribed by law and are necessary in a democratic society in the interests of public safety, for the protection of public order, health or morals, or for the protection of the rights and freedoms of others.

Therefore, both articles mention that a restriction must be prescribed by law and must be necessary in a democratic society for one or more of the aims described in the second paragraph of both these articles.

The purpose of the requirement 'prescribed by law' is, as Evans writes, 'to ensure that when rights are restricted by public authorities, this restriction is not arbitrary and has some basis in domestic law'.[61] Or, as Murdoch writes, 'this concept expresses the value of legal certainty which might be defined broadly as the ability to act within a settled framework without the fear of arbitrary or unforeseeable state interference'.[62] In *Sunday Times v United Kingdom*, the European Court of Human Rights explained the two requirements that flow from the expression 'prescribed by law' which is used in articles 9(2), 10(2) and 11(2) ECHR:

> Firstly, the law must be adequately accessible: the citizen must be able to have an indication that is adequate in the circumstances of the legal rules applicable to a given case. Secondly, a norm cannot be regarded as a 'law' unless it is formulated with sufficient precision to enable the citizen to regulate his conduct: he must be able – if need be with appropriate advice – to foresee, to a degree that is reasonable in the circumstances, the consequences which a given action may entail. Those consequences need not be foreseeable with absolute certainty: experience shows this to be unattainable.

---

61 Evans, M., *Manual on the Wearing of Religious Symbols in Public Areas* (Strasbourg, Council of Europe, 2009) 125.
62 Murdoch, J., *Freedom of Thought, Conscience and Religion. A Guide to the Implementation of Article 9 of the European Convention on Human Rights* (Human Rights Handbooks No. 9, Strasbourg, Council of Europe, 2007) 27.

Again, whilst certainty is highly desirable, it may bring in its train excessive rigidity and the law must be able to keep pace with changing circumstances. Accordingly, many laws are inevitably couched in terms which, to a greater or lesser extent, are vague and whose interpretation and application are questions of practice.[63]

Therefore, the legal rule must be accessible and sufficiently precise to make its effects foreseeable and the latter can be through the interpretation by the domestic courts, as the last sentence of the above quote suggests. In *Kervanci v France* and *Dogru v France*, the Court held that, according to its settled case law, 'the concept of "law" must be understood in its "substantive" sense, not its "formal" one. It therefore includes everything that goes to make up the written law, including enactments of lower ranks than statutes'.[64]

In *Handyside v the United Kingdom*, the European Court of Human Rights explained that 'necessary in a democratic society' in article 10(2) means that there must be a 'pressing social need' and this, in turn, means that the restriction must be proportionate to the legitimate aim pursued.[65] The Court considered that, 'necessary' is not synonymous with 'indispensable' but neither has it the flexibility of such expressions as 'admissible', 'ordinary', 'useful', 'reasonable' or 'desirable'.[66] And, in relation to article 9(2), the Court has also held that 'the Court's task is to determine whether the measures taken at national level were justified in principle – that is, whether the reasons adduced to justify them appear "relevant and sufficient" and are proportionate to the legitimate aim pursued'.[67] Establishing whether a restriction on freedom of expression and on the right to manifest one's religion is justified thus involves a proportionality test, a balancing of all the interests involved.

The second paragraphs of articles 9 and 10 ECHR sum up these legitimate aims. Article 9(2) mentions public safety, the protection of public order, health or morals, or the protection of the rights and freedoms of others as legitimate aims. These are all mentioned in article 10(2) as well, but that article also allows restrictions in the interests of national security and territorial integrity, for the prevention of disorder or crime, for the protection of the reputation of others, for preventing the disclosure of information received in confidence, or for maintaining the authority and impartiality of the judiciary. Therefore, in relation to the legitimate aims, article 10(2) is wider than article 9(2). The European Court of Human Rights has held that 'the exceptions to freedom of

---

63 *Sunday Times v the United Kingdom*, Application No. 6538/74, 26 April 1979, para 49. For a recent discussion of this see: *Delfi AS v Estonia*, Application No. 64569/09, 16 June 2015, paras 120–122.
64 *Kervanci v France*, Application No. 31645/04 and *Dogru v France*, Application No. 27058/05, both 4 December 2008, both para 52.
65 *Handyside v the United Kingdom*, supra note 3, paras 48 and 49.
66 Ibid. para 48.
67 *Dahlab v Switzerland*, Application No. 42393/98, 15 February 2001, 12.

religion listed in Article 9 § 2 must be narrowly interpreted, for their enumeration is strictly exhaustive and their definition is necessarily restrictive'.[68] The Court then continued:

> However, unlike the second paragraphs of Articles 8, 10, and 11, paragraph 2 of Article 9 of the Convention does not allow restrictions on the ground of national security. Far from being an accidental omission, the non-inclusion of that particular ground for limitations in Article 9 reflects the primordial importance of religious pluralism as 'one of the foundations of a 'democratic society' within the meaning of the Convention' and the fact that a State cannot dictate what a person believes or take coercive steps to make him change his beliefs.[69]

Therefore, the Court concluded that the interests of national security could not serve as a justification for an interference with the right to freely manifest one's religion. Rainey *et al.* write that 'in modern times, it looks anomalous that the interests of national security are not listed in article 9'.[70] National security could, indeed, be at risk when religious people manifest their religion by calling for violence against all people who do not believe as they do, but restrictions on such expressions could be brought under article 10 and there national security can be a legitimate aim. The same is true for laws banning expressions against (certain) religions or beliefs or against believers. Apart from national security, such restrictions could also have the legitimate aim of protecting public safety and public order or the rights of others to freely manifest their religion or belief. But even if these aims are considered legitimate, the restriction must also pass the proportionality test.

Margin of appreciation

The European Court of Human Rights has also held that 'by reason of their direct and continuous contact with the vital forces in their countries', states are better placed than the international judge to assess what is necessary in a democratic society and, therefore, they have a certain margin of appreciation to make the initial assessment of the reality of the pressing social need implied by the notion of 'necessity'. However, this margin is not unlimited and the Court is empowered to give the final ruling. The domestic margin of appreciation thus goes hand in hand with European supervision.[71] And, as the Court considered in *Handyside v the United Kingdom*, 'the Court's supervisory functions oblige it to pay the

---

68 *Nolan and K v Russia*, Application No. 2512/04, 12 February 2009, para 73.
69 Ibid.
70 Rainey, B., Wicks, E. and Ovey, C., *Jacobs, White and Ovey: The European Convention on Human Rights* (6th edn, Oxford, Oxford University Press, 2014) 314.
71 *Handyside v the United Kingdom*, supra note 3, paras 48 and 49.

utmost attention to the principles characterising a "democratic society"'.[72] The width of the margin of appreciation afforded to states is important because, if the Court affords states a wider margin of appreciation, it will scrutinise a restriction or limitation less closely.

But what margin of appreciation is applied to the restrictions under articles 9(2) and 10(2) ECHR? The European Court of Human Rights has consistently held that exceptions to the right to freedom of expression in article 10 ECHR 'must be narrowly interpreted and the necessity for any restrictions must be convincingly established'.[73] As mentioned above, the Court has often stressed the importance of political speech and speech on matters of public interest for a democratic society.[74] The Court therefore affords such speech strong protection and it will scrutinise restrictions on this very closely. In other words, it affords the state a narrow margin of appreciation when it comes to restrictions on such speech. However, the margin of appreciation is wider when it concerns speech on moral or religious issues. This is clear from *Wingrove v the United Kingdom*, where the Court stated that, whereas there is little scope for restrictions on political speech or on debate of questions of public interest:

> A wider margin of appreciation is generally available to the Contracting States when regulating freedom of expression in relation to matters liable to offend intimate personal convictions within the sphere of morals or, *especially, religion*. Moreover, as in the field of morals, and *perhaps to an even greater degree*, there is no uniform European conception of the requirements of 'the protection of the rights of others' in relation to attacks on their religious convictions. What is likely to cause substantial offence to persons of a particular religious persuasion will vary significantly from time to time and from place to place, especially in an era characterised by an ever growing array of faiths and denominations [emphasis added].[75]

Under article 9(2) ECHR, the width of the margin of appreciation is also generally wider than, for example, the restrictions under articles 8 (right to respect for private and family life), 10 and 11 (freedom of assembly and association), which all contain the condition that a restriction must be 'necessary in a democratic society'.[76] The European Court of Human Rights affords States a wide margin of appreciation in relation to article 9 because 'it is not possible to

---

72 Ibid. para 49.
73 See, for example, *Observer and Guardian v the United Kingdom*, Application No. 13585/88, 26 November 1991, para 59; *Oberschlick v Austria, No. 2*, Application No. 20834/92, 1 July 1997, para 29; *Ceylan v Turkey*, supra note 46, para 32; *Balsytė-Lideikienė v Lithuania*, supra note 46, para 75; *Perinçek v Switzerland*, supra note 46, para 196.
74 See the cases mentioned in footnotes 31 and 32.
75 *Wingrove v the United Kingdom*, Application No. 17419/90, 25 November 1996, para 58. See also: *Murphy v Ireland*, Application No. 44179/98, 10 July 2003, para 67.
76 See for example, Lewis, T., 'What not to Wear: Religious Rights, the European Court, and the Margin of Appreciation', 56 (2) *International and Comparative Law Quarterly* (2007) 397–401; Knights, supra note 48, 138.

discern throughout Europe a uniform conception of the significance of religion in society . . . even within a single country such conceptions may vary'.[77]

In conclusion, the margin of appreciation afforded to states is wider under article 9(2) than it is under article 10(2) ECHR and restrictions on the right to freedom of expression will generally be scrutinised more closely by the European Court of Human Rights although, even under article 10(2), expressions on moral or religious matters will be scrutinised less closely than restrictions on matters contributing to the public and political debate. It should be noted that the Court can always narrow the margin of appreciation if a more uniform conception, a consensus, emerges in Europe about certain aspects of religion or belief. But what level of scrutiny will be and should be applied to expressions criticising religions or beliefs or religious believers but which also contribute to the public and political debate? This will be analysed below.

It will be clear that articles 9(2) and 10(2) ECHR have a number of issues in common, but there are also some differences. Article 10(2) stresses that the exercise of freedom of expression 'carries with it duties and responsibilities', which is not mentioned in article 9(2). This suggests that the exercise of the freedom to manifest one's religion does not carry with it duties and responsibilities. This will be discussed below. Article 10(2) also seems to be wider in that it mentions 'formalities, conditions, restrictions or penalties' and in that it contains more 'legitimate aims' than article 9(2) does. On the other hand, the margin of appreciation afforded to states is wider under article 9(2) than it is under article 10(2) and restrictions on article 10 will thus generally be scrutinised more closely by the European Court of Human Rights. Even so, restrictions on both rights are allowed when these are prescribed by law and necessary in a democratic society, which means that they are subject to a proportionality test: the means used must be proportionate to the legitimate aim pursued. One of the legitimate aims in both articles, which could be important when analysing freedom of expression and religious hate speech, is the protection of the rights of others. But, should the freedom of expression of one person be restricted because the expression offends or insult someone else in their religious feelings? Does article 9 ECHR include a right to protection of one's religious feelings or a right not to be offended? This will be examined in the next part.

A right not to be offended?

Article 9 ECHR does not explicitly mention a right to protection of one's religious feelings, but can or should such a right be read in there? The Research Division of the European Court of Human Rights, in their 'Overview of the Court's Case-law on Freedom of Religion', states:

> Does article 9 protect the right to protection of religious feelings as an aspect of religious freedom? The scope of article 9 of the Convention is actually very broad, so that such a right does appear to be protected by that Article.[78]

---

77 *Otto-Preminger-Institut v Austria*, Application No. 13470/87, 20 September 1994, para 50.
78 Research Division, European Court of Human Rights, supra note 1, para 40.

This suggests that article 9 ECHR does provide protection of one's religious feelings. However, there is also case law from the Court which seems to suggest that there is no such right. First of all, the European Court of Human Rights has stated that the right to freedom of expression applies:

> Not only to 'information' or 'ideas' that are favourably received or regarded as inoffensive or as a matter of indifference, but also to those that offend, shock or disturb the State or any sector of the population. Such are the demands of that pluralism, tolerance and broadmindedness without which there is no 'democratic society'.[79]

As Barendt writes, 'the proscription of any type of speech on the ground of its offensiveness is, of course, very hard to reconcile with freedom of expression, for a right to express and receive only inoffensive opinions would hardly be worth having'.[80] And, as the dissenting judges in *Otto-Preminger-Institut v Austria* said, 'there is no point in guaranteeing this freedom only as long as it is used in accordance with accepted opinion'.[81] Moreover, the European Court of Human Rights has also held that:

> Those who choose to exercise the freedom to manifest their religion, irrespective of whether they do so as members of a religious majority or a minority, cannot reasonably expect to be exempt from all criticism. They must tolerate and accept the denial by others of their religious beliefs and even the propagation by others of doctrines hostile to their faith.[82]

This would suggest that a right not to be offended in one's religious feelings does not exist under article 9 ECHR. It is submitted that there is no such right, although the case law of the European Court of Human Rights has not always been very clear on this.[83] As Leigh writes, the Court has sometimes read into article 9 ECHR 'a right not to be offended where none is present in the text'.[84]

---

79 *Handyside v United Kingdom*, supra note 3, para 49.
80 Barendt, supra note 25, 44.
81 *Otto-Preminger-Institut v Austria*, supra note 77, dissenting opinion, para 3.
82 *Otto-Preminger-Institut v Austria*, supra note 77, para 47. See also on this: Evans, supra note 61, 49–50.
83 See for a discussion of this: Nathwani, N., 'Religious Cartoons and Human Rights – a Critical Legal Analysis of the Case Law of the European Court of Human Rights on the Protection of Religious Feelings and its Implications in the Danish Affair Concerning Cartoons of the Prophet Muhammad', 4 *European Human Rights Law Review* (2008) 488–507; Kapai, P. and Cheung, A., 'Hanging in the Balance: Freedom of Expression and Religion', 15 *Buffalo Human Rights Law Review* (2009) 41–79; Temperman, J., 'Protection against Religious Hatred under the United Nations ICCPR and the European Convention System' in Ferrari, S. and Cristofori, R. (eds) *Law and Religion in the 21st Century* (Farnham, Ashgate Publishing, 2010) 215–223; Leigh, supra note 44; Letsas, G., 'Is there a Right Not to be Offended in One's Religious Beliefs?' in Zucca, L. and Ungureanu, C. (eds) *Law, State and Religion in the New Europe* (Cambridge, Cambridge University Press, 2012) 239–260, available at SSRN: http://ssrn.com/abstract=1500291.
84 Leigh, supra note 30, 72.

For example, in *Otto-Preminger-Institut v Austria*, the European Court of Human Rights stated that:

> The manner in which religious beliefs and doctrines are opposed or denied is a matter which may engage the responsibility of the State, notably its responsibility *to ensure the peaceful enjoyment of the right guaranteed under Article 9* to the holders of those beliefs and doctrines. Indeed, in extreme cases the effect of particular methods of opposing or denying religious beliefs can be such as to inhibit those who hold such beliefs from exercising their freedom to hold and express them [emphasis added].[85]

The Court also mentioned that 'the *respect for the religious feelings of believers as guaranteed in Article 9* can legitimately be thought to have been violated by provocative portrayals of objects of religious veneration' [emphasis added].[86] The Court also accepted that the purpose of the measures taken by Austria in this case, which was 'to protect the right of citizens not to be insulted in their religious feelings by the public expression of views of other persons', served the legitimate aim of the protection of the rights of others.[87] All this appears to lead to the conclusion that the peaceful enjoyment of one's freedom of religion and the right to respect for one's religious feelings are part of the freedom of religion as guaranteed by article 9 ECHR. However, Edge, for example, suggests 'that *Otto-Preminger-Institut* should be treated with caution as an authority on the extent of Article 9 protection'.[88] It will become clear in the following why this is the case.

Support for the existence of a right not to be offended under article 9 ECHR can also be found in *I.A. v Turkey*, a case concerning a conviction for blasphemy. The applicant had published a fictional novel containing disparaging remarks about Islam and the Prophet Muhammad. The European Court of Human Rights did not find that his conviction violated his freedom of expression, because 'the present case concerns not only comments that offend or shock, or a "provocative" opinion, but also an abusive attack on the Prophet of Islam' and 'believers may legitimately feel themselves to be the object of unwarranted and offensive attacks'. The Court concluded that:

> The measure taken in respect of the statements in issue was intended to provide protection against offensive attacks on matters regarded as sacred by Muslims. In that respect it finds that the measure may reasonably be held to have met a 'pressing social need'.[89]

---

85 *Otto-Preminger-Institut v Austria*, supra note 77, para 47.
86 Ibid.
87 In the same vein: the Overview of the Research Division of the European Court of Human Rights, supra note 1, paras 40–41.
88 Edge, P., 'The European Court of Human Rights and Religious Rights', 47 (3) *International and Comparative Law Quarterly* (1998) 683.
89 *I.A. v Turkey*, Application No. 42571/98, 13 September 2005, para 29.

Therefore, in these two cases, the European Court of Human Rights appears to accept that a right to protection of one's religious feelings, a right not to be offended in one's religious belief is present in article 9 ECHR. Letsas points out that this presumes 'that *religious* offense grounds special kinds of reasons for state action, that are not co-extensive with reasons grounded by non-religious instances of offense'.[90] In other words, accepting the argument that article 9 contains a right not to be offended presupposes that religious offence is, in some way, different from other types of offence and that people who are offended in their religious feelings are more worthy of protection. Nathwani criticises this where she writes that 'the enjoyment of a certain freedom does not generally give others the duty to value the exercise of that freedom'[91] and that 'provocation and mockery have important roles in the competition of ideologies. . . . It is not clear why religion should be privileged over other ideologies; after all, religion could be understood as a particular type of ideology'.[92] This issue will be analysed in more detail in relation to religious hate speech in Chapter 3.

Moreover, there are also a number of arguments for accepting that no such right exists. First, it was already mentioned that such a right is 'not present in the text' of article 9 ECHR.[93] Second, support can be found in the fact that the judgments in both *Otto-Preminger-Institut v Austria* and *I.A. v Turkey* were majority judgments with a dissenting opinion in each case. The three dissenting judges[94] in *Otto-Preminger-Institut v Austria* clearly stated that 'the Convention does not, in terms, guarantee a right to protection of religious feelings. More particularly, such a right cannot be derived from the right to freedom of religion, which in effect includes a right to express views critical of the religious opinions of others'.[95] In *I.A. v Turkey*, three out of seven judges dissented and expressed the opinion that perhaps the time had come 'to "revisit" the case law, which in our view seems to place too much emphasis on conformism or uniformity of thought and to reflect an overcautious and timid conception of freedom of the press'.[96] Therefore, in both cases, the judgments were by no means unanimous and the judges were divided about the question whether there had been a violation of the right to freedom of expression.

Furthermore, although these two cases can be read as acceptance by the majority of judges of the existence of a right not to be offended in one's religious beliefs as part of the freedom of religion in article 9 ECHR, in a number of later cases,

90 Letsas, supra note 83, 4.
91 Nathwani, supra note 83, 498.
92 Ibid. 499.
93 Leigh, supra note 30, 72. For the same argument see also: Letsas supra note 83; Temperman, J., 'A Right to be Free from Religious Hatred? The Wilders Case in the Netherlands and Beyond', in Molnar, P. (ed.) *Free Speech and Censorship around the Globe* (Budapest/New York, Central European University Press, 2015) 528.
94 Six judges found that Article 10 had not been violated but the three dissenters found that it had.
95 *Otto-Preminger-Institut v Austria*, supra note 77, dissenting opinion, para 6.
96 Ibid. paras 7 and 8.

the European Court of Human Rights has held that such a right does not exist. In *Giniewski v France*, the applicant was convicted for publicly defaming a religious group and the Court found that this conviction violated his right to freedom of expression. The article in question contributed to a matter of public interest and, although the article contained conclusions and phrases that may offend, shock or disturb some people, this did not preclude the enjoyment of freedom of expression, according to the Court.[97] In *Klein v Slovakia*, a journalist had written an article in which he attacked an archbishop for suggesting that a film should be banned. The Court unanimously held that the conviction violated article 10 ECHR because it 'was not persuaded that the applicant had discredited and disparaged a sector of the population on account of their Catholic faith' and because 'the article neither unduly interfered with the right of believers to express and exercise their religion, nor did it denigrate the content of their religious faith'.[98]

In *Nur Radyo Ve Televizyon Yayıncılığı A.Ş. v Turkey*, the European Court of Human Rights found that a broadcasting ban imposed on the applicant broadcasting company violated article 10 ECHR. The ban had been imposed after the company had broadcast certain comments that an earthquake in Turkey in which thousands of people had died was a warning from Allah against the enemies of Allah. The Court noted that the remarks were of a proselytising nature in that they accorded religious significance to the earthquake. Although the remarks might have been shocking and offensive and might have led to superstition and intolerance, they did not in any way incite to violence and were not liable to stir up hatred against people.[99] In *Öllinger v Austria*, the Court repeated that 'those who choose to exercise the freedom to manifest their religion cannot reasonably expect to be exempt from all criticism'. The Court then appeared to limit the duty of the state to ensure the peaceful enjoyment of the right guaranteed in article 9 to instances 'where religious beliefs are opposed or denied in a manner which inhibits those who hold such beliefs from exercising their freedom to hold or express them'.[100] And, lastly, in *Vajnai v Hungary*, relating to a political expression rather than a religious expression – the applicant was convicted for wearing a red star, the symbol of the workers' movement, in public – the Court accepted that a symbol that was ubiquitous during the communist rule may create uneasiness among past victims and their relatives, but that this was not enough to limit the freedom of expression. According to the Court, restrictions on human rights applied to satisfy the dictates of public feeling do not meet a pressing social need, since a democratic society must remain reasonable in its judgement. 'To hold otherwise would mean that freedom of speech and opinion is subjected to the heckler's veto'.[101]

97 *Giniewski v France*, supra note 18, para 53.
98 *Klein v Slovakia*, Application No. 72208/01, 31 October 2006, paras 51 and 52.
99 *Nur Radyo Ve Televizyon Yayıncılığı A.Ş. v Turkey*, Application No. 6587/03, 27 November 2007, para 30. See also: Weber, supra note 6, 52.
100 *Öllinger v Austria*, Application No. 76900/01, 29 June 2006, para 39.
101 *Vajnai v Hungary*, Application No. 33629/06, 8 July 2008, para 57.

These later cases and the dissent in the earlier ones strongly suggest that there is no right not to be offended under (article 9 of) the ECHR, a view clearly supported by the literature.[102] For example, Bielefeldt *et al.* write:

> Freedom of religion or belief cannot generally shield religions against criticism, not even against polemical, offensive, or deeply ironic forms of criticism. Hence the fact that some individuals or groups may feel seriously offended by satirical or otherwise negative depictions of their faith, albeit understandably in many cases, does not suffice to justify State-imposed restrictions on freedom of expression.[103]

The argument that there is no right not to be offended is also supported by the statements of the Parliamentary Assembly of the Council of Europe that 'freedom of thought and freedom of expression in a democratic society must, however, permit open debate on matters relating to religion and beliefs' and that 'freedom of expression as protected under article 10 of the European Convention on Human Rights should not be further restricted to meet increasing sensitivities of certain religious groups'.[104] Van Dijk and van Hoof point out that a right not to be offended 'is not included in Article 9, but is on the contrary inconsistent with the "pluralism indissociable from a democratic society", embedded in Article 9'.[105] And, Grimm writes that 'a general prohibition against hurting religious feelings would put the public discourse at the mercy of the sensitivity of religious groups, and particularly the most militant amongst them'.[106] Here the importance of freedom of speech and the crucial role it plays in the formation of public opinion, one of the arguments for the right as distinguished above, can be seen. The role of the public discourse is analysed in the next part.

Gratuitously offensive

The above strongly suggests that just being offensive about beliefs or believers is, in itself, not enough to hold that an expression breached article 10 ECHR. On the other hand, article 10(2) states that the exercise of the freedom of expression brings with it 'duties and responsibilities' and the European Court of Human Rights has held that:

102 See the authors in footnote 83 supra.
103 Bielefeldt, H., Ghanea, N. and Wiener, M., *Freedom of Religion or Belief: An International Law Commentary* (Oxford, Oxford University Press, 2016) 493.
104 Parliamentary Assembly, Council of Europe, Resolution 1510 (2006) *Freedom of Expression and Respect for Religious Beliefs*, Articles 3 and 12, http://assembly.coe.int/nw/xml/XRef/Xref-XML2HTML-en.asp?fileid=17457&lang=en
105 Dijk, P. van and Hoof, F. van, *Theory and Practice of the European Convention on Human Rights* (London, Kluwer Law International, 1998) 551, with reference in Footnote to *Kokkinakis v Greece*, supra note 8.
106 Grimm, supra note 12, 19.

Amongst them – in the context of religious opinions and beliefs – may legitimately be included an obligation to avoid as far as possible expressions that are gratuitously offensive to others and thus an infringement of their rights, and which therefore do not contribute to any form of public debate capable of furthering progress in human affairs.[107]

Therefore, article 10(2) imposes a duty on those who exercise their right to freedom of expression to avoid being 'gratuitously offensive'.[108] This, however, raises some questions. First, what does the European Court of Human Rights mean by 'in the context of religious opinions and beliefs'? In the same case, the Court refers to 'the manner in which religious beliefs and doctrines are opposed or denied' and considers that 'the respect for the religious feelings of believers as guaranteed in article 9 can legitimately be thought to have been violated by provocative portrayals of objects of religious veneration'.[109] The Court thus appears to give a wide meaning to the terms 'in the context of religious opinions and beliefs' to include both criticism of beliefs and offence to believers.

The second question raised by the above quote is: what does 'gratuitously offensive' mean? And who determines this? In the eyes of religious believers, any critique of or aspersion on their religious beliefs will likely be seen as (gratuitously) offensive. Cram writes that, in the context of gratuitously offensive expression, 'two distinct meanings can be discerned. The first concerns offensive expression that is groundless, lacking an objective basis in fact or reason whilst the second involves some form of unnecessary or needless expression that offends members of the audience'.[110]

Considering the first meaning, Cram writes that 'the criticism of the speaker is that the facts do not lend any support whatsoever to his assertions'.[111] It is doubtful whether expressions about religions or beliefs or believers are assertions that could be supported by facts in any case so it is submitted that the second meaning of 'gratuitously offensive' speech distinguished by Cram is more in line with what the European Court of Human Rights said in the quote given, as the Court also mentions that 'gratuitously offensive' expressions do not contribute to the public debate and/or are not capable of furthering progress in human affairs. Therefore, a 'gratuitously offensive' expression appears to be an expression that is needlessly offensive, is made with the sole purpose of causing offence without serving any further purpose. An expression that contributes to the public debate and/or is

---

107 *Otto-Preminger-Institut v Austria*, supra note 70, para 49. The same or similar expressions have been used in other cases, see, for example: *Wingrove v the United Kingdom*, supra note 75, para 52; *Gündüz v Turkey*, supra note 34, para 37; *Giniewski v France*, supra note 18, para 43.
108 See also on this: Howard, E., 'Gratuitously Offensive Speech and the Political Debate', 6 *European Human Rights Law Review* (2016) 636–644.
109 *Otto-Preminger-Institut v Austria*, supra note 77, para 47.
110 Cram, supra note 26, 325.
111 Ibid.

capable of furthering progress in human affairs would thus not be 'gratuitously offensive'. Nathwani seems to read this quote in the same way as she writes about 'expressions that are "gratuitously offensive to others" and which therefore do not contribute to any form of public debate'.[112] She also points out that:

> The 'obligation to avoid gratuitously offensive expressions' expressed in *Otto-Preminger* is not easy to reconcile with the right to offend, shock and disturb postulated by the ECtHR [European Court of Human Rights] in *Handyside v United Kingdom*. . . The point is that gratuitously offensive expressions might be needed and justified as an expression of dissent or protest against a dominant group, ideology or religion.[113]

Nathwani thus appears to advocate that even gratuitously offensive expressions should attract the protection of article 10 ECHR, although the last sentence of the quote could also suggest that she sees this as part of the public debate. Whether this is what she means or not, all the above leads to the conclusion that expressions that contribute to the public and political debate and/or further progress in human affairs, would not be considered to be gratuitously offensive and thus that restrictions on such expressions would be held to violate the freedom of expression of the speaker or author.

More support for this can be found in the case law of the European Court of Human Rights. For example, in *Giniewski v France*, the Court held that the applicant 'had made a contribution, which by definition was open to discussion, to a wide-ranging and ongoing debate . . . without sparking off any controversy that was gratuitous or detached from the reality of contemporary thought'.[114] And, although the article contained conclusions and phrases that might offend, shock or disturb some people, this did not preclude the enjoyment of freedom of expression. The article was not gratuitously offensive or insulting and did not incite to disrespect or hatred. The Court thus found a violation of article 10 ECHR.[115]

The same finding was made in *Gündüz v Turkey*, where the European Court of Human Rights considered that the applicant contributed to a programme on a topic that was widely debated in the Turkish media. The programme was designed to encourage an exchange of views on the role of religion in a democratic society.[116] All this supports the argument that speech is not gratuitously offensive if it contributes to the public debate and/or is capable of furthering progress in human affairs. And, as Barendt points out, 'speech hostile to religious belief and the ridicule and abuse of religious practices forms part of . . . "public discourse"'.[117]

---

112 Nathwani, supra note 83, 493.
113 Ibid. footnote 44. A similar view is expressed by the dissenting judges in *I.A. v Turkey*, supra note 89, para 3.
114 *Giniewski v France*, supra note 18, para 50.
115 Ibid. paras 52 and 53.
116 *Gündüz v Turkey*, supra note 34, paras 43 and 44.
117 Barendt, supra note 25, 44.

Even exaggerated or provocative expressions are not gratuitously offensive if they contribute to the public debate, according to the European Court of Human Rights. In *Le Pen v France*, the Court stated that 'anyone who engages in a debate on a matter of public interest can resort to a degree of exaggeration, or even provocation, provided that they respect the reputation and the rights of others'.[118] This also includes a degree of immoderation.[119] These cases concerned a politician's expressions, but the Court has also held that journalistic freedom covers possible recourse to a degree of exaggeration, or even provocation.[120] And, in *I.A. v Turkey*, which concerned the publisher of a fictional novel, the Court held that the expressions in that case did not attract the protection of article 10 ECHR, because they went beyond 'comments that offend or shock, or a "provocative" opinion'.[121] According to the Court in *Morice v France*, when it concerns a matter of public interest, a degree of hostility and the potential seriousness of certain remarks do not obviate the right to a high level of protection.[122] Therefore, expressions that contribute to the public debate can exaggerate and provoke, be immoderate, hostile and potentially serious and still attract the protection of article 10(2).

One last problem with the term 'gratuitously offensive' is that the term is very subjective: one person might find something gratuitously offensive while another person might find the same expression acceptable.[123] As Leigh points out, 'gratuitously offensive speech is a vague category that is unpredictable in its application'.[124] And, Cram states that:

> This confers on the state wide and vaguely defined powers to prescribe the manner in which ideas and opinions are expressed. It constrains the speaker by ruling out emotively charged language which . . . might often constitute the most powerful communicative style available to him. The 'cleansing' of the public debate that results may please the squeamish but only at a cost to public discourse as the norms of a particular section of society are privileged.[125]

Therefore, the vagueness and uncertain meaning of the term 'gratuitously offensive' could lead to abuse by the state to suppress speech because of the way this is expressed. This is another reason why the term 'gratuitously offensive' should

---

118 *Le Pen v France*, Application No. 18788/09, 20 April 2010. See also on this: Voorhoof, D., *European Court of Human Rights Jean-Marie Le Pen v. France* (2010) http://merlin.obs. coe.int/iris/2010/7/article1.en.html
119 *Otegi Mondragon v Spain*, Application No. 2034/07, 15 March 2011, para 54.
120 *Lopez Gomes da Silva v Portugal*, Application No. 37698/97, 28 September 2000, para 34.
121 *I.A. v Turkey*, supra note 89, para 29.
122 *Morice v France*, Application No. 29369/10, 23 April 2015, para 125.
123 The same can be said of the term 'offensive speech'. See on this: O'Reilly, A., 'In Defence of Offence: Freedom of Expression, Offensive Speech, and the Approach of the European Court of Human Rights', 19 *Trinity College Law Review* (2016) 240.
124 Leigh, supra note 30, 71.
125 Cram, supra note 26, 327.

be interpreted very strictly and should not include expressions that contribute to the public debate. As the three dissenting judges in *Otto-Preminger-Institut v Austria* state, the terms of article 10(2) 'must be narrowly interpreted' and

> It should not be open to the authorities of the state to decide whether a particular statement is capable of 'contributing to any form of public debate capable of furthering progress in human affairs'; such a decision cannot but be tainted by the authorities' idea of 'progress'.[126]

Fostering intolerance

Based on the above, it appears that anyone who exercises their freedom of expression has, in the context of religious opinions and beliefs, an obligation to avoid as far as possible expressions that are gratuitously offensive. However, in some cases, the European Court of Human Rights appears to have imposed a further duty on politicians: a duty not to foster intolerance. In *Erbakan v Turkey*, the Court pointed out that combating all forms of intolerance was an integral part of human rights protection because tolerance and respect for equal dignity of all human beings constitute the foundations of a democratic pluralist society.[127] Therefore, the Court continued, it may, in principle, be considered necessary in democratic societies to sanction or prevent all forms of expression that spread, incite, promote or justify hatred based on intolerance, including religious intolerance, provided that the formalities, conditions, restrictions or sanctions are proportionate to the legitimate aim pursued.[128] So these restrictions still have to pass the justification test of article 10(2). The Court also held that it was crucially important that, in their public speeches, politicians should avoid making comments likely to foster such intolerance.[129] The Court also referred to this duty in *Féret v Belgium*, after stating that political speech that stirred up religious or ethnic hatred was a threat to social peace and political stability in democratic states.[130]

This suggests that politicians, when exercising their right to free speech, have a duty not to foster intolerance. But what does this mean? This is a very vague term that could be open to many different interpretations. In *Erbakan v Turkey*, the European Court of Human Rights also considered that 'it had not been established that at the time of his prosecution the speech in question had given rise to, or been likely to give rise to, a "present risk" and an "imminent danger"'[131] and, thus, a violation of Mr Erbakan's freedom of expression was found. This would suggest that combating mere intolerance is not sufficient to justify infringing the freedom of expression. The three dissenting judges, in *Féret v*

---

126 *Otto-Preminger-Institut v Austria*, supra note 77, dissenting opinion, para 3.
127 *Erbakan v Turkey*, supra note 31, para 56.
128 Ibid.
129 Ibid. para 64.
130 *Féret v Belgium*, supra note 41, paras 73 and 75.
131 *Erbakan v Turkey*, supra note 31, para 68.

Belgium, also argued that combating mere intolerance was not, in their view, sufficient to justify infringing the freedom of expression and that real – and not potential – impact on the rights of others needed to be demonstrated.[132] These three dissenters expressed their opinion that there had been a violation of Mr Féret's freedom of expression but the four majority judges came to the conclusion that there had not been a violation. Therefore, the Court is not very clear about the meaning of 'fostering intolerance'. In *Féret v Belgium*, the judges were divided over this issue, while *Erbakan v Turkey*, appears to suggest that the dissenters in *Féret v Belgium* are right and that real impact, present risk and imminent danger needs to be established. Any other interpretation would allow states to curtail (political) speech based on a hypothetical and unsubstantiated danger of fostering intolerance.

It is submitted that fostering mere intolerance is thus not enough to restrict the freedom of expression of politicians, especially because politicians play such a big role in the public debate. And, even if there is real impact or a clear danger, the restriction is still subject to the justification test in article 10(2) ECHR and the European Court of Human Rights should carefully examine whether the means used to achieve the aim of protecting national security or the rights of others are proportionate and necessary. This will be examined in more detail in Chapter 4.

Conclusion

In this Chapter, the two fundamental human rights that play a role in relation to the subject of this book – freedom of expression and freedom of religion – were analysed. The importance the European Court of Human Rights attaches to both these rights for the functioning of a democratic society was stressed.

Article 10 guarantees the freedom of expression and this right has both an active and a passive side: it includes not only the right to express one's own opinions but also the right to receive information. The right is an important freedom and the four arguments that are generally given for the existence of the right were discussed. These include the role the right plays in the discovery of the truth; in the self-development and self-fulfilment of the individual; in the maintenance of a democratic society and in the importance of open and public debate; and in the ability to show suspicion of the government. The argument most used by the European Court of Human Rights is the argument of the importance on free speech for political and public discourse in a democratic society.

Article 9 ECHR guarantees the freedom of thought, conscience and religion, which includes the freedom to change one's religion, and the freedom to freely manifest one's religion. Only the latter freedom can be restricted under certain circumstances set out in article 9(2). The meaning of 'religion' and 'belief' was examined and the conclusion was drawn that these terms are interpreted widely

---

132 *Féret v Belgium*, supra note 41, dissenting opinion. See also: Buyse, supra note 39, 499.

by the European Court of Human Rights. The case law has also explained how a manifestation can be established, although both the Commission of Human Rights and the Court have sometimes accepted that there is a manifestation without further examination and have moved straight to the question whether the interference can be justified under article 9(2).

Both articles 9 and 10 ECHR allow for restrictions on the rights guaranteed in certain prescribed circumstances. A restriction or limitation can be justified if this is prescribed by law and is necessary in a democratic society for one or more of the aims described in the second paragraph of both these articles. 'Necessary in a democratic society' has been interpreted by the European Court of Human Rights as meaning that there must be a 'pressing social need' and this, in turn, means that the restriction must be proportionate to the legitimate aim pursued.

The European Court of Human Rights has also held that states are better placed than the international judge to assess what is necessary in a democratic society and, therefore, they have a certain margin of appreciation to make the initial assessment. However, this margin is not unlimited and the Court is empowered to give the final ruling. The domestic margin of appreciation thus goes hand in hand with European supervision. The width of the margin of appreciation afforded to states is important because, if the Court affords states a wider margin of appreciation, it will scrutinise a restriction or limitation less closely. The margin of appreciation afforded to states is wider under article 9(2) than it is under article 10(2) ECHR and restrictions on the right to freedom of expression will generally be scrutinised more closely by the European Court of Human Rights although, even under article 10(2), expressions on moral or religious matters will be scrutinised less closely than restrictions on matters contributing to the public and political debate.

The question whether article 9 ECHR includes a right not to be offended in one's religious feelings was analysed and it was concluded that no such right exists. The European Court of Human Rights has stated that the right to freedom of expression also applies to expressions that offend, shock and disturb; and, that people who exercise their right to freely manifest their religion cannot expect to be exempt from criticism. However, the Court has not always been very clear regarding the existence of a right not to be offended in one's religious feelings. Some cases have suggested that such a right forms part of article 9, but later cases and the literature appear to support the conclusion that such a right does not exist.

The European Court of Human Rights has also held that the 'duties and responsibilities' that article 10(2) imposes on those who exercise the right to freedom of speech includes an obligation to avoid expressions that are gratuitously offensive in the context of religious opinions and beliefs. What 'gratuitously offensive' means was examined and the conclusion was drawn that 'gratuitously offensive' expressions are expressions that do not contribute to the public debate and/or are not capable of furthering progress in human affairs. An expression that contributes to the public debate and/or is capable of furthering progress in human affairs would thus not be 'gratuitously offensive'. Expressions that contribute to the public debate can still attract the protection of article 10, even if they are exaggerated, provocative, immoderate, hostile and potentially serious.

In the last part of the chapter, the question whether politicians have a duty not to foster intolerance when they exercise their right to free speech was examined. The case law of the European Court of Human Rights suggests that restrictions on expressions cannot be justified merely because they foster intolerance but that they require real, and not potential, impact on the rights of others. And even if this is present, the restriction is still subject to the justification test in article 10(2) ECHR and the Court should carefully examine whether the means used to achieve the aim of, for example, protecting national security, public order or the rights of others are proportionate and necessary.

Where a person criticises a religion or belief or offends religious believers, there could be a conflict between two human rights: the right to freedom of expression and the right to freedom of religion, but there could also be a clash between these two rights and the right to be free from (religious) discrimination. In Chapter 2, the question when such a conflict occurs and how to deal with the situation where it does occur, will be examined.

2 Conflicts of rights?

Introduction

In Chapter 1, the rights to freedom of expression and freedom of religion as laid down in articles 9 and 10 ECHR were examined. Both rights can be restricted under circumstances described in the second paragraph of each of these articles and a three part test is applied under both, which can be summed up as legality – is the restriction prescribed by law; necessity – is the restriction necessary in a democratic society; and proportionality – are the means used to achieve the legitimate aim proportionate and necessary. The legitimate aims in both articles include the protection of the rights of others. But, as argued in the previous chapter, the right to freely manifest one's religion under article 9 ECHR does not include a right to protection of one's religious feelings against criticism or offence, in other words, does not include a right not to be offended. However, under article 10 ECHR, there is a duty on those who exercise their right to freedom of expression not to be 'gratuitously offensive' in the context of religious opinions and beliefs. It was established that 'gratuitously offensive' expressions are expressions that do not contribute to the public debate and/or are not capable of furthering progress in human affairs. Therefore, an expression that contributes to the public debate and/or is capable of furthering progress in human affairs, would not be 'gratuitously offensive' and would attract the protection of article 10, even if they are exaggerated, provocative, immoderate, hostile and potentially serious, as was discussed in Chapter 1.

In the last part of Chapter 1, the duty of politicians when exercising their right to free speech was considered and the conclusion was that the case law of the European Court of Human Rights suggests that combating mere intolerance is not sufficient to justify infringing the freedom of expression and that real – and not potential – impact on the rights of others needed to be demonstrated. And, even if real impact is present, any restriction is still subject to the justification test in article 10(2) ECHR and the Court should carefully examine whether the means used to achieve the aims are proportionate and necessary.

This chapter analyses whether, in cases where a person uses expressions that criticise religions or beliefs or that are offensive to religious believers, there is a conflict between the rights to freedom of expression and to freedom of religion and, if there is, how this should be dealt with. A number of principles can be derived from the case law of the European Court of Human Rights to deal with situations of conflicting rights. The rights to freedom of expression and freedom of religion are, however, not the only rights that can be involved. Another human right that could be relevant is the right not to be discriminated against as laid down in article 14 ECHR and in article 1 Protocol 12 to the ECHR and this right will also be examined in this Chapter.

Conflict between freedom of expression and freedom of religion

When a person criticises a religion and/or offends religious believers, there appear to be two possible human rights involved: the right of the speaker or author to freedom of expression and the right of the religious believer, who is the target of the speech, to manifest their religion. The impression is often created that these rights are in conflict with each other when a person criticises a religion or belief or religious believers, but are they? Is a person's right to freely manifest their religion affected by someone else making offensive remarks about their religion or about the way they manifest that religion? If the believer's right is affected, then that would suggest that there is a right not to be offended implicitly present in article 9 ECHR. In Chapter 1, it was concluded that article 9 does not include such a right and, therefore, a person's freedom of speech cannot be restricted solely because it is offensive to religious believers. If it could, this would go against the freedom to change one's religion, which is also part of the freedom of religion and which requires open debates about religions and beliefs. This refers back to some of the arguments for or values of freedom of expression: the crucial role this right plays in the formation of public opinion, including opinions about religion or belief; the importance of discovering truth; and, the contribution free speech makes to an individual's self-development and self-fulfilment.

Kapai and Cheung argue that 'international case law to date has focused on respect for religion on the basis that insults, harassment and other defiling speech against religion should not be permissible if it impedes free exercise of religion, not on the basis that the substance of the religion deserves respect'.[1] It is submitted that, unless expressions prevent or deter any religious believers from believing what they wish, or from practising or manifesting their beliefs, the right to freely manifest one's religion is not engaged at all. As van Dijk and van Hoof write, 'freedom to manifest one's religion or belief does not in general imply a right to be exempted from criticism or ridicule by others, because these actions cannot generally be regarded as an interference with this freedom'.[2] Temperman expresses this as follows: 'criticism, ridicule, or insult of a religion or belief does not necessarily affect a person's freedom to have or adopt a religion or belief or

---

1 Kapai, P. and Cheung, A., 'Hanging in the Balance: Freedom of Expression and Religion', 15 *Buffalo Human Rights Law Review* (2009) 52.
2 Dijk, P. van and Hoof, F. van, *Theory and Practice of the European Convention on Human Rights* (London, Kluwer Law International, 1998) 551.

to freely exercise the religion or belief in question'. He submits that the onus is on the state to clearly establish that fully granting freedom of expression 'actually impedes or jeopardises the freedom of religion or belief of others' and that 'the sole reference to the likelihood of a group of religious believers being insulted' is not enough.[3] Temperman concludes that 'there is no abstract "clash" between freedom of expression and freedom of religion or belief', and, that the portrayal of these rights 'as being somehow perpetually at odds, as inevitably "clashing" whenever being implemented is a flawed and hazardous one'.[4]

Bielefeldt *et al.* write, under the heading 'antagonistic misconstructions', that the antagonism between the two rights

> Often rests on the false assumption that freedom of religion or belief abstractly promotes 'the cause of religion'. It is assumed that as soon as some religious interest comes into play, this could per se become a case for religious freedom. On a closer look, however, this is more than questionable.[5]

These authors continue that 'even some judgments of the European Court of Human Rights have nourished antagonistic perceptions of those two rights' and they discuss and criticise *Otto-Preminger-Institut v Austria*.[6] Leigh makes a similar argument in relation to the case law of the European Court of Human Rights where he writes:

> A fallacy lies at the heart of the ECtHR's anti-religious speech jurisprudence: that cases of this kind involve clashes between freedom of expression and religious liberty. For the most part, however, the religious offence caused by such attacks does not prevent or deter anyone from believing as they choose, or practising or manifesting their belief. The Strasbourg's Court's tendency to expand the scope of Article 9 by reference to illusory rights to 'respect' or 'peaceful enjoyment' of freedom of religion risks unbalancing the Convention scheme and reading-in a right not to be offended where none is present. When freedom of religion is properly understood, it is confined to tangible harm to specific victims. It follows that there is generally no clash between it and freedom of expression in most religious offence cases.[7]

---

3 Temperman, J., 'Blasphemy, Defamation of Religions and Human Rights Law', 26 (4) *Netherlands Quarterly of Human Rights* (2008) 527. See also: Temperman, J., 'Protection against Religious Hatred under the United Nations ICCPR and the European Convention System' in Ferrari, S. and Cristofori, R. (eds) *Law and Religion in the 21st Century* (Farnham, Ashgate Publishing, 2010) 222.

4 Temperman (2008), supra note 3, 544.

5 Bielefeldt, H., Ghanea, N. and Wiener, M., *Freedom of Religion or Belief An International Law Commentary* (Oxford, Oxford University Press, 2016) 492–493.

6 Ibid. 493. *Otto-Preminger-Institut v Austria*, Application No. 13470/87, 20 September 1994.

7 Leigh, I., 'Damned if They Do, Damned if They Don't: the European Court of Human Rights and the Protection of Religion from Attack', 17 (1) *Res Publica* (2011) 72.

Letsas also writes that if there is no right not to be insulted in one's religious beliefs, 'then there is no conflict with other rights, like free speech'.[8] And, Cram puts it thus: 'it is difficult to see how, outside of wholly exceptional circumstances, public insults and criticisms of religious belief and practices by others might engage Article 9 by effectively restraining believers' freedom of religion, or the public/private manifestation of religious belief'.[9]

All the above supports the argument that freedom of expression can only be limited if it prevents or deters an individual or group from exercising their freedom to manifest their religion or when there is tangible harm to a specific victim. Religious hate speech or speech against religion or religious believers could do both, but only if an expression deters someone from actually exercising their right to freedom of religion is there a clash between the two rights.

This raises the question: when does an expression actually interfere with the free manifestation of religion? Fenwick and Phillipson give as example a situation where a person bursts into a religious service and disrupts it by heckling and obscenities.[10] Benesch writes that 'if a non-believer flagrantly violates a basic tenet of a religion inside one of its houses of worship that could indeed interfere with freedom to worship' and gives two examples from Hitchins: the slaughtering of a pig in a synagogue or mosque or relieving oneself on a holy book.[11] Benesch continues:

> When the violation or mocking takes place, instead, in the public sphere, or in the pages of a magazine which the devout need not read, it is much less clear that their freedom of religion is compromised, and not their legally unprotected feelings or sense of dignity.[12]

In Chapter 1, it was discussed that the European Court of Human Rights, in the cases of *Otto-Preminger-Institut v Austria*,[13] and *I.A. v Turkey*,[14] appeared to accept, albeit in neither case unanimously, that a right to protection of one's religious feelings, a right not to be offended in one's religious belief is present in

---

8 Letsas, G., 'Is there a Right Not to be Offended in One's Religious Beliefs?' in Zucca, L. and Ungureanu, C. (eds) *Law, State and Religion in the New Europe* (Cambridge, Cambridge University Press, 2012) 239–260, available at SSRN: http://ssrn.com/abstract=1500291, 9.

9 Cram, I., 'The Danish Cartoons, Offensive Expression and Democratic Legitimacy', in Hare, I. and Weinstein, J. (eds) *Extreme Speech and Democracy* (Oxford, Oxford University Press, 2010) 319–320. In a footnote, Cram explains that by 'others' he means private individuals.

10 Fenwick, H. and Phillipson, G., *Media Freedom under the Human Rights Act* (Oxford, Oxford University Press, 2006) 501.

11 Benesch, S., 'Charlie the Freethinker: Religion, Blasphemy and Decent Controversy', 10 *Religion and Human Rights* (2015) 251. The reference to Hitchens is: Hitchens, C., 'Cartoon Debate: The Case for Mocking Religion', *Slate*, 4 February 2006, www.slate.com/articles/news_and_politics/fighting_words/2006/02/cartoon_debate.html

12 Benesch, supra note 11, 251.

13 *Otto-Preminger-Institut v Austria*, supra note 6.

14 *I.A. v Turkey*, Application No. 42571/98, 13 September 2005.

article 9 ECHR, although later cases seem to contradict this. In *Otto-Preminger-Institut v Austria*, a film that depicted the figures of Christ, God and Mary in a disparaging way had been seized and banned. The Court did not find a violation of article 10. It accepted that the purpose of the measures taken by Austria in this case, which was 'to protect the right of citizens not to be insulted in their religious feelings by the public expression of views of other persons', served the legitimate aim of the protection of the rights of others.[15] The Court did point out that 'in extreme cases the effect of particular methods of opposing or denying religious beliefs can be such as to inhibit those who hold such beliefs from exercising their freedom to hold and express them',[16] but it did not state whether this was so in this case. Looking at the facts, the religious people in this case (the Roman Catholic population of the region of Tyrol) were unlikely to be inhibited from manifesting their religion by the showing of the film. The three dissenting judges expressed the same opinion. They stated that the seizure and ban had been a violation of article 10 and considered that:

> The need for repressive action amounting to complete prevention of the exercise of freedom of expression can only be accepted if the behaviour concerned reaches so high a level of abuse, and comes so close to a denial of the freedom of religion of others, as to forfeit for itself the right to be tolerated by society.[17]

The dissenters considered that 'the film was to have been shown to a paying audience in an "art cinema" which catered for a relatively small public with a taste for experimental films. It is therefore unlikely that the audience would have included persons not specifically interested in the film'. Moreover, the applicant association had provided sufficient information and thus the audience had 'sufficient opportunity of being warned beforehand about the nature of the film'. There was, therefore, 'little likelihood in the instant case of anyone being confronted with objectionable material unwittingly'.[18] As Edge points out about this case, 'the material had to be sought out'.[19] In other words, anyone who thought they may be offended by the film could avoid this offence by not going to see it. O'Reilly refers to Feinberg and his concept of 'reasonable avoidability' in this context.[20] The dissenters also considered that the film was restricted by law to

---

15 *Otto-Preminger-Institut v Austria*, supra note 13, para 48.
16 Ibid. para 47.
17 Ibid. dissenting opinion, para 7.
18 Ibid. para 9.
19 Edge, P., 'The European Court of Human Rights and Religious Rights', 47 (3) *International and Comparative Law Quarterly* (1998) 682.
20 O'Reilly, A., 'In Defence of Offence: Freedom of Expression, Offensive Speech, and the Approach of the European Court of Human Rights', 19 *Trinity College Law Review* (2016), 253, referring to Feinberg, J., *The Moral Limits of the Criminal Law: Volume 2 Offense to Others* (Oxford, Oxford University Press, 1988) 48.

anyone over 17 years, and the announcement by the applicant association carried a notice to that effect. The dissenters therefore concluded 'that the applicant association acted responsibly in such a way as to limit, as far as it could reasonably have been expected to, the possible harmful effects of showing the film' and thus that the seizure and ban were not proportionate to the legitimate aim pursued.[21]

Fenwick and Phillipson comment on this case and express the opinion that:

> The right to religious freedom is violated if one is not free to choose, express or manifest one's religious beliefs: the right is not violated simply because one is not protected from mental suffering caused by verbal attacks upon one's religion or offensive portrayals of it.[22]

The majority judgment is also criticised by van Dijk and van Hoof, who write that the decision 'is mistaken. The screening of the film in no way would have limited or inhibited Roman Catholics in manifesting their religion and therefore did not restrict their rights under Article 9.'[23] And Temperman submits that 'it was very unlikely . . . that the screening of this film would have affected anyone's right freely to have or to adopt a religion or belief or freely practice that belief'.[24]

There is also some support in the case law of the European Court of Human Rights for the argument that freedom of expression can only be limited if it prevents or deters anyone from exercising their freedom to hold or manifest their religion or when there is tangible harm to a specific victim. The opinion of the three dissenting judges in *Otto-Preminger-Institut v Austria*[25] has been discussed already. In *Féret v Belgium*, there were also three dissenting judges and they argued that combating mere intolerance was not, in their view, sufficient to justify infringing the freedom of expression and that real, and not potential, impact on the rights of others needed to be demonstrated.[26] From the opinion, it is not clear whether they meant real impact on the right to freedom of religion or to freely manifest one's religion. These were dissenting opinions but there are also some (majority) judgments to support the argument here.

In *Klein v Slovakia*, a journalist had written an article in which he attacked an archbishop for suggesting that a film should be banned.[27] The European Court of Human Rights unanimously held that the conviction violated article 10 ECHR as it accepted that 'the article neither unduly interfered with the right of believers to express and exercise their religion, nor did it denigrate the content of their religious faith'.[28] And, in *Öllinger v Austria*, the Court appeared to limit the duty

---

21 Ibid. para 11.
22 Fenwick, and Phillipson, supra note 10, 505.
23 Van Dijk and Van Hoof, supra note 2, 551.
24 Temperman in Ferrari and Cristofori, supra note 3, 216–217.
25 *Otto-Preminger-Institut v Austria*, supra note 6, dissenting opinion.
26 *Féret v Belgium*, Application No. 15615/07, 16 July 2009, dissenting opinion.
27 *Klein v Slovakia*, Application No. 72208/01, 31 October 2006, para 51.
28 Ibid. para 52.

of the state to ensure the peaceful enjoyment of the right guaranteed in article 9 as formulated in the judgment in *Otto-Preminger-Institut v Austria*[29] to instances 'where religious beliefs are opposed or denied in a manner which inhibits those who hold such beliefs from exercising their freedom to hold or express them'.[30]

All this suggests that expressions that interfere with a person's right under article 9 ECHR could fall outside the protection of article 10, subject to the three part justification test in article 10(2). Therefore, if the interference is prescribed by law and the means used are proportionate, the right to freedom of expression could be limited to achieve the legitimate aim of the protection of the right of others to hold or manifest their beliefs. And, only when an expression interferes with a person's right to hold or to practice or to manifest a religion can it be said that there is a clash between the two ECHR rights. It is submitted, based on the above, that there was no clash of rights in *Otto-Preminger-Institut v Austria*, although the European Court of Human Rights did see this case as one of conflicting rights.[31] How the rare cases where there is a conflict between different rights are resolved is examined in the next part.

Dealing with situations of conflict between two fundamental rights

How does the European Court of Human Rights deal with situations where two ECHR rights are in conflict with each other? In a compilation of standards relating to freedom of religion, the Council of Europe writes:

> The Convention protects all these rights equally. . . . Although these rights are complementary, they may at times involve conflicting interests as a result of being exercised. In such situations the State will need to weight the competing rights against one another in order to strike a fair balance between them. The proper balancing of these rights in accordance with the principle of proportionality is subject to the Court's supervision.[32]

Tulkens, a former judge of the European Court of Human Rights, writes that where provisions of the same instrument, like the ECHR, contradict each other, as articles 9 and 10 sometimes do, 'the principle of proportionality is irrelevant' and the Court uses the approach of a balancing of interests to check whether the state has struck the right balance between the conflicting rights.[33] This appears to

---

29 *Otto-Preminger-Institut v Austria*, supra note 6, para 47. See on this also Chapter 1.

30 *Öllinger v Austria*, Application No. 76900/01, 29 June 2006, para 39.

31 *Otto-Preminger-Institut v Austria*, supra note 6, para 55.

32 Council of Europe, *Compilation of Council of Europe Standards Relating to the Principles of Freedom of Thought, Conscience and Religion and Links to other Human Rights* (Strasbourg, Council of Europe, 2015) 23.

33 Tulkens, F., 'Conflicts between Fundamental Rights: Contrasting Views on Articles 9 and 10 of the European Convention on Human Rights', in Venice Commission, *Blasphemy,*

follow what the European Court of Human Rights held in *Chauvy v France*, that, 'in the exercise of its European supervisory duties, the Court must verify whether the authorities struck a fair balance when protecting two values guaranteed by the Convention which may come into conflict with each other'.[34]

Tulkens' statement that 'the principle of proportionality is irrelevant' appears to contradict the Council of Europe Standards that the proper balancing of the conflicting rights should be done in accordance with the principle of proportionality. But it is submitted that this contradiction is more apparent than real. Tulkens explains that when there is a clash between two ECHR rights, 'we are no longer dealing with a freedom and the exceptions to it, but with an interpretative dialectic that must reconcile freedoms'.[35] Therefore, she suggests that proportionality applies when a restriction on a fundamental right is assessed, while a balancing of interests test applies when there are two ECHR rights involved. But is the proportionality test not also a 'balancing of interests' test? The proportionality test in articles 9(2) and 10(2) ECHR suggests that all interests at stake must be considered and balanced against each other: a fair balance needs to be struck between the rights of the individual and the interests of the state and the rights of others in restricting these rights. As Fenwick and Phillipson explain 'a key concern of proportionality is often the balancing of the seriousness of the interference with the right against the importance of the aim pursued'.[36] Evans writes that 'by proportionality measures the Court means measures taken by authorities that strike a fair balance between the interests of the community and the interests of the individual'.[37] It is argued here that, when the aim of the restriction on one person's fundamental right is for the protection of another person's fundamental right, this falls under the legitimate aim (in both articles 9(2) and 10(2)) of the protection of the rights of others. And, in the balancing that needs to be done under those paragraphs, the interests of both people exercising their respective rights must be taken into account and balanced against each other and against the interests of the community. Therefore, the tests are similar and, in all cases, all the interests involved must be taken into account and balanced against each other. A good example of this fair balancing under the proportionality test in article 10(2) ECHR can be found in *Tierbefreier EV v Germany*, where the European Court of Human Rights stated that:

> Having regard to the foregoing considerations and, in particular, to the careful examination of the case by the domestic courts, which fully acknowledged the impact of the right to freedom of expression in a debate on matters of

Insult and Hatred: Finding Answers in a Democratic Society, (Strasbourg, Council of Europe, Science and Technique of Democracy No. 47) 125 www.venice.coe.int/webforms/documents/?pdf=CDL-STD(2010)047-e

34 *Chauvy v France*, Application No. 64915/01, 29 June 2004, para 70.

35 Ibid.

36 Fenwick and Phillipson, supra note 10, 86.

37 Evans, M., *Manual on the Wearing of Religious Symbols in Public Areas* (Strasbourg, Council of Europe, 2009) 125.

public interest, the Court considers that the domestic courts struck a fair balance between the applicant association's right to freedom of expression and the C. company's interests in protecting its reputation. There has accordingly been no violation of Article 10 of the Convention taken separately.[38]

The case law of the European Court of Human Rights also shows that a balancing of interests is required in cases where there are two possibly conflicting Convention rights. In *Karaahmed v Bulgaria*, where the freedom of religion clashed with the freedom of assembly under article 11 ECHR, the Court explained that the two rights must 'be balanced against each other in a manner which recognises the importance of these rights in a society based on pluralism, tolerance and broadmindedness'.[39] And, in *Chassagnou and Others v France*, the Court held that:

> In the present case the only aim invoked by the Government to justify the interference complained of was 'protection of the rights and freedoms of others'. Where these 'rights and freedoms' are themselves among those guaranteed by the Convention or its Protocols, it must be accepted that the need to protect them may lead States to restrict other rights or freedoms likewise set forth in the Convention. It is precisely this constant search for a balance between the fundamental rights of each individual which constitutes the foundation of a 'democratic society'. The balancing of individual interests that may well be contradictory is a difficult matter, and Contracting States must have a broad margin of appreciation in this respect, since the national authorities are in principle better placed than the European Court to assess whether or not there is a 'pressing social need' capable of justifying interference with one of the rights guaranteed by the Convention.[40]

This case also suggests that the margin of appreciation afforded to the states in cases of conflict is wide. Support for this can be found in other case law. For example, in *Axel Springer AG v Germany*, there was a clash between the rights in articles 8 and 10 ECHR. The European Court of Human Rights stated that:

> Where the balancing exercise between those two rights has been undertaken by the national authorities in conformity with the criteria laid down in the Court's case-law, the Court would require strong reasons to substitute its view for that of the domestic courts.[41]

---

38 *Tierbefreier E.V. v Germany*, Application No. 45192/09, 16 January 2014, paras 59–60.
39 *Karaahmed v Bulgaria*, Application No. 30587/13, 24 February 2015, para 92.
40 *Chassagnou and Others v France*, Application Nos 25088/94, 28331/95 and 28443/95, 29 April 1999, para 113.
41 *Axel Springer v Germany*, Application No. 39954/08, 7 February 2012, para 88; this was repeated in *Annen v Germany*, Application No. 3690/10, 26 November 2015.

And, in *Eweida and Others v the United Kingdom*, it was stated that 'the Court generally allows the national authorities a wide margin of appreciation when it comes to striking a balance between competing Convention rights'.[42]

Therefore, a balancing in which the competing rights are weighed is needed at domestic level, with the European Court of Human Rights assessing whether a fair balance has indeed been struck but leaving a broad margin of appreciation to the states. Grimm makes an important point where he writes that 'it is not sufficient to consider only the detrimental effects speech may have on other equally important rights. The detrimental effects limitations of speech might have on democratic discourse must also be considered'.[43] This again shows the need for a balancing of all interests involved.

In relation to the proportionality test, the European Court of Human Rights takes a number of factors into account to assess whether the balance is struck fairly.[44] These include the extent of the interference with the right or freedom: does the restriction actually extinguish the right completely or does it leave some scope for its exercise? In other words, does it impair the very essence of the right? For example, in *Jacubowski v Germany*, the Court held that the interference with Mr Jacubowski's right to freedom of expression was not disproportionate because he 'retained the right to voice his opinions and to defend himself by any other means'.[45] In *Kovalkovs v Latvia*,[46] a prisoner claimed that the prison authorities had violated his article 9 right as he was not able to read religious literature or meditate and pray because he had been placed in a cell with other prisoners. The Court considered that 'what needs to be balanced is the degree of the interference with the applicant's right to manifest his religion on the one hand and the rights of other prisoners on the other hand'. It continued that 'the interference with the applicant's right is not such as to completely prevent him from manifesting his religion'. The Court considered that 'having to pray, read religious literature and to meditate in the presence of others is an inconvenience, which is almost inescapable in prisons . . . yet which does not go against the very essence of the freedom to manifest one's religion'. The Court then concluded that 'the balance between the legitimate aims sought to be achieved and the minor interference with the applicant's freedom to manifest his religion has clearly been achieved'.[47]

Another issue that is taken into account is the question whether the concern can be addressed in another, less restrictive way. For example, in *Campbell v the United Kingdom*, the applicant, a prisoner, complained that the prison authorities

---

42 *Eweida and Others v the United Kingdom*, Application Nos 48420/10, 59842/10, 51671/10 and 36516/10, 15 January 2013, para 106. See also: *Evans v the United Kingdom*, Application No. 6339/05, 10 April 2007, para 77.

43 Grimm, D., 'Freedom of Speech in a Globalized World', in Hare, I. and Weinstein, J. (eds) *Extreme Speech and Democracy* (Oxford, Oxford University Press, 2009) 13.

44 See on this: Lisbon Network, Council of Europe, *The Margin of Appreciation*, 3, www.coe.int/t/dghl/cooperation/lisbonnetwork/themis/echr/paper2_en.asp

45 *Jacubowksi v Germany*, Application No. 15088/89, 23 June 1994, para 29.

46 *Kovalkovs v Latvia*, Application No. 35021/05, 31 January 2012.

47 All ibid. para 67.

opened and read all correspondence between prisoners and their lawyers and that this was an interference with his right under article 8 ECHR. The prison service brought forward as justification that this was necessary to check whether the correspondence contained illicit disclosures. The Court rejected this and suggested an alternative, less restrictive way of dealing with the issue of illicit enclosures: opening but not reading the correspondence.[48]

There is no reason why these factors should not be applied to the balancing of interests required when two fundamental rights clash. The questions should then be applied to both the rights at stake. The first question would then be: does the restriction of the one right extinguish this right completely, or does not restricting the one right extinguish the other right completely? In *Delfi AG v Estonia*, the Court stated:

> Bearing in mind the need to protect the values underlying the Convention, and considering that the rights under Article 10 and 8 of the Convention deserve equal respect, a balance must be struck that retains the essence of both rights.[49]

The second question, whether the concern can be addressed in another, less restrictive way, would take account of the restriction on both the rights involved.

This can be illustrated by using the *Otto-Preminger-Institut v Austria*[50] case, which the Court saw, erroneously as was argued above, as a clash between freedom of expression and freedom of religion. Did the ban on the film extinguish the right to freedom of expression of the film association? Yes, it did, as they were not allowed to show the film at all and thus the very essence of the right was impaired. Moreover, would the right to freedom of religion of the Catholic population of Tyrol have been impaired by not restricting the film? This is highly unlikely as they could still fully and freely hold and manifest their religion. Less restrictive ways were available that would have limited the restriction on the freedom of expression while not restricting the freedom of religion: Austria did impose a minimum age requirement that stopped people under 17 from seeing the film. Austria could also have imposed clear requirements about advertising and describing the film. In fact, the dissenters held that the film association had done enough in this area.

Another principle from the case law of the European Court of Human Rights is important here. In *Karaahmed v Bulgaria*, the Court stated that, 'at the heart of this case is the exercise of two sets of competing fundamental rights. . . . The Convention does not establish any *a priori* hierarchy between these rights: as a matter of principle, they deserve equal respect'.[51] So there is no hierarchy of

---

48 See on this: *Campbell v the United Kingdom*, Application No. 13590/88, 25 March 1992, para 48. See also: Howard, E., 'Reasonable Accommodation of Religion and other Discrimination Grounds in EU law' 38 (3) *European Law Review* (2013) 360–375 and the cases referred to there.

49 *Delfi AS v Estonia*, Application No. 64569/09, 16 June 2015, para 110.

50 *Otto-Preminger-Institut v Austria*, supra note 6.

51 *Karaahmed v Bulgaria*, supra note 39, para 92. See also the Council of Europe Standards quote above that 'the Convention protects all rights equally', supra note 32, 23.

fundamental rights with one right being given more weight and thus trumping the other. Evans discusses the intersection of the right to freedom of religion or belief and the right to freedom of expression and argues that:

> It is both artificial and unhelpful to juxtapose them in an oppositional fashion or seek to determine a hierarchy of significance between them. Rather, it is necessary to identify the important contribution of both rights to the functioning of a tolerant, plural and democratic society and seek to ensure there is a maximising of both rights in situations of tension, rather than a relativising of the one in the interests of the other.[52]

And Boyle expresses the same where he writes that 'a human rights approach requires all – believers and non-believers – to seek harmony between these freedoms in practice, not one that *a priori* privileges one over the other, whether it is freedom of expression or freedom of religion'.[53]

Therefore, in situations of apparently competing rights, all interests involved need to be balanced against each other and this analysis is not a 'zero sum' game, in which a gain for one side in a conflict necessarily entails a corresponding loss for the other; rather, it is one in which compromise may be required from both sides and attempts should be made to give both rights as much room as possible with neither right being inappropriately sacrificed.[54]

Another issue needs to be highlighted. As Brems writes about conflicting human rights:

> Although both human rights are equally fundamental and *a priori* carry equal weight, they do not come before the judge in an equal manner. The right that is invoked by the applicant receives most attention, because the question to be answered by the judge is whether or not this right was violated. The arguments of the defendant may advance the theory that granting the applicant's claim would violate an additional human right. Through these arguments, the protection of that secondary right may find its way to the judge's reasoning, but it is not among the legal questions to be directly addressed.[55]

---

52 Evans, M., (2009) 'The Freedom of Religion or Belief and the Freedom of Expression', 4 (2–3) *Religion & Human Rights* (2009) 233.

53 Boyle, K., 'The Danish Cartoons', 24 (2) *Netherlands Quarterly of Human Rights* (2006) 188.

54 See also on this: Donald, A. and Howard, E., *The Right to Freedom of Religion or Belief and its Intersection with Other Rights* (A Research Paper for ILGA-Europe, January 2015) 7–9 (on the clash between freedom of religion and freedom of expression) and 16–19 (on the principles derived from the case law to assist in solving cases where the right to freedom of religion or belief appears to be in conflict with other rights): www.ilga-europe.org/sites/default/files/Attachments/the_right_to_freedom_of_religion_or_belief_and_its_intersection_with_other_rights__0.pdf

55 Brems, E., 'Conflicting Human Rights: An Exploration in the Context of the Right to a Fair Trial in the European Convention for the Protection of Human Rights and Fundamental Freedoms', 27 *Human Rights Quarterly* (2005) 305.

Tulkens concludes from what Brems writes that 'the test of necessity would tend to lean in favour of the applicant's right . . . this leads implicitly to establishing a presumption in favour of the right of the applicant'.[56] However, in *Axel Springer AG v Germany*, it was stated that:

> In cases such as the present one the Court considers that the outcome of the application should not, in principle, vary according to whether it has been lodged with the Court under Article 10 of the Convention by the publisher who has published the offending article or under Article 8 of the Convention by the person who was the subject of that article. Indeed, as a matter of principle these rights deserve equal respect. Accordingly, the margin of appreciation should in principle be the same in both cases.[57]

It is not clear whether this contradicts the quotes from Brems and Tulkens, because the Court seems to suggest that this applies to the application of the margin of appreciation. If this is the correct reading, then the point made by Brems and Tulkens is an important and valid point.

Tulkens also points out three particular difficulties with the balancing of interests test.[58] The first is the 'incommensurability of rights': balancing 'presupposes the existence of a common scale against which the respective importance or the weight of different rights could be measured, which is highly unrealistic'. The second difficulty is 'that of subjectivity. By using the metaphor of the balance, in fact one leaves the court great freedom of judgment and this can have formidable effects on judicial reasoning'. These two issues overlap: there is no objective scale that says which interest should be given more weight and, thus, the weight given to each interest to be balanced could be influenced by the Court's subjective view of which interests deserve to be protected more. And, also related to the first two points, the third difficulty described by Tulkens is 'that the parties are not in symmetrical positions and so the importance attributed to each of their rights may depend on their relative positions'. Tulkens uses the judgment of *Otto-Preminger-Institute v Austria*[59] to illustrate this. As she writes: 'whereas it was a private association that invoked freedom of expression, the freedom of religion was that of all persons of the Catholic faith who might feel offended by the images of the film.' So, Tulkens continues:

> The possibility cannot be ruled out that the balance of rights was influenced, more or less consciously, by the impression that an individual's freedom of expression had to be measured against the interests of all Catholics in the Austrian Province of Tyrol.

---

56 Tulkens, supra note 33, 124–125.
57 *Axel Springer AG v Germany*, supra note 41, para 87. See also: *Bédat v Switzerland*, Application No. 56925/08, 29 March 2016, para 52.
58 Tulkens, supra note 33, 125–127.
59 *Otto-Preminger-Institut v Austria*, supra note 6.

In other words, the rights might not be compared on the same plane.[60] It is submitted that it is important that the European Court of Human Rights is aware of these issues. The last one can be especially problematic, because it can unconsciously play a role and because it could mean that the majority view in a society would be given more weight, while it is often the minority views and interests that are most in need of protection by human rights law.

O'Reilly appears to give a similar warning, although she mentions this in relation to the European Court of Human Rights allowing a wide margin of appreciation when it concerns religious offensive speech.[61] She criticises the decisions of the Court in *Otto-Preminger-Institut v Austria*,[62] *Wingrove v the United Kingdom*[63] and *I.A. v Turkey*[64] because they give a wide margin of appreciation to the national authorities and this 'may permit censorship of unpopular minority views and insulate orthodoxies from critical scrutiny. It will generally result in the majority religion being significantly favoured' and 'will disproportionately impact minority religionists and non-believers, whose expressions may not accord with majority religious values'.[65] But maybe the Court is already aware of this, as it has emphasised that:

> The mere fact that the Evangelical Christian religion was practised by a minority of the town residents was not capable of justifying an interference with the rights of followers of that religion. It would be incompatible with the underlying values of the Convention if the exercise of Convention rights by a minority group were made conditional on its being accepted by the majority. Were it so a minority group's rights to freedom of religion, expression and assembly would become merely theoretical rather than practical and effective as required by the Convention.[66]

A last point that needs to be made in this part is that the assessment of the legitimacy of any restriction to the fundamental rights under the proportionality test and the balancing of interests test is very much dependent on the particular circumstances of each case. This means that the analysis is highly context-specific, as the European Court of Human Rights itself pointed out in *Perinçek v Switzerland*.[67] Evans writes that, because of the doctrine of the margin of appreciation,

> different responses to similar situations will be acceptable within the Convention framework, providing that they properly reflect a balancing up on the particular issues in the contexts in which they emerge. This means that the

60 Tulkens, supra note 33, 125–126.
61 O'Reilly, supra note 20, 249–254.
62 *Otto-Preminger-Institut v Austria*, supra note 6.
63 *Wingrove v the United Kingdom*, Application No. 17419/90, 25 November 1996.
64 *I.A. v Turkey*, Application No. 42571/98, 13 September 2005.
65 O'Reilly, supra note 20, 249–250.
66 *Barankevich v Russia*, Application No. 10519/03, 26 July 2007, para 31.
67 *Perinçek v Switzerland*, Application No. 27510/08, 15 October 2015, para 208.

decisions of the Court in relation to Article 9(2) must be treated with extreme caution: for example, just because a restriction on the wearing of a religious symbol has been upheld in one case does not mean that a similar restriction will be upheld in another, where the context may be very different.[68]

This means that it is not possible to make abstract and general determinations about the outcome of cases based on previous judgments of the Court.

The right not to be discriminated against

In relation to freedom of expression and religious hate speech, the subject of this book, another right that could possibly clash with the freedom of expression and the freedom of religion is the right to non-discrimination as guaranteed by article 14 ECHR. Freedom of expression can come into possible conflict with the right not to be discriminated against if, for example, the speaker or author of the expression discriminates against, or calls up others to discriminate against, people with or without a certain religion or belief. But these rights might also clash where a religious person expresses hate or calls for discriminatory treatment of people of other religions or beliefs, of women or of lesbian, gay, bisexual, transsexual or intersex people. Boyle, writing about freedom of speech and freedom from discrimination, asks the important question: 'what should a democratic society do when some groups seek to use their freedom of expression to advocate the denial of equality, discrimination, and exclusion of others?'[69] Whether the freedom of expression in such cases should be restricted by the state will be examined in subsequent chapters. Here the right not to be discriminated against as guaranteed by the ECHR will be analysed.

Article 14 ECHR reads:

> The enjoyment of the rights and freedoms set forth in this Convention shall be secured without discrimination on any ground such as sex, race, colour, language, religion, political or other opinion, national or social origin, association with a national minority, property, birth or other status.

This article contains an extensive list of discrimination grounds, which includes religion. Moreover, the words 'any ground such as' and 'or other status' indicate that this is an open-ended and non-exhaustive list and, therefore, the European Court of Human Rights can extend the list of grounds covered. The Court has called the list 'illustrative and not exhaustive'[70] and has, for example, held that discrimination on the ground of sexual orientation is covered.[71]

---

68 Evans, supra note 37, 21.
69 Boyle, K., 'Hate Speech: The United States versus the Rest of the World', 53 *Maine Law Review* (2001) 491.
70 *Engel and Others v The Netherlands*, Application Nos 5100/71, 5101/71, 5102/71, 5354/72 and 5370/72, 8 June 1976, para 72.
71 *Salgueiro da Silva Mouta v Portugal*, Application No. 33290/96, 21 December 1999, para 29.

The importance of the right to non-discrimination or equality should not be underestimated. Grimm points out that 'equality and dignity of human beings regardless of their gender, race, religion, and similar classifications are themselves democratic values'.[72] Moreover, if an individual is not equal, does not have access to fundamental rights on an equal basis and without discrimination, then a right or freedom is not much use to that individual. As Bielefeldt *et al.* write, 'without taking account of equality the rights of freedom would amount to privileges of the happy few'.[73] Article 2(2) of the UN Declaration on the Elimination of All Forms of Intolerance and of Discrimination Based on Religion or Belief clearly links equality and fundamental rights in this way as well.[74] It states that:

> For the purposes of the present Declaration, the expression 'intolerance and discrimination based on religion or belief' means any distinction, exclusion, restriction or preference based on religion or belief and having as its purpose or as its effect nullification or impairment of the recognition, enjoyment or exercise of human rights and fundamental freedoms on an equal basis.

However, article 14 ECHR only secures 'the enjoyment of the rights and freedoms set forth in this Convention' without discrimination. This means that discrimination can only be challenged in conjunction with other rights and a victim of discrimination cannot claim a violation of article 14 alone. For example, if Muslim employees are not allowed to take time off work to attend the mosque, but Jewish employees are allowed to take time off for religious reasons, then the Muslim employees would be discriminated against. But, at the European Court of Human Rights, they cannot simply claim a violation of article 14 because of religious discrimination, they have to claim a violation of article 14 in conjunction with, in this case, article 9. The right to non-discrimination is therefore said to be accessory and article 14 does not guarantee a freestanding right to discrimination.

In 2000, the Council of Europe adopted Protocol 12 to the ECHR to overcome this problem. Article 1(1) of this Protocol declares: 'The enjoyment of any right set forth by law shall be secured without discrimination on any grounds such as. . .' and then it mentions the same grounds as article 14 ECHR. This thus establishes a general, freestanding prohibition of discrimination that can be invoked without any other substantive provision of the ECHR. The Preamble of the Protocol refers to 'the fundamental principle according to which all persons are equal before the law and are entitled to equal protection of the law'. The Protocol came into force in 2005, but only 19 out of the 47 Council of Europe states have signed and ratified it.[75] For those countries that have not

72 Grimm, supra note 43, 13.
73 Bielefeldt *et al.*, supra note 5, 311.
74 *Declaration on the Elimination of All Forms of Intolerance and of Discrimination Based on Religion or Belief*, A/RES/36/55, 25 November 1981.
75 Protocol No. 12 of the ECHR, CETS No. 177, Status of Ratifications, http://conventions. coe.int/Treaty/Commun/ChercheSig.asp?NT=177&CM=1&DF=19/02/2011&CL=ENG

ratified Protocol 12, the main anti-discrimination provision to invoke before the European Court of Human Rights is thus article 14. The Court has held that Protocol 12 should be interpreted in the same way as article 14.[76] In *Savez crkava "Riječ života" and Others v Croatia*, the Court found a violation of article 14 in conjunction with article 9 and then held that it was 'not necessary to examine separately whether, in this case, there has also been a violation of Article 1 of Protocol No. 12 to the Convention'.[77]

The European Court of Human Rights has not very often made a decision on article 14 ECHR because it has to be invoked in conjunction with another article or articles and, if the Court has decided that there is a violation of the other article(s), it will usually find it unnecessary to consider whether there was also a breach of article 14. In *Dudgeon v the United Kingdom*, the Court held that:

> Where a substantive Article of the Convention has been invoked both on its own and together with Article 14 (art. 14) and a separate breach has been found of the substantive Article, it is not generally necessary for the Court also to examine the case under Article 14 (art. 14), though the position is otherwise if a clear inequality of treatment in the enjoyment of the right in question is a fundamental aspect of the case.[78]

The European Court of Human Rights has also held that article 14 can be violated even where the substantive article relied upon to invoke article 14 has not been violated.[79] But, despite this, in many cases the Court does not find it necessary to address the complaint under article 14 ECHR.[80] There have also been some recent cases where the articles were dealt with the other way around. For example, In *Church of Jesus Christ of the Latter-Day Saints v the United Kingdom*, the Court held that there had been no violation of article 14 in conjunction with article 9 and that there was no need to examine separately the complaints under article 9.[81] Sometimes, the article 14 claim is addressed but rejected because the discrimination is held to be reasonably and objectively justified on the same grounds on

---

76 *Sejdic and Finci v Bosnia and Herzogovina*, Application Nos 27996/06 and 34836/06, 22 December 2009, para 55.

77 *Savez crkava "Riječ života" and Others v Croatia*, Application No. 7798/08, 9 December 2010, para 115.

78 *Dudgeon v the United Kingdom*, Application No. 7525/76, 22 October 1981, para 67. See also: *Chassagnou and Others v France*, supra note 40, para 89.

79 See, for example, *Case Relating to Certain Aspects of the Laws on the Use of Languages in Education in Belgium v Belgium* Application Nos 1474/62; 1677/62; 1691/62; 1769/63; 1994/63; 2126/64, 23 July 1968, BI para 9. In the following referred to as the *Belgian Linguistics* case.

80 See for a recent example, where the European Court of Human Rights did not find it necessary to address the article 14 complaint see: *Österreichischer Rundfunk v Austria*, Application No. 35841/02, 7 December 2007, para 77.

81 *Church of Jesus Christ of the Latter-Day Saints v the United Kingdom*, Application No. 7552/09, 4 March 2014, paras 38–39. See also: *Vojnity v Hungary*, Application No. 29617/07, 12 February 2013, para 47.

which the claim under the substantive article was held to be justified.[82] However, some authors argue that the Court has recently become more willing to address a claimed violation of article 14 separately.[83] This appears to be confirmed by two cases, *Tierbefreier EV v Germany*, concerning articles 10 and 14 and *İzzettin Doğan and Others v. Turkey*, concerning articles 9 and 14, where the alleged violation of article 14 was addressed separately from the substantive claim.[84]

The above shows that article 14 allows for justification: the European Court of Human Rights has held that the principle of equal treatment is violated if the distinction made has no objective and reasonable justification. To be justified, a difference in treatment must pursue a legitimate aim and there must be a reasonable relationship of proportionality between the means employed and the aim sought to be realised.[85] This test is thus similar to the justification and proportionality test in articles 9(2) and 10(2) ECHR, especially because, here again, 'the Contracting States enjoy a certain margin of appreciation in assessing whether and to what extent differences in otherwise similar situations justify a different treatment'.[86]

The margin of appreciation afforded to the states under article 14 ECHR is linked to whether a discrimination ground is considered to be 'suspect' or not. The European Court of Human Rights will scrutinise differences in treatment on 'suspect' grounds more carefully and it will require very weighty reasons before it finds justification of discrimination on these grounds, while it leaves a wider margin of appreciation in the case of other grounds.[87] According to Rainey *et al.*, this applies to grounds 'where there is recognition that discrimination on such grounds is especially demeaning for those affected'.[88] For the subject of this book, the following 'suspect grounds' are relevant: religion[89] and nationality and race.[90]

A good example to illustrate all the above is *Eweida and Others v the United Kingdom*.[91] Here, three of the four applicants, Eweida, Chaplin and McFarlane, claimed violations of article 9 and article 14 in conjunction with article 9.

82 See, for example, *Evans v the United Kingdom*, supra note 42, para 95.
83 See, for example, Rainey, B., Wicks, E. and Ovey, C., *Jacobs, White and Ovey: The European Convention on Human Rights* (6th edn, Oxford, Oxford University Press, 2014) 572–576; O'Connell, R., 'Cinderella comes to the Ball: Article 14 and the Right to Non-Discrimination in the ECHR', 29 (2) *Legal Studies* (2009) 211–229. Further discussion of this is beyond the subject of this book. For more information, the reader is referred to these authors.
84 *Tierbefreier E.V. v Germany*, supra note 38; and *İzzettin Doğan and Others v. Turkey*, 62649/10, 26 April 2016.
85 *Belgian Linguistics* case, supra note 79, BI para 10.
86 *Willis v the United Kingdom*, Application No.36042/97, 11 June 2002, para 39.
87 For the 'very weighty reasons' test, see, for example, *Schuler-Zgraggen v Switzerland*, Application No. 14518/89, 24 June 1993, para 67; *Van Raalte v the Netherlands*, Application No. 20060/92, 21 February 1997, para 39.
88 Rainey *et al.*, supra note 83, 581.
89 *Vojnity v Hungary*, Application No. 29617/07, 12 February 2013, para 36.
90 Nationality: *Gaygusuz v Austria*, Application No. 17371/90, 16 September 1996, para 42; race: *Timishev v Russia*, Application Nos 55762/00 and 55974/00, 13 December 2005, para 58.
91 *Eweida and Others v the United Kingdom*, supra note 42.

The Court, in relation to Eweida, found a violation of article 9 and did 'not consider it necessary to examine separately the applicant's complaint under article 14 taken in conjunction with article 9'.[92] In relation to Chaplin, the Court did not find a violation of article 9 and then considered that:

> The factors to be weighed in the balance when assessing the proportionality of the measure under article 14 taken in conjunction with Article 9 would be similar, and that there is no basis on which it can find a violation of Article 14 either in this case.[93]

The Court's conclusion on McFarlane's claim was simply that it 'does not consider that the refusal by the domestic courts to uphold Mr McFarlane's complaints gave rise to a violation of Article 9, taken alone or in conjunction with Article 14'.[94]

The fourth applicant, Ladele, only claimed a breach of article 14 in conjunction with article 9. The European Court of Human Rights 'recalls that in its case-law under Article 14 it has held that differences in treatment based on sexual orientation require particularly serious reasons by way of justification'.[95] Sexual orientation is thus a suspect ground. It then explained how to deal with situations where there is a conflict between articles 9 and 14. It considered that 'the consequences for the applicant were serious' but that, on the other hand, 'the local authority's policy aimed to secure the rights of others which are also protected under the Convention' and then it repeated that 'the Court generally allows the national authorities a wide margin of appreciation when it comes to striking a balance between competing Convention rights'. The Court came to the conclusion that the state had not exceeded its margin of appreciation in balancing the applicant's rights to freely manifest her religion with the rights of others not to be discriminated against and thus that there was no violation of article 14 in conjunction with article 9.[96]

What happens if the rights to freedom of expression or religion come into conflict with the right to be free from discrimination? There is no reason to treat these types of situations differently from situations where other fundamental rights clash, so, here too, a balancing of all interests involved needs to be performed and the role of the European Court of Human Rights is to assess whether this balancing has been done fairly, while leaving a wide margin of appreciation to the national authorities. This will be clear from the above and especially from what was said about the case of *Eweida and Others v the United Kingdom*. Sottieaux suggests that the balancing exercise should be informed by other values underlying the Convention, which are, in the case of hate speech, the principles

---

92 Ibid. para 95.
93 Ibid. para 101.
94 Ibid. para 110.
95 Ibid. para 105.
96 Ibid. para 106.

of equality and dignity.[97] This is also confirmed by Grimm where he writes that 'protecting people's personality rights [equality and dignity of all human beings] against offensive speech seems, therefore, to be a democratically legitimate cause for limitations. In the final analysis, everything depends on a fair balance between the rights and interests at stake'.[98]

One last point needs to be made: Grimm, in the quote above, mentions 'the dignity of all human beings'. In *Perinçek v Switzerland*, a Turkish politician was convicted, in Switzerland, for expressing the view that the mass deportations and massacres of Armenians in 1915 and following years did not amount to genocide.[99] The Court held that the dignity of the victims and the dignity and identity of modern day Armenians were protected by article 8 ECHR and thus that it had to measure the extent to which the applicant's statements affected those rights.[100] Therefore, the right to freedom of expression could also clash with the right under article 8 to respect for private and family life, home and correspondence. In this case, as in all cases of clashes between two or more Convention rights, a balancing of all interests involved needs to be performed.

Conclusion

In this Chapter, possible conflicts between the rights to freedom of expression, freedom of religion and freedom from discrimination were examined. It was argued that there is no conflict between the rights to freedom of expression and freedom of religion in cases where a person uses expressions that criticise religions or beliefs or which are offensive to religious believers, unless the expressions prevent or deter any religious believers from believing what they wish, or from manifesting their beliefs. In most instances where someone uses expressions about a religion or belief or about religious believers, this is not the case and then the right to freely manifest one's religion is not engaged at all and thus there is no conflict between these rights.

In the few situations where the rights do clash, the European Court of Human Rights has explained that its role is to verify whether the national authorities struck a fair balance.[101] Therefore, a balancing in which the competing rights are weighed is needed at domestic level, with the Court assessing whether a fair balance has indeed been struck. The Court leaves the states a broad margin of appreciation in deciding cases of conflicting rights.

An important principle derived from the case law of the European Court of Human Rights in cases of conflicting rights was that all rights deserve equal respect and that there is no hierarchy of rights. In situations of apparently competing rights,

---

97 Sottieaux, S., '"Bad Tendencies" in the ECtHR "Hate Speech" Jurisprudence', 7 (1) *European Constitutional Law Review* (2011) 46.
98 Grimm, supra note 43, 13.
99 *Perinçek v Switzerland*, supra note 67.
100 Ibid. para 251.
101 *Chauvy v France*, supra note 34, para 70.

all interests involved need to be balanced against each other. However, the Court has to decide the question whether the right of the applicant has been violated, which might mean that the balancing of interests test might favour the applicant.

Three particular difficulties with the balancing of interest test, all interlinked and overlapping, were highlighted. First, the test presupposes that the importance and weight of each right can be measured in each case, which might not be realistic as there is no common scale to measure this against. Second, the test leaves great freedom to the judges and thus the results could be influenced by the Court's subjective view of which interests deserve to be protected more. And, third, the parties are not in symmetrical positions and so the rights might not be compared on the same plane. The importance attributed to each of the rights may depend on their relative positions, with the view of the majority in society given more weight. It was submitted that it is important that the European Court of Human Rights is aware of these issues.

Another point that was made is that the assessment of the legitimacy of any restriction to the fundamental rights under the proportionality test and the balancing of interests test is very much dependent on the particular circumstances of each case. This means that the analysis is highly context-specific and that it is not possible to make abstract and general determinations about the outcome of cases based on previous judgments of the Court.

The last part of this Chapter analysed the right to freedom from discrimination as laid down in article 14 and article 1, Protocol 12 of the ECHR, as this right can also come into conflict with the rights to freedom of expression and freedom of religion. The difference between article 14 ECHR and article 1, Protocol 12 was explained. Article 14 is an accessory right that cannot be invoked without another, substantive ECHR right, while article 1, Protocol 12 provides a free-standing right to non-discrimination. But, Protocol 12 has only been signed and ratified by 19 out of the 47 member states of the Council of Europe so for most member states the protocol does not apply. However, in the states where it does apply, the case law under article 14 is also applicable to article 1, Protocol 12 as the European Court of Human Rights has held that article 1 must be interpreted in the same way as article 14.[102]

The European Court of Human Rights has held that the principle of equal treatment is violated if the distinction made has no objective and reasonable justification. To be justified, a difference in treatment must pursue a legitimate aim and there must be a reasonable relationship of proportionality between the means employed and the aim sought to be realised.[103] And, here again, 'the Contracting states enjoy a certain margin of appreciation in assessing whether and to what extent differences in otherwise similar situations justify a different treatment'.[104] This justification test is thus quite similar to the justification tests under articles 9(2) and 10(2) ECHR.

---

102 *Sejdic and Finci v Bosnia and Herzogovina*, supra note 76, para 55.
103 *Belgian Linguistics* case, supra note 79, BI para 10.
104 *Willis v the United Kingdom*, supra note 86, para 39.

In situations where the rights to freedom of expression or religion come into conflict with the right to be free from discrimination, the same rules that are used in other situations of conflicts of Convention rights applies and, here too, a balancing of all interests involved needs to be performed and the role of the European Court of Human Rights is to assess whether this balancing has been done fairly, while leaving a wide margin of appreciation to the national authorities.

In the next chapter, a number of concepts will be examined, including hate speech and religious hate speech, the differences between hate speech and blasphemy and the difference between criticising religions or beliefs and offending believers. When an expression becomes hate speech will also be analysed. The arguments for and against the enactment of laws against hate speech or against incitement to hatred will be evaluated together with the question whether such laws are useful and necessary in a democratic society.

3 Religious hate speech and religious hate speech laws

Introduction

In Chapter 2, situations of possible clashes between the rights to freedom of expression, freedom of religion and freedom from discrimination were examined. It was argued that, in cases where a person uses expressions that criticise religions or beliefs or that are offensive to religious believers, there is only a conflict between the rights to freedom of expression and freedom of religion if the expressions prevent or deter any religious believers from believing what they wish, or from manifesting their beliefs. In most instances, this is not the case and then the right to freely manifest one's religion is not engaged at all and thus there is no conflict between these rights.

In exceptional situations where these rights do clash, with each other or with other human rights guaranteed by the ECHR, the European Court of Human Rights has explained that its role is to verify whether the authorities struck a fair balance between the different fundamental rights involved.[1] Therefore, a balancing in which the competing rights are weighed is needed at domestic level, with the European Court of Human Rights assessing whether a fair balance has indeed been struck. The Court leaves the states a wide margin of appreciation in deciding cases of conflicting rights.

The case law of the European Court of Human Rights in cases of conflicting rights also showed that all rights deserve equal respect and that there is no hierarchy of rights. The difficulties with the balancing of interest test were highlighted as was the fact that the assessment of the legitimacy of any restriction to the fundamental rights under the proportionality test and the balancing of interests test is very much dependent on the particular circumstances of each case. This means that the analysis is highly context-specific and that it is not possible to make abstract and general determinations about the outcome of cases based on previous judgments of the Court.

The right to freedom from discrimination as laid down in article 14 and article 1, Protocol 12 of the ECHR was also examined in Chapter 2, because this right can also come into conflict with the rights to freedom of expression and freedom of religion. Article 14 is an accessory right that cannot be invoked without another substantive ECHR right, while Protocol 12 provides a freestanding right

1 *Chauvy v France*, Application No. 64915/01, 29 June 2004, para 70.

to non-discrimination. The European Court of Human Rights has held that the principle of equal treatment is violated if the distinction made has no objective and reasonable justification. To be justified, a difference in treatment must pursue a legitimate aim and there must be a reasonable relationship of proportionality between the means employed and the aim sought to be realised.[2] 'The Contracting States enjoy a certain margin of appreciation in assessing whether and to what extent differences in otherwise similar situations justify a different treatment.'[3] This justification test is thus quite similar to the justification tests under articles 9(2) and 10(2) ECHR.

In situations where the rights to freedom of expression or religion come into conflict with the right to be free from discrimination, the same rule that is employed in other situations of conflicts of Convention rights applies and, here too, a balancing of all interests involved needs to be performed and the role of the European Court of Human Rights is to assess whether this balancing has been done fairly, while leaving a wide margin of appreciation to the national authorities.

In this Chapter, the concepts of hate speech and of religious hate speech are analysed and the question when an expression becomes hate speech will be examined. The differences between hate speech and blasphemy and between insulting religions or beliefs and offending religious believers will be explained. The Chapter will finish with an analysis of the arguments for and against the enactment of hate speech laws, including the question whether such laws are useful and necessary in a democratic society.

Hate speech

What is meant by the term 'hate speech'? Boyle writes that hate speech is also termed 'hate propaganda'. He defines it as speech 'that involves the advocacy of hatred and discrimination against groups on the basis of their race, colour, ethnicity, religious beliefs, sexual orientation, or other status'.[4] According to Leigh, 'there is no generally accepted definition of "incitement to hatred" or "hate speech"',[5] although he refers to the Committee of Ministers of the Council of Europe, which has stated that hate speech covers:

> All forms of expression which spread, incite, promote or justify racial hatred, xenophobia, anti-Semitism or other forms of hatred based on intolerance, including intolerance expressed by aggressive nationalism and ethnocentrism, discrimination and hostility against minorities, migrants and people of immigrant origin.[6]

---

2 *Case Relating to Certain Aspects of the Laws on the Use of Languages in Education in Belgium v Belgium*, Application Nos 1474/62; 1677/62; 1691/62; 1769/63; 1994/63; 2126/64, 23 July 1968, BI para 10.
3 *Willis v the United Kingdom*, Application No.36042/97, 11 June 2002, para 39.
4 Boyle, K., 'Hate Speech – the United States versus the Rest of the World', 53 (2) *Maine Law Review* (2001) 489.
5 Leigh, I., 'Damned if They Do, Damned if They Don't: the European Court of Human Rights and the Protection of Religion from Attack', 17 (1) *Res Publica* (2011) 63.
6 Committee of Ministers, Council of Europe, Recommendation No. R(97)20 on "Hate Speech".

Another Council of Europe body, the European Commission against Racism and Intolerance, describes hate speech as

> Advocacy, promotion or incitement, in any form, of the denigration, hatred or vilification of a person or group of persons, as well as any harassment, insult, negative stereotyping, stigmatization or threat in respect of such a person or groups of persons and the justification of all the preceding types of expression, on the ground of 'race', colour, descent, national or ethnic origin, age, disability, language, religion or belief, sex, gender, gender identity, sexual orientation and other personal characteristics or status.[7]

The latter definition appears to be much wider than the other two and includes harassment, insult, negative stereotyping and threats. Tulkens asks the question whether a European legally binding definition of hate speech is possible or desirable. According to her, 'some argue that hate speech has vague boundaries and does not have a clear-cut definition. So what constitutes hate speech varies from country to country. Others have a different view'. But, she continues, 'hate speech has a common denominator: it is speech that intentionally attacks a person or a group based on race, ethnicity, gender, disability, sexual orientation, religion, or any other prohibited criterion'.[8] So, according to Tulkens, there must be an 'intentional attack'. There is thus no consensus on what hate speech or incitement to hatred is, although all definitions appear to include hate speech on the ground of religion or belief. The definition of the Council of Ministers does not mention religion or belief explicitly, but it is submitted that 'other forms of hatred based on intolerance' and 'hostility against minorities' include hatred against people because of their religion or belief.

But does this lack of definition matter for the subject of this book? What is of interest here is the questions whether hate speech or incitement to hatred is covered by the protection provided by article 10 ECHR and whether legal prohibitions of (religious) hate speech or incitement to (religious) hatred violate that article. Barendt writes that 'there is little doubt that hate speech, even extreme racist speech, is an exercise of freedom of speech, and is rightly regarded as covered by free speech or freedom of expression clauses'.[9] Keane states:

> The issue of hate or xenophobic speech engages both Article 10 and Article 17 of the ECHR. Article 10 seems to protect all types of expression under paragraph 1. The onus is therefore on the State to show that the interference was justified under paragraph 2.[10]

---

7 European Commission against Racism and Intolerance, General Policy Recommendation No. 15, on *Combating Hate Speech*, CRI(2016) 15, Recital, 3.
8 Tulkens, F., *The Hate Factor in Political Speech: Where do Responsibilities Lie?* (2013) point 11, https://rm.coe.int/CoERMPublicCommonSearchServices/DisplayDCTMContent?documentId=09000016800c170e
9 Barendt, E., *Freedom of Speech* (2nd edn, Oxford, Oxford University Press, 2005) 172.
10 Keane, D., 'Attacking Hate Speech under Article 17 of the European Convention on Human Rights', 25 (4) *Netherlands Quarterly of Human Rights* (2007) 642.

Hate speech thus appears to attract the protection of article 10 ECHR but article 17 can also apply. Article 17 will be discussed further in Chapter 4.

However, this does not mean that all prohibitions on hate speech are considered to be a violation of article 10. In *Gündüz v Turkey*, the European Court of Human Rights has stated that:

> The present case is characterised, in particular, by the fact that the applicant was punished for statements classified by the domestic courts as 'hate speech'. Having regard to the relevant international instruments . . . and to its own case-law, the Court would emphasise, in particular, that tolerance and respect for the equal dignity of all human beings constitute the foundations of a democratic, pluralistic society. That being so, as a matter of principle it may be considered necessary in certain democratic societies to sanction or even prevent all forms of expression which spread, incite, promote or justify hatred based on intolerance (including religious intolerance), provided that any 'formalities', 'conditions', 'restrictions' or 'penalties' imposed are proportionate to the legitimate aim pursued.[11]

A number of conclusions can be drawn from this. First, the Court stresses that tolerance and respect for the equal dignity of all human beings constitute the foundations of a democratic, pluralistic society. As we saw in Chapter 1, the Court has said the same about freedom of expression[12] and freedom of religion.[13] Second, the Court follows the definition given by the Committee of Ministers and, in fact, it refers to this definition in an earlier paragraph.[14] Third, laws prohibiting hate speech can, in the Court's opinion, be compatible with article 10 ECHR. And, fourth, it is clear that such laws are only compatible with that article if they satisfy the justification and proportionality test in paragraph 2. Therefore, some forms of hate speech are protected but others are not and all laws against hate speech, whatever definition of the term 'hate speech' one uses, need to satisfy the justification and proportionality test in article 10(2) ECHR. As we shall see in Chapter 4, an exception to this is hate speech which falls under article 17 ECHR.

It is submitted that, for the subject of this book, whether legal prohibitions of religious hate speech violate the right to freedom of expression in article 10 ECHR, a precise definition of the term 'hate speech' is thus not important as all restrictions on such speech must satisfy the justification and proportionality test in article 10(2). And, as we have seen in Chapter 2, this test is dependent on the specific circumstances of each case. For example, if a law prohibits hate speech and uses a wide definition of the term to include speech that merely insults or

11 *Gündüz v Turkey*, Application No. 35071/97, 4 December 2003, para 40. See also: *Erbakan v Turkey*, Application No. 59405/00, 6 July 2006, para 56.
12 *Handyside v the United Kingdom*, Application No. 5493/72, 7 December 1976, para 49.
13 *Kokkinakis v Greece*, Application No. 14307/88, 25 May 1993, para 31.
14 *Gündüz v Turkey*, supra note 11, para 22.

offends some people because of their religion, restrictions on the latter speech would not satisfy the test because, as we have pointed out in Chapter 1, the right to freedom of religion in article 9 ECHR does not include a right not to be offended in one's religious feelings. From the above it is also clear that the term 'incitement to hatred' is sometimes used instead of the term 'hate speech' and, in the following, these terms will be used as being interchangeable and as having the same meaning.

Although this book concentrates on the ECHR, when analysing hate speech, article 20(2) of the International Covenant on Civil and Political Rights (ICCPR) must be mentioned. The Covenant guarantees freedom of expression in article 19 (1) and (2) in similar terms to article 10(1) ECHR. Article 19(3) ICCPR allows for restrictions on this right similar to article 10(2) ECHR and subject to a justification and proportionality test. But the ICCPR also contains an obligation for states to prohibit by law 'any propaganda for war' (article 20(1)) and 'any advocacy of national, racial or religious hatred that constitutes incitement to discrimination, hostility or violence' (article 20(2)). So, this imposes a duty on states to have laws against hate speech, a duty that is not found in the ECHR. The Covenant does not give a definition of hate speech but, according to Temperman, 'the threshold for this extreme-speech provision is very high. The Article's complex and qualified formulation leaves no doubt as to the extreme nature of the speech required to trigger the ban'.[15] Despite this, during the drafting of article 20 ICCPR 'fears were expressed that its adoption might lead to abuse and would be detrimental to freedom of expression' and 'several states parties made reservations and declarations concerning Article 20.'[16] The Human Rights Committee, which oversees the ICCPR, has stated that:

> Articles 19 and 20 are compatible with and complement each other. The acts that are addressed in article 20 are all subject to restriction pursuant to article 19, paragraph 3. As such, a limitation that is justified on the basis of article 20 must also comply with article 19, paragraph 3.[17]

So, not only is article 20 limited to extreme cases of hate speech or incitement to hatred, but laws enacted under this article must still meet the justification and

15 Temperman, J., 'Blasphemy versus Incitement: An International Law Perspective', in Beneke, C., Grenda, C. and Nash, D. (eds) *Profane: Sacrilegious Expression in a Multicultural Age* (Oakland, University of California Press, 2014), 5, available at SSRN: http://ssrn.com/abstract=2712702. See also: *Rabat Plan of Action on the Prohibition of Advocacy of National, Racial or Religious Hatred that Constitutes Incitement to Discrimination, Hostility or Violence*, 5 October 2012, para 22, www.ohchr.org/Documents/Issues/Opinion/SeminarRabat/Rabat_draft_outcome.pdf

16 Boerefijn, I. and Oyediran, J., 'Article 20 of the International Covenant on Civil and Political Rights', in Coliver, S. (ed.) *Striking a Balance Hate Speech, Freedom of Expression and Discrimination* (London, Article 19, 1992) 29.

17 Human Rights Committee, General Comment No. 34, *Article 19: Freedoms of Opinion and Expression*, CCPR/C/GC/34, 12 September 2011, para 50.

proportionality test of article 19(3) ICCPR, which, as explained above, is the same for laws against hate speech or incitement to hatred under article 10 ECHR.[18]

Religious hate speech

In the above, it was argued that the terms 'hate speech' and 'incitement to hatred' do not need precise definitions for the purpose of this book. However, the term 'religious hate speech' needs further discussion. Religious hate speech can simply be described as speech that incites to hatred on the ground of the religion or belief of the targets of the hate speech, of the victims. A good example can be found in *Norwood v the United Kingdom*, where, according to the European Court of Human Rights, all Muslims were linked to the terrorist attacks in September 2001.[19] Therefore, laws against religious hate speech protect persons holding religious beliefs. As was mentioned in the introduction to this book, the term 'religious hate speech' will be used in this way. It will not include instances where religion or belief acts as a source of hate speech, provides the motivation for the perpetrator for inciting hatred against people because of other characteristics, for example sex or sexual orientation. It will, therefore, for example, not include religious preaching against equality between the sexes or against same-sex relationships.

In Chapter 1, it was discussed that there is no right not to be offended present in article 9 ECHR. But even if there is no such right, are there any other reasons why religious hate speech deserves different protection than other forms of hate speech? Nathwani suggests that restrictions on religious offence should not be given more protection, where she points out:

> Human beings have a right to have a religion under the ECHR, but they equally have a right not to have any. Therefore, it is difficult to reason that, under freedom of religion, religious feelings deserve or merit special protection against those who do not share them.[20]

She also writes that 'it is not clear why religion should be privileged over other ideologies; after all, religion could be understood as a particular type of ideology'.[21]

Some authors have mentioned that religious hate speech is different from, for example, racial hate speech because race is an immutable characteristic, while

---

18 For more information on the situation under international human rights law the reader is referred to: Temperman, J., *Religious Hatred and International Law: The Prohibition of Incitement to Violence or Discrimination* (Cambridge: Cambridge University Press, 2016).

19 *Norwood v the United Kingdom*, Application No. 23131/03, 6 November 2004. The case is discussed in more detail below.

20 Nathwani, N., 'Religious Cartoons and Human Rights – a Critical Legal Analysis of the Case Law of the European Court of Human Rights on the Protection of Religious Feelings and its Implications in the Danish Affair Concerning Cartoons of the Prophet Muhammad', 4 *European Human Rights Law Review* (2008) 498.

21 Ibid. 499.

religion is not, although most also admit that this distinction is not as clear as it might seem.[22] Barendt mentions this difference and writes that 'racist hate speech hits people harder because it targets a feature of their personality – their colour or race – which they cannot change'.[23] Vrielink writes about 'the (alleged) fact of one's racial identity being something one is born with, while one's religion is something one chooses'. But he continues that 'to begin with, this distinction might not be as clear as it might seem. For one thing, the vast majority of adherents to a religion never actively choose their beliefs, but are instead "born into them"'.[24] Cox expresses the same opinion even more strongly where he writes that 'for many religious devotees their religion is immutable'.[25] In any case, with Vrielink we can ask 'why the choice factor should legitimate a differential treatment for the purposes of free speech'.[26] O'Reilly also expresses that the fact that 'religion is an immutable characteristic may not be the safest ground on which to criticise the special protection afforded to it'.[27]

But are there any other reasons why religious hate speech is different from racial hate speech from a free speech perspective? Both O'Reilly and Vrielink point to other reasons.[28] Vrielink, for example, writes that:

> Religion is primarily a matter of beliefs, ideas, values and morality, while race could be said to lack content in this regard. Religious ideas and beliefs can be appraised and argued over, as in fact they are: religious perspectives are frequently at the centre of political and societal debates.[29]

Hare mentions that 'religious adherence is a matter of choice' and that 'the law usually does not provide the protection of the criminal law for vilification based upon the life choices of its citizens'.[30] Hare then gives a number of additional

---

22   See, for example, Hare, I., 'Blasphemy and Religious Hatred: Free Speech Dogma and Doctrine', in Hare, I. and Weinstein, J. (eds) *Extreme Speech and Democracy* (Oxford, Oxford University Press, 2009) 308; Barendt, E., 'Religious Hatred Laws: Protecting Groups or Belief?', 17 (1) *Res Publica* (2011) 46; Plant, R., 'Religion, Identity and Freedom of Expression', 17 (1) *Res Publica* (2011) 12; Vrielink, J., 'Islamophobia and the Law: Belgian Hate Speech Legislation and the Wilful Destruction of the Koran', 14 (1) *International Journal of Discrimination and the Law* (2014) 57. Especially Plant discusses whether religion is really self-chosen. For a discussion of this see also: Cox, N., 'Blasphemy, Holocaust Denial, and the Control of Profoundly Unacceptable Speech', 62 *American Journal of Comparative Law* (2014) 760–763.
23   Barendt, supra note 22, 46.
24   Vrielink, supra note 22, 57. In the same vein, Plant, supra note 22.
25   Cox, supra 22, 745.
26   Vrielink, supra note 22, 57.
27   O'Reilly, A., 'In Defence of Offence: Freedom of Expression, Offensive Speech, and the Approach of the European Court of Human Rights', 19 *Trinity College Law Review* (2016) 248.
28   O'Reilly, supra note 27; Vrielink, supra note 22, 57.
29   Vrielink, supra note 22, 57.
30   Hare, supra note 22, 308.

reasons why 'greater latitude should be given to free discussion on religious matters than on those concerning race'.[31] First of all, 'a substantial part of the aim of most religions is to persuade and convert new adherents. Thus, religions are in a competitive position with regard to one another'. Hare's second point, which is similar to that of Vrielink above, is that religions inevitably make competing and often incompatible claims that are not mirrored in racial discourse.[32] Hare's third point is that many religious groups, unlike other minority groups subject to racial incitement, are highly organised and well-funded and are thus able to counter extreme speech against them. Hare's fourth argument echoes what Vrielink writes about religious groups contributing to the public debate on matters of profound public controversy.[33] These arguments clearly reflect what was said in Chapter 1, that in a democratic society, open debates about religions and beliefs and religious beliefs are essential to make the right to change one's belief effective. This is thus linked to three of the arguments given for freedom of speech in Chapter 1: the importance of this right for the finding of truth, for self-development, self-fulfilment and moral autonomy and for democracy.

All these arguments brought forward in the literature appear to suggest that, if religious hate speech should be treated differently from racial hate speech from a free speech perspective, then restrictions on racial hate speech should be held to be justified more easily than restrictions on religious hate speech. An exception to this is Cox, who writes that, because religion is immutable for many religious devotees and because it provides their primary ground of self-identification, 'for such persons, gross irreverence can be as insidious and unacceptable offensive as can unspeakable racism in modern Western society'.[34]

Barendt uses the difficulties in distinguishing between criticising religions or beliefs and offending believers to argue against laws banning religious hate speech.[35] As mentioned above, Barendt writes that racist speech hits people harder because they cannot change their colour or race. He then continues that the distinction between racial and religious hate speech is important because it explains why it is fundamentally wrong to ban religious hate speech, even if it may be right to proscribe, or at least regulate, racist hate speech. Barendt bases this on the fact that 'religious hate speech cannot in principle (or in practice) be distinguished from abuse or ridicule of the beliefs and practices of members of the targeted community which must be treated . . . as an exercise of the right to freedom of expression' and that 'there is no comparable difficulty in the case of racist hate speech'.[36] Barendt, therefore, argues that religious hate speech should not be banned by law. However, the European Court of Human Rights holds that laws banning (religious) hate speech, can, under certain circumstances, be

31 Ibid.
32 Hare, supra note 22, 308; Vrielink, supra note 22, 57.
33 Vrielink, supra note 22, 57.
34 Cox, supra note 22, 745.
35 Barendt, supra note 22, 46.
36 Ibid.

compatible with article 10(2) ECHR and this will be analysed in Chapter 4. However, this raises another issue: whether religious hate speech targets religions or beliefs or religious believers and whether a distinction can be made between criticising or insulting religions or beliefs and criticising or insulting believers. This will be analysed next.

Beliefs and believers

As mentioned in Chapter 1, the right to freedom of expression also applies to expressions that offend, shock or disturb[37] and religious believers 'cannot reasonably expect to be exempt from all criticism. They must tolerate and accept the denial by others of their religious beliefs and even the propagation by others of doctrines hostile to their faith'.[38] It was argued, in Chapter 1, that the right to choose a religion or belief, to change religion or belief or to choose not to hold or practise a religion or belief can only become real if open debates about religions and beliefs can take place, with room for criticism and denial of other people's religions or beliefs. It was also explained that trying to convert others is part of the right to freely manifest one's religion. This might include, as Temperman expresses, 'the right to manifest beliefs that may be heretical, defamatory or blasphemous to another person'.[39] Therefore, the right to freedom of expression 'implies that it should be allowed to scrutinise, openly debate, and criticise, even harshly and unreasonably, belief systems, opinions and institutions, as long as this does not amount to advocating hatred against individuals or groups', according to the Council of Europe's Venice Commission.[40] And Vrielink writes that 'allowing hostile criticism, ridicule and even "desecration" of religious tenets and beliefs is a necessary price of living in a free society'.[41]

The above suggests that religions or beliefs as such are not protected by the right to freedom of religion. This is confirmed by Bielefeldt *et al.* where they discuss the misconception that freedom of religion or belief abstractly promotes 'the cause of religion' and that, as soon as some religious interest comes into play, this would become a case of religious freedom. But, they continue, this is 'more than questionable' because freedom of religion protects human beings, not religions.[42] And, Leigh explains that 'religions do not have rights because ideas do not have rights. Groups of religious believers . . . do have rights'.[43]

---

37 *Handyside v the United Kingdom*, supra note 12, para 49.
38 *Otto-Preminger-Institut v Austria*, Application No. 13470/87, 20 September 1994, para 47.
39 Temperman, supra note 15, 3.
40 European Commission for Democracy through Law (Venice Commission), *Report on the Relationship between Freedom of Expression and Freedom of Religion: the Issue of Regulation and Prosecution of Blasphemy, Religious Insult and Incitement to Religious Hatred* (Strasbourg, Council of Europe, 2008, Study No. 406/2006, CDL-AD(2008)026) www.venice.coe.int/webforms/documents/?pdf=CDL-AD%282008%29026-e
41 Vrielink, supra note 22, 57.
42 Bielefeldt, H., Ghanea, N. and Wiener, M., *Freedom of Religion or Belief: An International Law Commentary* (Oxford, Oxford University Press, 2016) 492–493.
43 Leigh, supra note 5, 68.

Therefore, criticism of religions and beliefs is protected by the right to freedom of speech and restrictions on expressions criticising religions or beliefs should be considered to violate that right. But is the same true for criticism or offence of religious believers? It was argued in Chapter 1, that there is no right not to be offended and the mere fact that an expression is seen as offensive by (some) religious believers is not sufficient to justify interference with the freedom of speech of the speaker or author. As recounted in Chapter 1, the Parliamentary Assembly of the Council of Europe expressed that 'freedom of expression as protected under Article 10 of the European Convention on Human Rights should not be further restricted to meet increasing sensitivities of certain religious groups'.[44] Moreover, as O'Reilly points out, what gives offence is inherently subjective: what one person finds offensive, another might find entertaining and the European Court of Human Rights 'should be mindful of the difficulty in conceptualising objectively offensive expression, and the potential for the imposition of uncertain and unforeseeable standards on individuals'.[45]

However, the absence of a right not to be offended does not mean that speech that offends people can never be restricted. It cannot be restricted just because it causes offence, but it can be restricted if this is justified under the three part test of article 10(2) ECHR. It was argued, in Chapter 2, that one of the circumstances when an interference with the right to freedom of expression can be justified is when it stops people from holding or manifesting their religion or belief. It will be argued in Chapter 4, that the only other situation where it can be restricted is when the expression incites to hatred and violence and violence is likely to follow imminently.

Therefore, criticism of religions or beliefs is protected by the freedom of expression and should not be subject to restrictions, but limitations on expressions criticising or offending religious believers can, under certain limited circumstances, be justified. However, there is another issue here: can you distinguish clearly between criticism of a religion or belief and criticism of the believers? The boundaries between the two are not always easy to draw. As Horton writes, 'it is often hard . . . clearly to separate the belief from the believer'.[46] Heinze writes that 'the Danish or *Charlie Hebdo* cartoon controversies show how the boundary between assailing a religion's idea and its members remains controversial'.[47] And, as mentioned above, Barendt uses the fact that

---

44 Parliamentary Assembly, Council of Europe, Resolution 1510 (2006) *Freedom of Expression and Respect for Religious Beliefs*, para 12 http://assembly.coe.int/nw/xml/XRef/Xref-XML2HTML-en.asp?fileid=17457&lang=en

45 O'Reilly, supra note 27, 240.

46 Horton, J., 'Self-censorship', 17 (1) *Res Publica* (2011) 103.

47 Heinze, E., *Hate Speech and Democratic Citizenship* (Oxford, Oxford University Press, 2016) 23. This refers to the fact that, in 2005, a Danish newspaper published a series of cartoons of the prophet Muhammad and this led to violent protests and demonstrations by Muslims in Denmark and subsequently in other places around the world. In 2015, staff members of the French satirical magazine *Charlie Hebdo* were killed by Muslim extremists for also publishing cartoons of the prophet Muhammad.

'religious hate speech cannot in principle (or in practice) be distinguished from abuse or ridicule of the beliefs and practices of members of the targeted community' to argue against bans on religious hate speech.[48] This is confirmed by his conclusion, drawn from *Otto-Preminger-Institut v Austria* and *I.A. v Turkey*,[49] that

> The reasoning in the Strasbourg cases shows that there is little or no distinction between safeguarding of religious communities against offensive and insulting speech and protection of religious dogma or belief. Limits on freedom of expression should not be upheld as necessary to prevent offence to religious groups, for this is often a thin disguise for the imposition of restrictions on the open discussion of religious truths and beliefs.[50]

This would suggest that the European Court of Human Rights does not distinguish between offending believers and criticising religions or beliefs, and, indeed, the cases mentioned by Barendt, *Otto-Preminger-Institut v Austria* and *I.A. v Turkey*, seem to support that. However, the European Court of Human Rights in those cases came to the opposite conclusion to Barendt: the latter argues that religions or beliefs should be open to discussion and debate and thus that speech criticising or attacking them cannot be restricted under article 10(2) ECHR; and, that, because it is difficult to distinguish criticism of religions or beliefs from offending or attacking religious believers, restrictions on the latter can also not be justified under article 10(2).

In contrast, the European Court of Human Rights in the two cases seems to hold that laws against offending religious believers by criticising or attacking their beliefs can be compatible with article 10 ECHR. This might suggest that laws prohibiting attacks on a religion or belief can also be compatible with the right to freedom of expression. However, this does not appear to be what the Court meant as, in *Otto-Preminger-Institut v Austria*, it also held that 'those who choose to exercise the freedom to manifest their religion . . . must tolerate and accept the denial by others of their religious beliefs and even the propagation by others of doctrines hostile to their faith'.[51] Therefore, Barendt and the European Court of Human Rights appear to agree that criticism of religions or beliefs cannot be restricted under article 10(2) ECHR, but they disagree on expressions that criticise religious believers. From the quote from *Gündüz v Turkey* above, it is clear that the European Court of Human Rights holds that 'expressions which spread, incite, promote or justify hatred based on intolerance (including religious intolerance)', in other words hate speech against religious believers, may be

---

48 Barendt, supra note 22, 46.
49 *Otto-Preminger-Institut v Austria*, supra note 38; *I.A. v Turkey*, Application No. 42571/98, 13 September 2005. As discussed in Chapter 1, these were the cases that seem to suggest that there is a right not to be offended in one's religious feelings present in Article 9 ECHR.
50 Barendt, supra note 22, 53.
51 *Otto-Preminger-Institut v Austria*, supra note 38, para 47.

restricted subject to the three part test in article 10(2).[52] But the Court has also expressed that it is for the Court to give the final ruling on the compatibility with article 10(2) and that the Court's supervision

> Can be considered to be all the more necessary given the rather open-ended notion of respect for the religious beliefs of others and the risks of excessive interferences with freedom of expression under the guise of action taken against allegedly offensive material.[53]

In conclusion, the European Court of Human Rights does appear to hold that religious hate speech laws, laws against expressions of hate that target religious believers, can be compatible with the guarantee of freedom of expression in Article 10 ECHR, as long as they pass the three part justification test in article 10(2), as determined by the Court. This will be analysed in Chapter 4.

Blasphemy and religious hate speech

Some countries have blasphemy laws. This raises the question where these laws fit into in relation to the subject of this book. Are such law different from laws against religious hate speech? Leigh writes that 'the essence of blasphemy is showing contempt or insult to God or anything considered sacred'.[54] He distinguishes this from religious insult, which focuses on insulting those who belong to a specific religion or their religious feelings; and, from religious hatred, which 'is a stronger form of conduct that may or may not be accompanied by intention to promote discrimination or violence against members of a religion'. So, as Leigh sums up, 'in principle blasphemy protects religious ideas per se whereas religious insults and religious hatred protect the persons holding religious beliefs'.[55]

Hill and Sandberg write about the offence of blasphemy as it existed in Britain until 2008:

> The offence comprised publishing 'blasphemous' material in any form, by which the content had to be contrary to the tenets of the Church of England and couched in indecent or offensive terms likely to shock and outrage the feelings of the general body of believers.[56]

Thus, 'decent and reasonable criticism was not blasphemous' and 'if the decencies of controversy are observed, even the fundamentals of religion might be attacked'.[57]

---

52 *Gündüz v Turkey*, supra note 11, para 40.
53 *Murphy v Ireland*, App. No. 44179/98, 10 July 2003, para 68.
54 Leigh, supra note 5, 57.
55 Ibid.
56 Hill, M. and Sandberg, R., 'Blasphemy and Human Rights: An English Experience in a European Context', *IV Derecho y Religión* (2009) 148.
57 Sandberg, R. and Doe, N., 'The Strange Death of Blasphemy', 71 (6) *Modern Law Review* (2008) 973.

This suggests that the blasphemy law in the UK protected the dominant religion. This is similar in many states, as Temperman writes 'blasphemy prohibitions in States with a population that predominantly adheres to a specific religion have traditionally been brought into being and enforced so as to protect that dominant religion especially'.[58] Temperman also writes that the bans on blasphemy 'came to be used to solely counter intentionally insulting speech or publication that are meant to shock or harm the feelings of the dominant religious community'.[59] This suggests that the offence of blasphemy does not protect religions or beliefs as such, it only protects against offensive attacks on these religions or beliefs. This raises the question whether such laws are compatible with article 10 ECHR, as criticism or denial of religions or beliefs cannot be restricted by that article, as discussed above.

In 2007, the Parliamentary Assembly of the Council of Europe brought out a Recommendation on 'blasphemy, religious insults and hate speech against persons on grounds of their religion'. In this recommendation, the Assembly stated that:

> With regard to blasphemy, religious insults and hate speech against persons on the grounds of their religion, the state is responsible for determining what should count as criminal offences within the limits imposed by the case law of the European Court of Human Rights. In this connection, the Assembly considers that blasphemy, as an insult to a religion, should not be deemed a criminal offence.[60]

In the same Recommendation, the Assembly recommends that 'in view of the greater diversity of religious beliefs in Europe and the democratic principle of the separation of state and religion, blasphemy laws should be reviewed by the governments and parliaments of the member states'.[61] This suggests that the Parliamentary Assembly is against blasphemy laws because they ban expressions insulting religions. The Council of Europe's Venice Commission also concluded that 'the offence of blasphemy should be abolished (which is already the case in most European States) and should not be reintroduced'.[62] Similar views have been expressed in the literature. For example, Boyle writes that in the aftermath of the Danish cartoons affair 'there should be serious scrutiny of surviving offences of blasphemy in Europe'.[63] And, Nathwani states that 'blasphemy laws appear as the leftovers from a bygone age. They do not make sense under modern conditions'.[64] The reasons for rejecting blasphemy laws appears to be that such

58 Temperman, J., 'Blasphemy, Defamation of Religions and Human Rights Law', 26 (4) *Netherlands Quarterly of Human Rights* (2008) 518.
59 Ibid.
60 Parliamentary Assembly, Council of Europe, Recommendation 1805 (2007) *Blasphemy, Religious Insults and Hate Speech against Persons on Grounds of their Religion*, para 4 http:// assembly.coe.int/nw/xml/XRef/Xref-XML2HTML-en.asp?fileid=17569&lang=en
61 Ibid. para 10.
62 European Commission for Democracy through Law, supra note 40, para 89c.
63 Boyle, K., 'The Danish Cartoons' (2006) 24 *Netherlands Quarterly of Human Rights*, 189.
64 Nathwani, supra note 20, 498.

laws prohibit offensive attacks on religions as such and this goes against the need for open debates on religions and beliefs in democratic states.[65] As mentioned in Chapter 1, one of the arguments for and values of having a right to freedom of expression was the crucial role it plays in the formation of public opinion in a democratic society. Blasphemy laws were enacted 'to prevent challenge to State endorsed Christian truth and to punish error and heresy',[66] and thus they are no longer necessary 'in view of the greater diversity of religious beliefs in Europe and the democratic principle of the separation of state and religion'.[67] As the Venice Commission in the above quote already pointed out, blasphemy offences have been abolished in many European states in recent years[68] and, where they still exist, they are rarely prosecuted.[69]

Another argument brought forward against blasphemy laws, which appears to be implicit in the above mentioned 'greater diversity of religious beliefs', is that, if they only protect the dominant religion in a country against offensive attacks, they are discriminatory against other religions. Two cases have been brought against the United Kingdom where this was argued, but the European Commission held both inadmissible because freedom of religion under article 9 does not confer a right to bring any specific form of proceedings against those who, by authorship or publication, offend the sensitivities of an individual or of a group of individuals.[70] In *Wingrove v the United Kingdom*, the European Court of Human Rights recognised that 'the English law of blasphemy only extends to the Christian faith' but that 'the uncontested fact that the law of blasphemy does not treat on an equal footing the different religions practised in the United Kingdom does not detract from the legitimacy of the aim pursued in the present context'.[71] This appears rather short and dismissive of an important issue. As Temperman writes, 'the issue of the (il)legitimacy of discriminatory laws as a basis for grounds for limitations of fundamental rights certainly merits more elaborate discussion than this meagre if not empty phrase'.[72] Temperman also submits that 'if a blasphemy law discriminates on the basis of religion such certainly does detract from the legitimacy of the aim pursued'.[73]

---

65 Parliamentary Assembly, supra note 60, para 5.
66 Boyle, supra note 63, 189.
67 Parliamentary Assembly, supra note 60, para 5; See also: Nathwani, supra note 20, 498; Boyle, supra note 63, 189.
68 The exception to this is Ireland, where a new blasphemy law was introduced in Section 36 of the Defamation Act 2009.
69 Parliamentary Assembly, supra note 60, para 4; European Commission for Democracy through Law, supra note 40, para 26.
70 *X ltd and Y v the United Kingdom*, Application No. 8710/79, 7 May 1982 (Admissibility Decision) and *Choudhury v the United Kingdom*, Application No. 17439/90, 5 March 1991 (Admissibility Decision).
71 *Wingrove v the United Kingdom*, Application No. 17419/90, 25 November 1996, para 50.
72 Temperman, supra note 58, 538.
73 Ibid. 539.

Apart from rather skimming over the discriminatory aspect of the blasphemy law in question in *Wingrove v the United Kingdom*, the Court also held that blasphemy laws can be compatible with article 10 ECHR. The Court considered that

> There is as yet not sufficient common ground in the legal and social orders of the member States of the Council of Europe to conclude that a system whereby a State can impose restrictions on the propagation of material on the basis that it is blasphemous is, in itself, unnecessary in a democratic society and thus incompatible with the Convention.[74]

But the Court also considered that this does not exclude European supervision, which is 'all the more necessary given the breadth and open-endedness of the notion of blasphemy and the risks of arbitrary or excessive interferences with freedom of expression under the guise of action taken against allegedly blasphemous material'.[75] The Court was thus clearly aware that blasphemy laws could be used in an arbitrary way to suppress freedom of expression. It stressed that the law of blasphemy in question had to satisfy the justification test given in article 10(2) ECHR.[76]

However, it must be noted that the decision of the European Court of Human Rights was not unanimous and that two dissenting judges found that there had been a violation of the applicant's freedom of expression.[77] Moreover, earlier the European Commission of Human Rights had held, with a majority of 14 votes to 2, that there had been a violation.[78] It must also be pointed out that the case was decided 20 years ago. It could be that the Court would come to a different conclusion now. Then, the majority of judges considered that there was 'as yet' not sufficient common ground among the member states to hold a blasphemy law to be incompatible with the Convention, but as mentioned, this has changed as many European states have now abolished such laws.

Support for this can be found in the case law of the European Court of Human Rights. Although the Court, in 2005, in *I.A. v Turkey*,[79] held that a conviction for blasphemy did not violate article 10(2) ECHR, this was not a unanimous decision: four judges held the blasphemy law in question to be compatible with article 10(2), three dissenting judges found a violation. The three dissenters suggested that perhaps the time had come 'to "revisit" the case law'.[80] In 2006, in *Giniewski v France*, the Court found that a conviction for defamation of the

74 *Wingrove v the United Kingdom*, supra note 71, para 57.
75 Ibid. para 58. This echoes what the European Court of Human Rights said in *Murphy v Ireland*, supra note 53, para 68 in relation to 'the open-ended notion of respect for the religious beliefs of others' and 'allegedly offensive material'.
76 *Wingrove v the United Kingdom*, supra note 71, para 59.
77 Ibid. dissenting opinions.
78 Ibid. para 33.
79 *I.A. v Turkey*, Application No. 42571/98, 13 September 2005.
80 Ibid, dissenting opinion, paras 7 and 8.

Christian religion did violate the right to freedom of expression of the convicted person.[81] Therefore, within the Council of Europe and even within the European Court of Human Rights, opinions appear to be divided about blasphemy laws and their compatibility with article 10 ECHR, but there seems to be a move away from accepting bans on blasphemy, on expressing criticism or insult of (majority) religions. It is submitted that it is, indeed, time to revisit the case law on this.

Another argument for revisiting the case law is that the Human Rights Committee, which, as was mentioned above, oversees the ICCPR, has held that 'prohibitions of displays of lack of respect for a religion or other belief system, including blasphemy laws, are incompatible with the Covenant except in the specific circumstances envisaged in article 20, paragraph 2, of the Covenant'. As also mentioned above, article 20(2) ICCPR obliges states to prohibit by law 'any advocacy of national, racial or religious hatred that constitutes incitement to discrimination, hostility or violence'. Therefore, according to the Human Rights Committee, laws against blasphemy, laws that criminalise expressions that defame or insult a religion, are a violation of the freedom of expression, but laws against incitement to religious hatred, hatred of people because they belong to a certain religion or belief, are not. This suggests that article 19 ICCPR does not protect religions against offence. It is submitted that the European Court of Human Rights should follow this and that religious beliefs as such should not be protected against offence. Therefore, blasphemy laws should be considered as incompatible with the ECHR because they violate the right to freedom of expression.

The conclusion from the above is that laws that prohibit or punish attacks on or criticism of religions or beliefs, including blasphemy laws, should be considered to be incompatible with article 10 ECHR, because such laws prohibit open discussions and debates about religions and beliefs and, thus, interfere with the proper functioning of a democratic society. On the other hand, laws against hate speech, against speech that incites to hatred against believers, can, under certain limited circumstances as laid down in article 10(2) ECHR, be compatible with freedom of expression and these circumstances will be analysed in Chapter 4. In exceptional cases, the European Court of Human Rights has dealt with hate speech laws under article 17 ECHR, which prohibits the abuse of Convention rights. Article 17 will also be examined in Chapter 4.

Laws against hate speech

Laws against (religious) hate speech or against incitement to (religious) hatred exist in many European countries[82] and, as mentioned above, the European Court of Human Rights has held that such laws can be compatible with the guarantee of freedom of expression. But, why would a state enact such laws? Barendt writes that, 'verbal and written attacks on racial and other groups have generally been

---

81 *Giniewski v France*, Application No. 64016/00, 31 January 2006, para 53.
82 See Weber, A., *Manual on Hate Speech* (Strasbourg, Council of Europe, 2009) 3.

subjected to greater restriction in the last fifty years'.[83] He gives an explanation of why this is so. 'The repercussions of the vicious abuse of Jews (and other ethnic groups) encouraged by the Nazi regime suggested, to put it mildly, that there are worse evils than the suppression of free speech'.[84] Barendt appears to be writing here about laws against racial hate speech. As mentioned above, he is against enacting laws against religious hate speech.[85]

According to Buyse, three main justifications have usually been brought forward for enacting hate speech laws.[86] The first is 'the prevention of breaches of the peace and protecting public order'; the second is 'the protection of the targeted group, both regarding its members' feelings and physical safety;' and, the third argument is that 'the curtailment of speech through law can have a symbolic and declaratory function by reflecting what society deems inappropriate'.[87] These three arguments are clearly interlinked and overlap. The first argument, that hate speech laws are necessary to preserve public order or, as Barendt puts it, 'to preserve order between different groups',[88] can be linked to the fact that hate speech incites to hatred and violence against certain groups and this might lead to disturbances of the public order. This argument clearly reflects one of the legitimate aims for restrictions on freedom of expression in article 10(2) ECHR: 'the prevention of disorder and crime'. The European Court of Human Rights has held, in a number of cases concerning article 10(2) ECHR, that 'it remains open to the competent State authorities to adopt, in their capacity as guarantors of public order, measures, even of a criminal-law nature, intended to react appropriately and without excess to such remarks'.[89] Therefore, this is a justification for hate speech laws that is recognised by the Court.

Barendt phrases the second argument in a slightly different way where he writes that 'bans on hate speech also protect members of minority racial, ethnic, and other groups from psychological injury and damage to their self-esteem, or they may be seen as necessary to reflect their right to equality'.[90] This argument appears to be based on the legitimate aim of 'the protection of the rights of others' in article 10(2), for example, the right to security of the person as laid down in

83 Barendt, supra note 9, 170–171.
84 Ibid.
85 Barendt, supra note 22, 46.
86 Buyse, A., 'Dangerous Expressions: the ECHR, Violence and Free Speech', 63 (2) *International and Comparative Law Quarterly* (2014) 493.
87 Ibid.
88 Barendt, supra note 9, 171.
89 See, for example, *Castells v Spain*, Application No. 11798/85, 23 April 1992, para 46; *Incal v Turkey*, Application No. 22678/93, 9 June 1998 (Grand Chamber), para 54; *Balsytė-Lideikienė v Lithuania*, Application No. 72596/01, 4 November 2008, para 81; and, a number of cases against Turkey that were all heard by the Grand Chamber, and where the judgment came out on the same day, 8 July 1999, *Ceylan v Turkey*, Application No. 23556/94, para 17; *Erdoğdu and Ince v Turkey*, 25067/94 and 25068/94, para 50; *Sürek v Turkey* No 2, Application No. 24122/94, 8 July 1999, para 34.
90 Barendt, supra note 9, 171.

article 5 and the right to be free from discrimination, as laid down in article 14 and Protocol 12. However, under article 10(2), the European Court of Human Rights will have to perform a careful balancing exercise between the right of the speaker or author to freedom of expression and the rights of others, as was mentioned in Chapter 2 above. In this balancing exercise, it must be kept in mind that there is, as was established in Chapter 1, no right not to be offended in one's religious feelings present in article 9 ECHR. So, an expression cannot be limited merely because it gives offence to some people. Or, as Barendt warns:

> Legislation should be drafted carefully to ensure that only speech which is really wounding to the dignity of the targeted group is caught by criminal law. It is the responsibility of the courts to ensure that this boundary is not crossed to permit the proscription of speech which is merely offensive either to minority groups or to the majority.[91]

In Chapter 2, the case of *Otto-Preminger-Institut v Austria* was discussed and criticised. It is submitted that the majority judges in the European Court of Human Rights, by finding that the ban on the film in that case was not a violation of the freedom of expression of the film makers but was justified for the protection of the rights of others, namely the Catholic population of Tyrol, did not ensure that the boundary was not crossed but allowed the proscription of speech which was merely offensive to the majority population of that area of Austria. In Chapter 1, we saw that the Court itself, in later cases, confirmed that there is no right not to be offended.[92]

The third argument is that hate speech laws have a symbolic or declaratory value because they show that society regards such speech as inappropriate. Hate speech laws thus show that society rejects such speech and fights against the spreading of hate between groups. Some of the academic comments to the introduction, in British law, of an offence of stirring up religious hatred by the Racial and Religious Hatred Act 2006 pointed out the symbolic value of this legislation. Sandberg, for example, calls the law 'little more than political posturing; a simple statement that religious hatred is wrong'.[93] This suggests that the symbolic value of the act was its only value. Jeremy is slightly more positive, but still refers to the symbolic value of the Act where he writes that 'the difficulty in proving the essential elements of the offence of religious hatred may suggest that the 2006 legislation is essentially symbolic' but that the legislation serves an important purpose in supporting groups in society who are afraid for their safety, that the laws condemn bias, prejudice and hatred and 'send a signal to potential offenders that society will punish such conduct severely'.[94] Noorloos, writing about the adoption of hate speech offences in the Netherlands in 1971, mentions that 'hate

---

91 Ibid. 175.
92 See Chapter 1 and the cases referred to there.
93 Sandberg, R., *Law and Religion* (Cambridge, Cambridge University Press, 2011) 144.
94 Jeremy, A., 'Practical Implications of the Enactment of the Racial and Religious Hatred Act 2006', 9 (2) *Ecclesiastical Law Journal* (2007) 200.

speech legislation was rather viewed as a symbolic means of upholding the norm of equality'.[95] The Council of Europe's European Commission for Democracy through Law also points out that 'the pan-European introduction of sanctions against incitement to hatred has a very strong symbolic value'.[96]

Barendt explains that 'to tolerate speech abusing racial or ethnic groups is to lend respectability to racist attitudes. Such attitudes may foster an eventual breakdown of public order'[97] thus linking the third argument with the first. However, the same author also makes the point that 'the suppression of propaganda may in the long run be as likely to expose society to a risk of violence as tolerance of its dissemination'. Barendt mentions another problem: accepting this argument would mean that the state legally prohibits speech because it fears that this will affect popular attitudes or that individuals will respond to it 'in disapproved ways – thinking less well of members of different ethnic groups and refusing to mix with them'.[98] This is in conflict with the idea behind guarantees of freedom of speech, that listeners are, generally, able 'to make rational assessments of the credibility of the claims made to them, whether in the course of election campaigns or in other contexts'.[99] This is linked to and would also conflict with some of the arguments brought forward in Chapter 1 for having a right to freedom of expression: discovery of the truth, individual self-development and the effective participation in the forming of public opinion in a democracy.

After discussing the justifications for enacting hate speech laws, the potential dangers of such laws must also be analysed. Buyse sums these up as follows: first, 'such laws can and have been used merely to quash the rights of opponents of those in power or have been applied arbitrarily'; second, hate speech laws can lead to self-censorship; third, 'criminal trials can provide an additional public platform for those whose speech one wants to curtail by prosecuting them'; and, fourth, there are other, more effective and less problematic ways of dealing with such speech from a human rights perspective.[100] The last point will form the subject of Chapter 5, but the first three arguments will be analysed in more detail here.

The first argument is that hate speech laws can be used by governments to stop opponents from speaking, in other words, can be used to stifle opposition. Or, 'restrictions on freedom of expression enacted under cover of containing hate speech actually allow those who wield power greater leeway to suppress dissenting voices by codifying them as hateful', as Rorke expresses it.[101] The European Commission for Democracy through Law warns that:

---

95 Noorloos, M. van, 'The Politicisation of Hate Speech Bans in Twenty-first Century Netherlands: Law in a Changing Context', 40 (2) *Journal of Ethnic and Migration Studies* (2014) 251.
96 European Commission for Democracy through Law, supra note 40, para 57.
97 Barendt, supra note 9, 171.
98 Ibid. 173.
99 Ibid.
100 Buyse, supra note 86, 493.
101 Rorke, B., 'Free to Hate? Anti-Gypsyism in 21-Century Europe', in Molnar, P. (ed.) *Free Speech and Censorship around the Globe* (Budapest-New York, Central European University Press, 2015) 235.

The application of hate legislation must be measured in order to avoid an outcome where restrictions which potentially aim at protecting minorities against abuses, extremism or racism, have the perverse effect of muzzling opposition and dissenting voices, silencing minorities, and reinforcing the dominant political, social and moral discourse and ideology.

The European Commission against Racism and Intolerance recommends that prosecutions for hate speech 'are not used in order to suppress criticism of official policies, political opposition or religious beliefs'.[102] The European Court of Human Rights is aware of this as it has held that restrictions on expressions by opposition politicians call for the closest scrutiny by the Court.[103]

The second argument brought forward against hate speech laws is that these can lead to self-censorship. This is often referred to as the 'chilling effect' on freedom of speech.[104] Allowing for restrictions on freedom of expression through hate speech laws, especially when they involve the imposition of criminal sanctions, will 'chill' speech, will mean that people might not speak out at all and this would have serious consequences for the free and open public debate that is necessary in a democratic society. This is even more so if it stops politicians, especially opposition politicians, and journalists from expressing themselves. Boyle points out that the Danish cartoon affair has led to 'a vast expansion of self-censorship in the media over Islam'.[105] And, Grimm writes that 'the detrimental effects limitations might have on democratic discourse must also be considered. "Chilling effects" that speech regulation is likely to have on speech ought to be avoided'.[106]

In *Koç and Tambaş v Turkey*, the European Court of Human Rights observed that the suspended sentence imposed on the applicants had the effect of censoring their profession, compelling them to refrain from publishing anything likely to be considered to be contrary to the interests of the state.[107] In *Erbakan v Turkey*, the Court considered that the severe sanction in that case invariably produced a dissuasive effect.[108] This shows that the Court is not only aware of the possible chilling effect hate speech laws may have on freedom of expression, but also that it takes the severity of the sanction into account.

102 European Commission against Racism and Intolerance, supra note 7, Recommendation 10c. See also article 171 of the same Recommendation.
103 *Castells v Spain*, para 42 and *Incal v Turkey*, para 46, both supra note 89.
104 See on this, for example, Barendt, supra note 9, 32 and 175; European Commission for Democracy through Law, supra note 40, para 76; Grimm, D., 'Freedom of Speech in a Globalized World', in Hare, I. and Weinstein, J. (eds) *Extreme Speech and Democracy* (Oxford, Oxford University Press, 2009) 13; Cram, I., 'The Danish Cartoons, Offensive Expression and Democratic Legitimacy', in ibid. 324; Chan, S., 'Hate Speech Bans: An Intolerant Response to Intolerance', 14 *Trinity College Law Review* (2011), 84.
105 Boyle, supra note 63, 190.
106 Grimm, supra note 104, 13.
107 *Koç and Tambaş v Turkey*, Application No. 50934/99, 21 March 2006, para 39.
108 *Erbakan v Turkey*, supra note 11, para 68.

Cram summarises this argument in relation to the Danish cartoons and comments about Islam following these, where he writes that, if the European Court of Human Rights does not scrutinise national restrictions on expressions about Islamic links to terrorist activity very strictly then

> There will likely be self-censorship on the part of commentators with the result that the violent protests on behalf of those who have been 'insulted' will have succeeded in creating a 'chill' on freedom of expression that robs the public domain of a range of opinions concerning the links between religious fundamentalism and terrorism.[109]

The third argument made against hate speech laws is that prosecution under such laws create an extra platform for those people whose speech is targeted. As Buyse writes, 'such trials may lead to more rather than less attention for the contested expression'.[110] This is because a trial, especially a trial of an opposition politician, attracts huge media attention and gives the person on trial more air time and more opportunities to publicise their views. It also allows them to paint themselves as 'free speech martyr', as being on trial for exercising their freedom of expression. The Commission for Democracy through Law expresses that too activist an attitude on the part of the prosecuting authorities 'may place the suspect person or groups in the position of underdog, and provide them and their goal with propaganda and public support (the role of martyrs)'.[111] Barendt expresses this as follows: 'a prosecution and trial may have the effect of giving hate speech wider currency than it would otherwise enjoy, and indeed make the speaker or publisher a martyr to the cause of free speech'.[112] And, Chan points out that hate speech laws 'glorify the hate speaker whilst at the same time providing greater exposure and publicity for his message', and 'prosecutions merely provide a public platform for hate speakers who, if convicted could claim martyrdom and if acquitted could claim vindication'.[113]

There is another argument against hate speech laws that is linked to the argument of self-censorship: prohibiting hate speech might create a wolf in sheep's clothing. Hate speech laws might cause people to water down or temper their expressions, to use more moderate language, but this does not change what they think or, in case of politicians, what they will try to achieve as soon as they get the power to do so. It may even make the person more stubborn in their convictions. It may also drive these feelings underground and make them more dangerous. Heinze describes the view that 'punishing hate speakers serves . . . only to tutor them in dissimilation, either pushing them underground or teaching them how

109 Cram, supra note 104, 324.
110 Buyse, supra note 86, 493.
111 European Commission for Democracy through Law, supra note 40, para 67.
112 Barendt, supra note 9, 175.
113 Chan, supra note 104, 87–88.

to affect a deceptively mainstream veneer'.[114] In this sense you could say that a politician becomes a 'wolf in sheep's clothing'.[115] Driving feelings of hate underground and making a person more stubborn and hardened in their convictions, might mean that 'hate speech offences tend to have perverse effects in promoting rather than combating bigotry and intolerance', as Lester points out.[116]

As mentioned, the last argument put forward by Buyse, that 'there are other, more effective and less problematic ways of dealing with such speech from a human rights perspective'[117] will be discussed in Chapter 5. However, Callamard points out a slightly different problem with laws against hate speech which is that 'at national level, hate speech regulations, including on religious grounds, suffer the world over from very similar problems: being overly broad, offering little legal clarity and certainty, and underpinned by often contradictory jurisprudence'.[118] This could be seen as another argument against hate speech laws, although it could also be seen as an argument for improving existing hate speech laws. However, it does indicate the difficulty in defining hate speech and in enacting prohibitions against it in, especially, criminal law. Criminal law requires legal clarity and certainty and it might not be possible to achieve this in criminal laws against hate speech.

The developments that led to the British Racial and Religious Hatred Act 2006 can be used to illustrate some of the problems with putting down a provision against religious hate speech into criminal law.[119] The Act added a new part 3A to the Public Order Act 1986, entitled 'Hatred against persons on religious grounds'. Two previous attempts to extend the existing offence of racial hatred to include religious hatred had failed.[120] The Act prescribes three requirements for the offence: an act directed at a group; words behaviour, material or images that are threatening; and, an intention to stir up religious hatred.

---

114 Heinze, supra note 47, 148.
115 Brink, J. van den, 'Discriminatieverbod vs. Vrijheid van Meningsuiting 1–0? EHRM doet Uitspraak in Féret tegen Beligië', (Prohibition of Discrimination v Freedom of Expression 1–0? The European Court of Human Rights brings out its Judgment in Féret v Belgium), 2732 *Media Report* (2009), www.mediareport.nl/persrecht/29072009/discriminatiever bod-vs-vrijheid-van-meningsuiting-1-0-ehrm-doet-uitspraak-in-feret-tegen-belgie/
116 Lester, A., 'The Right to Offend', in: Casadevall, J., Myjer, E., O'Boyle, M. and Austin, A., (eds) *Freedom of Expression, Essays in Honour of Nicolas Bratza* (Oisterwijk, the Netherlands, Wolf Legal Publishers, 2012), 305.
117 Buyse, supra note 86, 493.
118 Callamard, A., 'Religion, Terrorism and Speech in a "Post-Charlie Hebdo" World', 10 (3) *Religion and Human Rights* (2015) 216.
119 For more information on this see: Howard, E. 'Freedom of Expression, Blasphemy and Religious Hatred: a View from the UK' in Temperman, J. and Koltay, A. (eds) *Blasphemy and Freedom of Expression* (Cambridge, Cambridge University Press, 2017, forthcoming) and the references in there.
120 Anti-Terrorism, Crime and Security Bill 2001, part 5 www.publications.parliament. uk/pa/cm200102/cmbills/049/2002049.pdf; and, the Serious Organised Crime and Police Bill 2004-2005, Section 119 www.publications.parliament.uk/pa/cm200405/ cmbills/005/2005005.pdf

The original proposal for the 2006 Act would have just added the offence of stirring up religious hatred to the existing offence of stirring up racial hatred like the two previous proposals did. However, the British Upper Chamber, the House of Lords, made four significant changes to the proposed law. First, the new offence of incitement to religious hatred got its own legislative provision, rather than just being added to the existing offence of incitement to racial hatred. Second, the wording of the offence of incitement to religious hatred was changed and the act now requires that the words, behaviour or material is threatening rather than 'abusive, insulting or threatening'. Third, the act now requires intention to stir up hatred and it is not enough that the words, material or behaviour are likely to stir up hatred. Fourth, and the most far-reaching change made by the House of Lords, was the addition of a so-called 'free speech clause'. This was added as a reaction to the strong criticism the proposed Bill had attracted because of its effects on freedom of expression. Article 29J of the Racial and Religious Hatred Act 2006, under the heading 'Protection of freedom of expression', reads:

> Nothing in this Part shall be read or given effect in a way which prohibits or restricts discussion, criticism or expressions of antipathy, dislike, ridicule, insult or abuse of particular religions or the beliefs or practices of their adherents, or of any other belief system or the beliefs or practices of its adherents, or proselytising or urging adherents of a different religion or belief system to cease practising their religion or belief system.

In the debates in the House of Lords on the Racial and Religious Hatred Bill, the 'encroachment not only of religious thought police but also of self-censorship' and the chilling effect of the proposed legislation were mentioned.[121] The amendments made in the House of Lords were approved by the House of Commons by a majority of one and thus became part of the Act. The four amendments to the original Bill have made it very difficult to prove the requirements for the offence and thus to secure a conviction under the Act.[122] There have, indeed been very few prosecutions since the act came into force.[123]

Returning to the arguments against hate speech laws, some authors have also pointed out that, partly because of the problems flagged up by Callamard and

---

121 House of Lords, Debates, Column 1072–1073 and 1074, 25 October 2005 www. publications.parliament.uk/pa/ld200506/ldhansrd/vo051025/text/51025-04. htm#51025-04_head2

122 See, for example, Hare, I. 'Crosses, Crescents and Sacred Cows: Criminalising Incitement to Religious Hatred', *Public Law* (2006) 521–538; Goodall, K., 'Incitement to Religious Hatred: All Talk and No Substance?' 70 (1) *Modern Law Review* 89–113; Jeremy, supra note 94; Hare, supra note 22; Barendt, supra note 22.

123 Memorandum to the Home Affairs Committee, Post-legislative Scrutiny of the Racial and Religious Hatred Act 2006, CM 8164, 2011 www.gov.uk/government/uploads/system/uploads/attachment_data/file/238156/8164.pdf

also linked to the argument that such laws create a wolf in sheep's clothing, hate speech laws have little practical impact and could even be counterproductive especially in a viral communication age where expressions can be distributed around the world within seconds.[124] How the European Court of Human Rights has dealt with hate speech laws will be examined in the next Chapter.

One more argument, specifically against criminal hate speech laws, can be made: as was mentioned in Chapter 2, the proportionality test which needs to be done under article 10(2) ECHR includes an examination of the question whether less restrictive means can be used to achieve the legitimate aim of a restriction. In many situations, using the criminal law to restrict speech might well not be the least restrictive means of dealing with such speech.

Conclusion

In this Chapter, the concept of hate speech was analysed and it was concluded that there is a lack of consensus as to what this term means, but that this is not a problem for the subject of this book because what is of interest here is the question whether and under what circumstances religious hate speech or expressions inciting to religious hatred attract the protection given to freedom of speech in article 10 ECHR. It was concluded that hate speech can attract the protection of article 10(2) ECHR. This also applied to religious hate speech, which was defined as hate speech motivated by the religion or belief of the targeted party, the victim of the hate speech.

However, not all prohibitions on hate speech are considered to be a violation of article 10 ECHR; such laws can be compatible with article 10(2) according to the European Court of Human Rights, but they have to satisfy the justification and proportionality test in that article. Therefore, some forms of hate speech are protected but others are not and all laws against hate speech, whatever definition of the term 'hate speech' one uses, need to satisfy the justification and proportionality test in article 10(2) ECHR.

The question whether religious hate speech deserves different, either more or less, protection than other forms of hate speech was examined and it was established that religious hate speech can be distinguished from race hate speech, but that most authors see in this a reason to give less protection to religious hate speech rather than more protection.

The difference between speech criticising religions or beliefs and criticising or offending religious believers was also part of the analysis in this Chapter. It was argued that religions or beliefs as such are not protected by the right to freedom of religion and that, therefore, criticism of religions and beliefs is protected

---

124 See, for example, Barendt, supra note 9, 172; Belavusau, U., 'A *Dernier Cri* from Strasbourg: An Ever Formidable Challenge of Hate Speech (*Soulas and Others v France, Leroy v France, Balsytė-Lideikienė v Lithuania*)', 16 (3) *European Public Law* (2010), 387; Chan, supra note 104, 84, 88 and 95; Rorke, supra note 101, 235; and Heinze, supra note 47, 145.

by the right to freedom of expression and restrictions should be considered to violate this right. But this was different with speech criticising or offending religious believers. Although there is no right not to be offended in one's religious feelings, as was established in Chapter 1, speech that offends religious people can be restricted if this is justified under the three part test of article 10(2) ECHR. It was suggested that there are only two situations under which free speech restrictions would be justified: when it stops people from holding or manifesting their religion or belief, as argued in Chapter 2, and when the expression incites to hatred and violence and violence is likely to follow imminently, as will be argued in Chapter 4.

The next issue discussed was whether blasphemy laws are compatible with the right to freedom of speech. Blasphemy was defined as 'showing contempt or insult of God or anything sacred'.[125] So, blasphemy 'protects religious ideas per se'.[126] Blasphemy laws usually protect the majority religion in a state and they protect this only against offensive attacks. Although the European Court of Human Rights has held that blasphemy laws can be compatible with article 10 ECHR, there appears to be difference of opinion within the Court and the Council of Europe on this, and there appears to be a move towards abolishing such laws in many European states. Moreover, where such laws still exist, they seldom lead to prosecutions. It was submitted that it is time for the Court to revisit the case law in this area and hold that blasphemy laws are not compatible with article 10 ECHR.

This Chapter finished with an examination of the arguments brought forward for and against enacting hate speech laws. The three arguments for enacting such laws were: that they protect the public order and prevent breaches of the peace; that they protect the group(s) targeted; and, that they have a symbolic and declaratory function by declaring what society finds inappropriate. The arguments raised against enacting hate speech laws were: that such laws are open to abuse and that states can use them to stifle opposition; that they have a chilling effect and lead to self-censorship; that they give speakers or publishers an extra platform for propaganda; that they create a 'wolf in sheep's clothing' because they might lead to people moderating their expressions but this does not change their views; and, that there might be other, more efficient ways of dealing with hate speech. Criminal laws against hate speech were described as particularly problematic, because they lack clarity and certainty, two requirements of criminal laws. The British Racial and Religious Hatred Act 2006 was used to illustrate this. Before we discuss other ways of dealing with hate speech (in Chapter 5), Chapter 4 will examine how the European Court of Human Rights has dealt with (religious) hate speech laws.

125 Leigh, supra note 5, 57.
126 Ibid.

4 Restrictions on freedom of expression to spare religious feelings

Introduction

In Chapter 3, the term 'hate speech' was examined and it was concluded that (religious) hate speech can attract the protection of article 10 ECHR and that legal prohibitions of such speech must satisfy the justification test in article 10(2), whatever definition of hate speech one uses. Therefore, it was submitted that the lack of consensus that exists about the meaning of the term did not present a problem for the question that is the focus of this book: when restrictions on hate speech can be justified and when they cannot.

The question whether religious hate speech deserves different protection than other forms of hate speech was also examined and it was concluded that many authors distinguish religious hate speech from race hate speech and then argue that, because of the difference, race hate speech should attract more protection. Chapter 3 also contained a discussion of the difference between speech criticising religion or beliefs and speech criticising or offending religious believers and the difficulties in making this distinction. It was argued that expressions criticising religions and beliefs are protected by the right to freedom of expression and that restrictions on such speech should be considered to violate this right. However, speech criticising or offending religious believers can be restricted if this is justified under the three part justification test of article 10(2) ECHR. Blasphemy laws were also discussed and it was submitted that the European Court of Human Rights should revisit its own case law on this and should hold that such laws are not compatible with article 10 ECHR.

The last part of Chapter 3 analysed the arguments in favour of and against enacting hate speech laws. Three arguments for enacting such laws were discussed: such laws protect public order, they protect the targeted individual or group, and they have an important symbolic value as they indicate that such speech is wrong. On the other hand, there were also arguments advanced against enacting such laws: they are open to abuse by the state; they have a chilling effect on freedom of speech; they create an extra platform for the speaker or author; and, they could just force people to moderate their language without changing their views. A last argument against such laws was that there are other, more efficient ways of dealing with hate speech.

But how has the European Court of Human Rights dealt with hate speech laws? The Court has approached these laws in two ways: either through article 17 ECHR, which contains an abuse of rights clause. If the Court uses this, it rejects a complaint of interference with a ECHR right without requiring evidence from the state that such interference is justified. Alternatively, the Court examines hate speech laws under the three part justification test of article 10(2) ECHR. In this Chapter, article 17 will be examined first, and this is followed by an analysis of the Court's case law on hate speech under article 10(2), including an examination of the factors the Court takes into account when it has to decide whether an interference with a person's freedom of expression is justified. It will be argued in this Chapter that (religious) hate speech should only be restricted when the expression incites to hatred and violence and violence is likely to follow imminently. The reasons why this is argued will form part of the discussion in this Chapter.

Article 17 ECHR

Laws on (religious) hate speech can be seen as an interference of the speaker or author's right to freedom of expression. In determining whether this interference is justified, the European Court of Human Rights has employed two different approaches, using either article 17 or article 10(2) ECHR.[1] Article 17 ECHR, which is headed 'prohibition of abuse of rights', states that:

> Nothing in this Convention may be interpreted as implying for any State, group or person any right to engage in any activity or perform any act aimed at the destruction of any of the rights and freedoms set forth herein or at their limitation to a greater extent than is provided for in the Convention.

In *Lawless v Ireland No. 3*, the European Court of Human Rights explained that article 17 meant that no person can take advantage of the provisions of the ECHR to perform acts aimed at destroying any of the rights and freedoms laid down in the Convention.[2]

In *Norwood v the United Kingdom*, the European Court of Human Rights explained that the purpose of this provision is 'to prevent totalitarian or extremist groups from justifying their activities by referring to the Convention'.[3] The Court continued that 'the freedom of expression guaranteed under article 10 of the

---

1 On this see: Keane, D., 'Attacking Hate Speech under Article 17 of the European Convention on Human Rights', 25 (4) *Netherlands Quarterly of Human Rights* (2007) 641–663; A. Weber (2009) *Manual on Hate Speech* (Strasbourg: Council of Europe).

2 *Lawless v Ireland, No. 3*, Application No. 332/57, 1 July 1961, para 7 (under 'the law'). Article 30 of the United Nations Universal Declaration of Human Rights contains a similar abuse of rights clause.

3 *Norwood v the United Kingdom*, Application No. 23131/03, 16 November 2004 (Admissibility Decision). Repeated in, for example: *Ždanoka v Latvia*, Application No. 58278/00, 17 June 2004 (Chamber), para 109.

Convention may not be invoked in a sense contrary to Article 17'.[4] Therefore, a person cannot invoke their right to freedom of speech to defend expressions that are aimed at the destruction of any of the ECHR rights and freedoms.[5] According to Keane:

> Article 17 has a significant effect on the regulation of hate and xenophobic speech – it serves to remove that speech from the protection of Article 10(1), purely on the basis of content. It eliminates the need for a 'balancing process' that characterises the Court's approach under Article 10.[6]

Therefore, no balancing of interests takes place under article 17 and it forms the 'outer limit to the protection of Article 10'.[7] This is confirmed in the Court's factsheet on hate speech which states that '[T]here is no doubt that any remark directed against the Convention's underlying values would be removed from the protection of Article 10 [freedom of expression] by Article 17 [prohibition of abuse of rights] (. . .)'.[8] Therefore, some (extreme) forms of hate speech fall outside the protection of article 10 ECHR altogether because they go against or are aimed at destroying the rights and freedoms guaranteed by the ECHR.

The European Court of Human Rights has applied article 17 in cases of Holocaust denial[9] and anti-Semitism.[10] In *Lehideux and Isorni v France*, for example, the Court stated that 'there is no doubt that, like any other remark directed against the Convention's underlying values . . . the justification of a pro-Nazi policy could not be allowed to enjoy the protection afforded by Article 10'.[11] And, in *Pavel Ivanov v Russia*, the applicant was convicted of public incitement to ethnic, racial and religious hatred because he had published a series of articles portraying the Jews as the source of evil in Russia. He had accused Jews of plotting a conspiracy against the Russian people and had ascribed Fascist ideology to the Jewish leadership. The Court declared the application inadmissible. It held that 'such a general and vehement attack on one ethnic group is in contradiction with the Convention's underlying values, notably tolerance, social peace and non-discrimination'. The Court concluded that 'by reason of Article 17 of the Convention, the applicant may not benefit from the protection afforded by Article 10 of the Convention'.[12]

---

4 *Norwood v the United Kingdom*, ibid.
5 This is the same under Article 5(1) of the International Covenant on Civil and Political Rights.
6 Keane, supra note 1, 643.
7 Buyse, A., 'Dangerous Expressions: the ECHR, Violence and Free Speech', 63 (2) *International and Comparative Law Quarterly* (2014) 494.
8 European Court of Human Rights, *Factsheet – Hate Speech*, June 2016, 2, www.echr.coe. int/Documents/FS_Hate_speech_ENG.pdf
9 See, for example, *Garaudy v France*, Application No. 65831/01, 24 June 2003; and a recent decision where the application was declared inadmissible based on Article 17: *M'Bala M'Bala v France*, Application No. 25239/13, 20 October 2015.
10 *Pavel Ivanov v Russia*, Application No. 35222/04, 20 February 2007.
11 *Lehideux and Isorni v France*, Application No. 24662/94, 23 September 1998, para 53.
12 Ibid.

In *Norwood v the United Kingdom*,[13] the applicant, who was a regional organiser for the British National Party (BNP), had displayed a large poster, supplied by the BNP, in his window that showed a photograph of the twin towers in flame and the words 'Islam out of Britain – Protect the British People' and a symbol of a crescent and star in a prohibition sign. Applicant complained that his conviction for causing alarm and distress was a violation of his freedom of speech. The European Court of Human Rights held that:

> The words and images on the poster amounted to a public expression of attack on all Muslims in the United Kingdom. Such a general, vehement attack against a religious group, linking the group as a whole with a grave act of terrorism, is incompatible with the values proclaimed and guaranteed by the Convention, notably tolerance, social peace and non-discrimination. The applicant's display of the poster in his window constituted an act within the meaning of Article 17, which did not, therefore, enjoy the protection of Articles 10 or 14.

This case has been strongly criticised in the literature.[14] Hare, for example, writes that the decision is contrary to the free speech principle because 'speech on matters of public controversy (such as race and religion) . . . is generally regarded as entitled to the highest level of protection' and that 'the mere fact that such views are expressed in crude and offensive language does not deprive them of this high level of protection'.[15] The poster in question in this case certainly expressed a matter of public controversy and an issue that was very much in the public debate at that time (the poster was put up in November 2001, so not long after the events of the 11th of September 2001 when the twin towers in New York were attacked by Islamist terrorists). As an expression that contributed to the public debate, the expression should have been given a very high level of protection as was discussed in Chapter 1. Hare writes that 'it is also broadly acknowledged that the hostile reaction of an audience to certain speech or the likelihood that they will be offended by it cannot be used as justifications for restrictions'[16] and, that the decision in *Norwood v the United Kingdom* is 'inconsistent with, or at least gravely undermines, the Court's oft-repeated statements that Article 10 also

---

13 *Norwood v the United Kingdom*, supra note 3.
14 See for example: Foster, S., 'Case Comment: Racist Speech and Articles 10 and 17 of the European Convention on Human Rights', 10 (1) *Coventry Law Journal* (2005) 94–95; Hare, I., 'Crosses, Crescents and Sacred Cows: Criminalising Incitement to Religious Hatred', *Public Law* (2006); Cannie, H. and Voorhoof, D., 'The Abuse Clause and Freedom of Expression in the European Human Rights Convention: An Added Value for Democracy and Human Rights Protection?', 29 (1) *Netherlands Quarterly of Human Rights* (2011) 63 and 77–78; Buyse, supra note 7, 495; O'Reilly, A., 'In Defence of Offence: Freedom of Expression, Offensive Speech, and the Approach of the European Court of Human Rights', 19 *Trinity College Law Review* (2016) 242–243.
15 Hare, supra note 14, 527. In a similar vein, O'Reilly, supra note 14, 243.
16 Hare, supra note 14, 528.

applies to expressions which offend, shock and disturb'.[17] Again, this reason has already been part of the discussions in Chapter 1: that merely causing offence to some people is not enough to justify an interference with article 10 and there is no right not to be offended in the ECHR.

But, apart from being contrary to the free speech principle on the above grounds, Hare's other arguments are also worth mentioning. He writes that the decision 'has the effect of removing the speech in question from the protection of Art. 10 altogether', which is 'particularly dangerous since it eliminates the requirement that the state has to justify the interference with Convention rights and drastically reduces the Court's role in ensuring that any limitations are narrowly construed and convincingly established'.[18] Article 17 is, therefore, sometimes referred to as a 'guillotine' provision.[19] Villiger expresses this as follows:

> By applying Article 17 directly, the Court actually pre-empts its own conclusion: it immediately arrives at its results without first analysing and balancing the content of the views expressed, as would normally be required under Article 10 para 2 of the Convention.[20]

Villiger also mentions the reluctance of the Court to invoke article 17 and concludes that 'extreme ideas may well eventually render the application inadmissible, but as part of the freedom of expression they at least deserve a certain scrutiny as to their content'.[21]

The most frequently raised objection against the use of article 17 is, therefore, that article 17 does not leave room for a balancing exercise.[22] For example, Buyse also mentions that the Court's jurisprudence on article 17 'has been criticised for the very reason that it does not allow for a balancing of rights and interests'.[23] He writes that, from a human rights perspective, reviewing applications under article 10 'is to be preferred since it explicitly evaluates arguments for and against

---

17 Ibid. 530. See also: O'Reilly, supra note 14, 243. See for a discussion of this argument also: Weinstein, J., 'Extreme Speech, Public order, and Democracy: Lessons from *The Masses*', in Hare and Weinstein, supra note 14, 23–61. Weinstein criticises the UK case of *Norwood v DPP* [2003] EWHC 1564, the domestic procedure before the case went to the European Court of Human Rights.

18 Hare, supra note 14, 530.

19 Tulkens, F., 'When to Say is to Do: Freedom of Expression and Hate Speech in the Case-law of the European Court of Human Rights', in Casadevall, J., Myjer, E., O'Boyle, M. and Austin, A., (eds) *Freedom of Expression, Essays in Honour of Nicolas Bratza* (Oisterwijk, the Netherlands, Wolf Legal Publishers, 2012) 284.

20 Villiger, M., Article 17 ECHR and Freedom of Speech in Strasbourg Practice', in Casadevall *et al.*, supra note 19, 329.

21 Ibid.

22 See for example, Grimm, D., 'Freedom of Speech in a Globalized World', in Hare and Weinstein supra note 14, 78; Buyse, supra note 7, 495; Foster, supra note 14, 94–95; Cannie and Voorhoof, supra note 14, 73–78.

23 Buyse, supra note 7, 495.

the prohibition of punishment of specific expressions'.[24] Foster also suggests 'that restrictions on free speech should be dealt with under article 10(2) of the Convention' because 'in that way a full discussion as to the legitimacy and necessity of any violation can be engaged in'.[25] In fact, Buyse points out that Norwood himself had tried to convince the Court to do a balancing exercise and had pointed out that he lived in 'a rural area not greatly affected by racial or religious tension and there was no evidence that a single Muslim had seen the poster',[26] something that would surely have been taken into account if the Court had done a balancing exercise under article 10(2) ECHR, as will become clear below.

It is submitted that supervision by the Court and a balancing of all the interests involved is, indeed, to be preferred to stop states from arbitrarily imposing restrictions on expressions, especially expressions of dissent. This is expressed as follows by Hare in another point of criticism about the decision in *Norwood v the United Kingdom*:

> The decision creates a serious risk that the state will (especially in times of particular religious or cultural sensitivity) be able to restrict or prohibit with impunity the expression of unpopular views by those who do not espouse mainstream liberal positions. If this is permitted to occur, the essential contribution which pluralism, tolerance and broadmindedness make to the definition of a democratic society under the Convention is substantially negated.[27]

In other words, article 17 would then be used to negate or undermine democracy, rather than protecting it. Foster expresses this as follows:

> Article 17 obviously plays an essential role in upholding the fundamental principles of democracy, equality and tolerance, but if it is used too widely its effect may be detrimental to the rule of law and the control of arbitrary interference with human rights.[28]

In *Féret v Belgium,* dissenting judge Sajó expressed his opinion that invoking the spirits of the ECHR failed to provide unambiguous standards and opened the door to abuse, because personal convictions, including those of judges, can influence our ideas about what is actually dangerous.[29]

Cannie and Voorhoof point out that 'application of the abuse clause removes the need for member States to pertinently and sufficiently justify interference and drastically reduces the European Court's role in ensuring that limitations are narrowly construed and convincingly established', and this 'could provoke

---

24 Ibid. 496.
25 Foster, supra note 14, 94–95.
26 Buyse, supra note 7, 495.
27 Hare, supra note 15, 530.
28 Foster, supra note 14, 94.
29 *Féret v Belgium*, Application No. 15615/07, 16 July 2009, Dissenting Opinion Judge Sajó.

a decreasing impact of European free speech guarantees at the domestic level'.[30] Therefore, the use of article 17 should only be applied in very limited circumstances and cases of hate speech should be considered under the three part justification test of Article 10(2). This fits in with the European Court of Human Rights own explanation about the purpose of Article 17.

Another reason why Hare criticises the decision in *Norwood v the United Kingdom* is that it is:

> Contrary to earlier statements from the European Commission on Human Rights to the effect that Art. 17 is strictly confined to those situations which threaten the democratic system of the state itself and even then is limited to the extent that the restriction is proportionate to the seriousness and duration of the threat.[31]

Again, it is suggested that this is a valid point of criticism. In the case of *Norwood v the United Kingdom* itself, the European Court of Human Rights stated that the purpose of article 17 is 'to prevent totalitarian or extremist groups from justifying their activities by referring to the Convention'.[32] This statement was made in earlier cases[33] as well as being repeated in later cases such as *Kasymakhunov and Saybatalov v Russia*.[34] Further support for the argument that article 17 is limited to extreme cases can be found in *Soulas v France*, where the applicants were convicted for inciting hatred and violence against Muslim communities through the publication of a book entitled *The Colonisation of Europe*, with the subtitle *Truthful remarks about immigration and Islam*. They complained about a breach of their freedom of expression under article 10.[35] Although the book intended to give readers a feeling of rejection and antagonism, used military language, described Muslims as the main enemy, and wanted the readers to share the solution recommended in the book, which was a war of ethnic conquest, the Court held that the disputed passages were not sufficiently serious to justify the application of article 17 ECHR.[36] The Court was even clearer in *Paksas v Lithuania*, where it considered that article 17 'is applicable only on an exceptional basis

---

30 Cannie and Voorhoof, supra note 14, 72.
31 Hare, supra note 14, 530. Hare refers to the Commission Decision of *De Becker v Belgium*, Application No. 214/56, 27 March 1962.
32 *Norwood v the United Kingdom*, supra note 3, para 109.
33 See, for example, *Glimmerveen and Hagenbeek v the Netherlands*, Application Nos 8348/78 and 8406/78, 11 October 1979; *W.P. and Others v Poland*, Application No 42264/98, 2 September 2004.
34 *Kasymakhunov and Saybatalov v Russia*, Application Nos 26261/05 and 26377/06, 14 March 2013, para 103.
35 *Soulas v France*, Application No. 15948/03, 10 July 2008, paras 1–8.
36 Ibid. paras 40–49. Similarly, in *Leroy v France*, Application No 36109/03, 2 October 2008, the conviction of the creator of a cartoon for complicity in condoning terrorism was considered. The European Court of Human Rights held that the message of the applicant, the destruction of American imperialism, was not aimed at the negation of fundamental rights and that the cartoon and the accompanying text were not so unequivocal a justification of terrorism that the applicant should be deprived of the protection of Article 10 (para 27).

and in extreme cases, as indeed is illustrated by the Court's case-law'.[37] And, in *Perinçek v Switzerland*, the Court stated that:

> Article 17 is, as recently confirmed by the Court, only applicable on an exceptional basis and in extreme cases. Its effect is to negate the exercise of the Convention right that the applicant seeks to vindicate in the proceedings before the Court. In cases concerning Article 10 of the Convention, it should only be resorted to if it is immediately clear that the impugned statements sought to deflect this Article from its real purpose by employing the right to freedom of expression for ends clearly contrary to the values of the Convention.[38]

So, the Court in both these cases clearly limited the application of article 17 to exceptional and extreme cases and decided that article 17 did not apply in either case. Rainey *et al.* write that 'the object of Article 17, therefore, is to limit the rights guaranteed only to the extent that such limitation is necessary to prevent their total subversion, and it must be quite narrowly constructed in relation to this object'.[39] *Norwood v the United Kingdom* does appear, therefore, to be an exception to this general rule. As Buyse writes, 'hateful utterances are not often considered under Article 17: the Court addresses the majority of such instances through substantive assessments' and 'one of the rare exceptions is the case of Norwood'.[40] It is suggested that *Norwood v the United Kingdom* was not an exceptional and extreme case and thus it should not have been dismissed under article 17. Instead, it should have been considered under article 10 and a balancing of interests should have taken place. Rainey *et al.* appear to agree with this as they comment that 'the Court does not always seem to be consistent in its use of Article 17. In recent times, it has been used to dismiss an application without elaboration of possible justifications for a repressive measure taken by a Contracting Party. A good example is the Norwood case'.[41] But maybe *Norwood v the United Kingdom* was decided as it was because the poster referred to, and was put up shortly after, such a serious and world-shocking event. A recent case where the application of article 17 led to an inadmissibility decision can be found in *Hizb Ut-Tahrir and Others v Germany*, where applicants denied the State of Israel's right to exist and called for the violent destruction of Israel and for the banishment and killing of all its inhabitants.[42]

---

37 *Paksas v Lithuania*, Application No. 34932/04, 6 January 2011, para 87. Para 88 gives a good summary of some of the case law of the European Court of Human Rights on Article 17.
38 *Perinçek v Switzerland*, Application No. 27510/08, 15 October 2015 (Grand Chamber), para 114.
39 Rainey, B., Wicks, E. and Ovey, C., *Jacobs, White and Ovey The European Convention on Human Rights* (6th edn, Oxford, Oxford University Press, 2014) 121.
40 Buyse, supra note 7, 495.
41 Rainey *et al.*, supra note 39, 124.
42 *Hizb Ut-Tahrir and Others v Germany*, Application No. 31098/08, 12 June 2012.

One more point needs to be made and that is the link between article 17 and a democratic society, which will be clear from some of the above. As was explained in Chapter 1, there is a clear connection between the ECHR and democracy and that 'democracy thus appears to be the only political model contemplated by the Convention and, accordingly, the only one compatible with it'.[43] Article 17 is, according the European Commission on Human Rights, 'designed to safeguard the rights listed therein by protecting the free operation of democratic institutions'.[44] Weber states that 'the aim of Article 17 is to guarantee the permanent maintaining of the system of democratic values underlying the Convention'.[45] In *Kasymakhunov and Saybatalov v Russia*, the applicants were both members of *Hizb Ut-Tahrir*. The European Court of Human Rights explained that 'in view of the very clear link between the Convention and democracy, no one may be authorised to rely on the Convention's provisions in order to weaken or destroy the ideals and values of a democratic society'.[46] The Court in that case defined

> The limits within which political organisations can continue to enjoy the protection of the Convention while conducting their activities. It has found that a political organisation may promote a change in the law or the legal and constitutional structures of the State on two conditions: firstly, the means used to that end must be legal and democratic; secondly, the change proposed must itself be compatible with fundamental democratic principles. It necessarily follows that a political organisation whose leaders incite to violence or put forward a policy which fails to respect democracy or which is aimed at the destruction of democracy and the flouting of the rights and freedoms recognised in a democracy cannot lay claim to the Convention's protection against penalties imposed on those grounds.[47]

The Court referred to its decision in *Hizb Ut-Tahrir and Others v Germany*,[48] and concluded that 'the dissemination of the political ideas of Hizb Ut-Tahrir by the applicants clearly constitutes an activity falling within the scope of Article 17 of the Convention'.[49]

Therefore, article 17 ECHR should only be applied in exceptional and extreme cases where the fundamental democratic principles and values of the state are at stake. If this is not the case, restrictions on the freedom of expression should be scrutinised under the three part justification test of article 10(2). It will be clear that this accords with the importance of the right to freedom of expression for

---

43 *United Communist Party of Turkey and Others v Turkey*, Application No. 19392/92, 30 January 1998, para 45.
44 *German Communist Party v Germany*, Application No. 250/57, 20 July 1957.
45 Weber, supra note 1, 22.
46 *Kasymakhunov and Saybatalov v Russia*, supra note 34, para 104.
47 Ibid. para 105.
48 *Hizb Ut-Tahrir and Others v Germany*, supra note 42.
49 *Kasymakhunov and Saybatalov v Russia*, supra note 34, para 113.

a democratic society that has been stressed throughout previous chapters. The following part of this Chapter looks at article 10(2).

Article 10(2) ECHR

In Chapter 1, it was made clear that the right to freedom of expression in article 10(1) ECHR is not an absolute right. It can be restricted under certain circumstances which are described in article 10(2): any limitation or restriction must be prescribed by law; and, must be necessary in a democratic society for one or more of the aims described in article 10(2). The European Court of Human Rights has explained that 'necessary in a democratic society' in article 10(2) means that there must be a 'pressing social need' and this, in turn, means that the restriction must be proportionate to the legitimate aim pursued.[50] Article 10(2) sums up the legitimate aims: the interests of national security, territorial integrity or public safety, the prevention of disorder or crime, the protection of health or morals, the protection of the reputation or rights of others, the prevention of disclosure of information received in confidence, or the maintenance of the authority and impartiality of the judiciary.

It was also explained in Chapter 3, that laws against (religious) hate speech, laws that prohibit incitement to (religious) hatred, can, according to the European Court of Human Rights, be compatible with article 10 ECHR as long as they fulfil the three part justification test in article 10(2).[51] So, convictions for hate speech under such laws will not always be held to violate the right to freedom of expression.

Cases relating to hate speech usually reach the European Court of Human Rights when someone is convicted under national hate speech or incitement laws and then applies to the Court claiming that their conviction is a violation of their right to freedom of expression under article 10 ECHR. But in some cases, the expression is stopped before it takes place, in other words, in those cases 'prior restraint' takes place. A good example is *Wingrove v the United Kingdom,* which related to a film called 'visions of ecstasy', a film depicting erotic visions of St Teresa of Avilla, a sixteenth century nun. The British Board of Film Classification refused to give the film a classification which meant that the film could not be shown or released on video.[52] Despite the fact that the Court was aware that the measures taken by the authorities amounted to a complete ban on the film's distribution[53] and, despite the fact that it stated that cases of prior restraint called for special scrutiny by the Court,[54] it held that the restraint in this case

50 *Handyside v the United Kingdom,* Application No. 5493/72, 7 December 1976, paras 48 and 49.
51 *Gündüz v Turkey,* Application No. 35071/97, 4 December 2003, paras 40–41. See also: *Erbakan v Turkey,* Application No. 59405/00, 6 July 2006, para 56.
52 *Wingrove v the United Kingdom,* Application No. 17419/90, 25 November 1996.
53 Ibid. para 64.
54 Ibid. para 58.

was justified, to avoid a criminal conviction under the laws of blasphemy and, thus, the national authorities had not overstepped their margin of appreciation.[55] Therefore, according to the European Court of Human Rights, hate speech laws and even prior restraints on expressions that incite to hatred can be compatible with the right to freedom of expression as guaranteed by article 10 ECHR. But where are the limits to such restrictions? This will be examined here.

In Chapter 1, it was mentioned that the European Court of Human Rights appears to have imposed a duty on politicians not to foster intolerance. In *Erbakan v Turkey,* Erbakan, the leader of a political party and previous Prime Minister of Turkey, had been convicted for incitement to hatred and hostility for remarks made in a public speech about distinctions between religions, races and regions. The speech had been made in an area that had been subject to terrorist attacks. The European Court of Human Rights held that combating all forms of intolerance was an integral part of human rights protection and that it was crucially important that in their speeches politicians should avoid making comments likely to foster such intolerance.[56]

In *Féret v Belgium,* a politician was convicted of incitement to discrimination and hatred. His party had, during the run-up to an election, distributed leaflets that he had written and posters presenting non-European migrant communities in Belgium, including Moroccans and Muslims, as criminally-minded, inferior to Belgian and European people and keen to exploit the Belgian benefits system. The European Court of Human Rights held that political speech that stirred up hatred based on religious, ethnic or cultural prejudices was a threat to social peace and political stability in democratic states.[57] Politicians, when expressing themselves in public, had to avoid fostering intolerance and should exercise particular caution because fostering the exclusion of foreigners was a fundamental attack on their rights. Thus, Féret's conviction was held not to interfere with article 10 ECHR.[58]

This would suggest, as was discussed in Chapter 1, that politicians have a duty not to foster intolerance when exercising their freedom of speech and that national (criminal) laws that prohibit expressions that 'foster intolerance' would be compatible with the ECHR. However, the term 'fostering intolerance' is very vague and open to a very broad interpretation, and thus to abuse, by states. Many expressions, especially if they are criticising a religion or belief or religious believers, can be seen as intolerant to the religious group targeted. It would then only be a small step to claim that such expressions foster intolerance between this group and others in society and thus must be prohibited. It also seems to come close to accepting a right not to be offended in one's religious feelings, which, as argued before, is not present in article 9 ECHR.

It is submitted that accepting that mere fostering intolerance is enough to prohibit hate speech puts the threshold for justification under article 10(2) too low,

---

55 Ibid. paras 61 and 64.
56 *Erbakan v Turkey,* supra note 51, para 64.
57 *Féret v Belgium,* supra note 29, para 73.
58 Ibid. para 75.

especially in relation to speech about issues contributing to the public debate. In fact, in *Erbakan v Turkey*, the European Court of Human Rights followed its consideration about the duty of politicians not to foster intolerance with a confirmation that free political debate was fundamental in a democracy and that there should be very serious reasons for an interference with political expressions.[59] The Court found a violation of Erbakan's right to freedom of expression.[60] A number of factors played a role in the Court's decision, including the fact that the prosecution was not instigated until more than four years after the event and the very high penalty imposed. The Court also considered that it had not been established that, at the time of his prosecution, the speech in question had given rise to, or been likely to give rise to, a 'present risk' and an 'imminent' danger.[61] A similar consideration can be found in *GÜl and Others v. Turkey*, where the Court pointed out that there was no 'clear and imminent danger' that required an interference with the right to freedom of expression of the applicant.[62] This will be analysed further below, but it already suggests that mere fostering intolerance is not enough to justify a restriction.

Despite the fact that the European Court of Human Rights, in both *Erbakan v Turkey*[63] and in *Féret v Belgium*,[64] referred to the duty of politicians not to foster intolerance through their speeches, the outcome of both cases was different. Erbakan's conviction was held to violate article 10, but Féret's conviction was held not to do so. This difference could be based on the fact that the criminal proceedings against Erbakan were instigated more than four years after the expressions were made, while there was no such delay in *Féret v Belgium*. Another explanation could be that Erbakan's remarks targeted a religion and religious groups, while Féret's expressions had a racist undertone. The European Court of Human Rights might have considered the latter more serious for this reason. As mentioned in Chapter 3, racist hate speech is seen by some as more serious than religious hate speech and, thus, racist hate speech should be punished more severely and restrictions on such speech are thus more likely to pass the justification test in article 10(2) ECHR. It is unclear whether the fact that different countries were involved in the cases also played a role in the decisions of the Court.

Whatever the reason for the different decisions in these cases, the European Court of Human Rights held that politicians were under a duty to avoid fostering intolerance, although, in *Erbakan v Turkey*, the Court appeared to indicate that 'present risk' or 'imminent danger' of violence is required. The one dissenting judge in *Erbakan v Turkey* pointed out that the impact of Erbakan's words could only be measured over time but that his speech was, in her view, a harmful

---

59   *Erbakan v Turkey*, supra note 51, para 65.
60   Ibid. para 71.
61   Ibid. para 68.
62   *GÜl and Others v. Turkey*, Application No. 4870/02, 8 June 2010, para 42. This echoes the 'clear and present danger' test used in the US. This will be discussed in Chapter 5.
63   *Erbakan v Turkey*, supra note 51, para 68.
64   *Féret v Belgium*, supra note 29.

contribution to a climate of intolerance nourishing primitive prejudice and cleavages in society.[65] But taking this to its logical conclusion, it would suggest that fostering intolerance or even contributing to the growth of intolerance over time would be enough to prohibit certain expressions. However, this is very difficult to put down in criminal law or to take into account in a criminal case and it raises problems with causation, proof and culpability.[66] Moreover, it would mean that someone could be prosecuted and punished because their expressions could or might have some effect, might be harmful in the future. People are not usually punished 'for things that *could within some imaginable scenario* result from their actions' [emphasis in original], and it is precisely to avoid this happening that the rule of law was created.[67] Bonello expresses this well where he writes that:

> The criminalization of incitement is a very special, almost unique, type of offence. It criminalizes anticipatory, not the act of incitement itself, but the evil consequences which are believed might flow from the act. In basic terms, it renders a human action criminal by guesswork, because words are in themselves harmless, and only their anticipated effect can cause social injury. . . . It punishes prospectively what could be harmless retrospectively.[68]

Therefore, punishing expressions for the effect they might have in the future presents huge problems from a criminal law point of view.

On the other hand, the European Court of Human Rights, in *Féret v Belgium*, did seem to hold that mere fostering intolerance is enough.[69] As Sottieaux writes, 'the real test the Strasbourg Court uses to justify the suppression of "hate speech" is . . . the dangerous tendency of the impugned discourse'.[70] Both these suggest that the Court accepts punishment of expression based on the effect it can have in the future. However, the judges in *Féret v Belgium* were sharply divided: four of the judges (the majority) held that Féret's conviction had not been a violation of article 10(2) ECHR on the above grounds, but the three dissenting judges did not agree with this. The dissenters stated that there had been an interference with Féret's right to freedom of expression and that combating mere intolerance was not, in their view, sufficient to justify infringing the freedom of expression of the applicant. *Real – and not potential – impact* on the rights of others needed to be demonstrated [emphasis added].[71] The dissenters also remarked that the idea of 'dangerous discourse' without more precise definition would lead to a rapid

---

65 *Erbakan v Turkey*, supra note 51, dissenting Opinion Judge Steiner, para 2.
66 See on this: Buyse, supra note 7, 499.
67 Heinze, E., *Hate Speech and Democratic Citizenship* (Oxford, Oxford University Press, 2016) 170.
68 Bonello, G., 'Freedom of Expression and Incitement to Violence', in Casadevall *et al.*, supra note 19, 352.
69 *Féret v Belgium*, supra note 29.
70 Sottieaux, S., '"Bad Tendencies" in the ECtHR "Hate Speech" Jurisprudence', 7 (1) *European Constitutional Law Review* (2011) 54.
71 *Féret v Belgium*, supra note 29, dissenting opinion.

extension of the list of prohibited speech.[72] Sottieaux also argues that the Court should abandon this 'bad tendency' approach, as he calls it.[73]

It is submitted that, in this, the judgment in *Erbakan v Turkey*[74] and the opinion of the dissenters should be followed and laws against incitement to hatred or violence should only be held to be compatible with the ECHR if there is real impact, present risk and imminent danger of violence. The reasons for this are, first, that the term 'fostering intolerance' is too vague, brings legal uncertainty and is, therefore, open to abuse by states; and, second, because the European Court of Human Rights has, as has been mentioned in previous chapters, always held that freedom of speech, because of the very important role this right plays in a democratic society, includes expressions that offend, shock or disturb.[75] As Buyse writes, the dissenters in *Féret v Belgium*:

> Pointed out the difference between incitement – with direct effect – and the long-term consolidation of prejudice and intolerance. Such potential future dangers should not be presented as an apocalyptic scenario which warrants limits on freedom of expression in the present. To do so would limit free political debate and deny the power of counter-arguments and the independent formation of opinions.[76]

Voorhoof criticises the European Court of Human Rights in *Féret v Belgium*, for not clearly differentiating between the different political pamphlets at issue in that case. By doing so, the Court could have avoided holding that punishment of political criticism is protected by the right to freedom of expression in article 10. The pamphlets that criticised a minister, a political party, the money-wasting government and their integration policies should have attracted the extensive protection given to political speech, while other pamphlets, that incited to hatred of foreigners, should not have done so, according to Voorhoof.[77] He also writes that the Court's argument to legitimise the criminal conviction that political speech that stirred hatred was a threat to social peace and political stability in democratic states is far-fetched and difficult to reconcile with the wide freedom of speech given to expressions contributing to the political debates especially during elections.[78]

An expression by a politician should, therefore, not be held against the law merely on the ground that it fosters intolerance because of the important

72 Ibid.
73 Sottieaux, supra note 70, 58.
74 *Erbakan v Turkey*, supra note 51.
75 *Handyside v the United Kingdom*, supra note 50, para 48.
76 Buyse, supra note 7, 499–500.
77 Voorhoof, D., 'Polticus die Haat Zaait is Strafbaar', Noot onder Féret/Belgie, EHRM 16 juli 2009 (*Appl. No. 15615/07*) (Politician who sows Hatred can be Punished, Case Comment *Féret/Belgium*, European Court of Human Rights, 16 July 2009) *Media Forum* 2009/11, para 10 (in Dutch, translation by author).
78 Ibid.

role politicians play in the political and public debate. Real impact or present danger should be required to restrict the right to freedom of expression and, even then the restriction is still subject to the justification test in article 10(2) ECHR.

The Parliamentary Assembly of the Council of Europe considers that 'national law should only penalise expressions about religious matters which intentionally and severely disturb public order and call for public violence'.[79] This also suggests that more than mere fostering intolerance is required.

Support for this can be found in both literature and case law. For example, Lester mentions that 'advocacy of religious hatred can properly be punished or suppressed only when it constitutes imminent incitement to unlawful acts of discrimination, hostility or violence'.[80] Kapai and Cheung write that incitement to hatred and violence should only be accepted if 'it is likely that violence will indeed occur'.[81] And, Cannie and Voorhoof criticise the European Court of Human Rights in *Le Pen v France*,[82] for not examining whether there was any actual violence as a consequence of the speech.[83] Bonello criticises the Court's decision in *Zana v Turkey* because there is 'not a trace of a "clear and present danger" analysis',[84] and opines that 'the suppression of freedom of expression is justifiable in a democratic society only when the words reproved would beget immediate lawless action', thereby echoing the US approach to hate speech.[85]

Apart from in *Erbakan v Turkey*,[86] some support for the argument that only hate speech that has real impact and that is likely to lead to violence can be restricted without violating article 10(2) ECHR can be found in the case law of the European Court of Human Rights as well. In *Hocaoğulları v Turkey*, the Court held:

> The language of the author, who was targeting young people and explaining to them that no revolution was possible without loss of life, could not be regarded as calling for peace or the peaceful settlement of political problems. On the whole, the tenor of the article could be construed as *incitement to violence, armed resistance or an uprising*. This article in particular was capable of *stirring up violence in Turkey*; it could not be regarded as compatible with

---

79 Parliamentary Assembly, Council of Europe, Recommendation 1805 (2007) *Blasphemy, Religious Insults and Hate Speech against Persons on Grounds of their Religion*, para 15 http://assembly.coe.int/nw/xml/XRef/Xref-XML2HTML-en.asp?fileid=17569&lang=en

80 Lester, A., *Free Speech and Religion – The Eternal Conflict in the Age of Selective Modernization*, keynote speech, 2006, 2 www.odysseustrust.org/lectures/274_Hungarytalk.pdf

81 Kapai, P. and Cheung, A., 'Hanging in the Balance: Freedom of Expression and Religion', 15 *Buffalo Human Rights Law Review* (2009) 77.

82 *Le Pen v France*, Application No. 18788/09, 20 April 2010 (Admissibility Decision).

83 Cannie and Voorhoof, supra note 14, 76, footnote 87.

84 Bonello, supra note 68, 350. *Zana v Turkey*, Application No. 18954/91, 25 November 1997.

85 Bonello, supra note 68, 359.

86 *Erbakan v Turkey*, supra note 51.

the spirit of tolerance and went against the fundamental values of justice and peace expressed in the Preamble to the Convention [emphasis added].[87]

In *Soulas and Others v France*, the European Court of Human Rights mentioned that the style of the book in question was polemic; it used military language; it presented the effects of immigration as close to catastrophic; and, it led the readers to share the solution recommended by the author, namely a war of ethnic re-conquest. Because of this, the conviction of the authors was not considered to have violated their right to freedom of expression.[88]

On the other hand, in a number of cases, the Court has held that the words used, although they have a hostile tone, do not encourage or incite violence.[89] In *Arslan v Turkey*, for example, the Court held that the book in question painted an extremely negative picture of the population of Turkish origin and had a hostile narrative, but that it did not constitute an incitement to violence, armed resistance or an uprising.[90] In *Dicle v Turkey*, the Court considered that certain particularly acerbic passages of the article had portrayed the state in a most negative light, so that it carried hostile undertones, but it had not encouraged the use of violence, armed resistance or insurrection and *did not constitute hate speech* [emphasis added].[91] And, in *Gündüz v Turkey*, the Court considered that 'the mere fact of defending sharia, without calling for violence to establish it cannot be regarded as "hate speech"'.[92]

The European Court of Human Rights was even clearer in *Vajnai v Hungary*, where a politician who was Vice-President of the Workers Party was convicted of wearing a totalitarian symbol in public. The applicant had worn a red star as symbol of the international workers movement at a legal demonstration.[93] The Court considered that there was no evidence that there was a 'real and present danger' and that the government, prior to enacting the ban in question, had not shown the existence of such a threat.[94] The Court also expressed the view that 'the containment of a mere speculative danger, as a preventive measure for the protection of democracy, cannot be seen as a "pressing social need"'.[95]

---

87 *Hocaoğulları v Turkey*, Application No 77109/01, 7 March 2006, paras 39 and 40.

88 *Soulas and Others v France*, supra note 35, paras 41 and 43.

89 See, for example: *Arslan v Turkey*, Application No. 23462/94, 8 July 1999, para 48; *Polat v Turkey*, Application No. 23500/94, 8 July 1999, para 47; *Duzgoren v Turkey*, Application No. 56827/00, 9 November 2006, para 31; *GÜl and Others v Turkey*, Application No. 4870/02, 8 June 2010, para 42.

90 *Arslan v Turkey*, supra note 89, para 48.

91 *Dicle v Turkey*, Application No. 46733/99, 11 April 2006, para 33. See also: *Duzgoren v Turkey*, supra note 89, para 31, *Erdal Taş v Turkey*, Application No. 77650/01, 19 December 2006, para 38; *Faruk Temel v Turkey*, Application No. 16853/05, 1 February 2011, para 62.

92 *Gündüz v Turkey*, supra note 51, para 51.

93 *Vajnai v Hungary*, Application No. 33629/06, 8 July 2008.

94 Ibid. para 49.

95 Ibid. para 55.

Therefore, only (religious) hate speech that has 'real impact', that carries a 'present risk' or 'imminent danger' that violence will follow, should fall outside the protection of article 10(2) ECHR. Any speech that falls short of this should be protected. In Chapter 2, it was argued that speech that prevents religious believers exercising their right to freedom of religion or to manifest their religion should not attract the protection of article 10(2) either. This is linked to the point above, because incitement to hatred and violence which is very likely to lead to violence, can have such an effect. It is argued here that the freedom of expression of politicians should only be limited in these two circumstances: where it constitutes hate speech and there is a real likelihood that violence will occur imminently or where it factually stops people from holding, manifesting or practising their religious beliefs. And, even then, both restrictions are still subject to the three part justification test in article 10(2) ECHR and the European Court of Human Rights should scrutinise carefully whether the means used to restrict the right to freedom of expression are proportionate to the aim of protecting the rights of others. And, just 'fostering intolerance' or 'offending religious feelings' should never be enough to justify restrictions. Laws banning hate speech should thus be scrutinised very strictly. Another argument for very strict scrutiny is given by Chan, where he writes that 'there is no conclusive evidence for the proposition that hate speech is a significant cause of violence or discrimination, nor any evidence to show that hate speech bans reduce incidents of intolerance in society'.[96] Chan concludes from this that it is imperative that alternatives to hate speech bans are considered,[97] something which will be examined in Chapter 5. In the last part of this Chapter, the factors the European Court of Human Rights takes into account when assessing whether a restriction on the right to freedom of expression under article 10(2) ECHR is justified are analysed.

Factors playing a role in justification under article 10(2) ECHR

First, in order to determine whether a form of expression can legitimately be restricted under article 10(2) ECHR, the European Court of Human Rights will look at the case as a whole.[98] The Court will examine the particular circumstances of the case and take a number of issues into account, including the aim pursued by the speaker or author; the content of the expression; the context in which it was disseminated and the potential impact of the remarks; the status and role in society of the maker and of the target of the statement; and, the nature and seriousness of the interference, including the severity of the penalty.[99] All these issues are linked and interrelated and it is, according to

---

96 Chan, S., 'Hate Speech Bans: An Intolerant Response to Intolerance', 14 *Trinity College Law Review* (2011), 93.

97 Ibid.

98 See, for example, *Jersild v Denmark*, Application No. 15890/89, 23 September 1994, para 31; *Ceylan v Turkey*, Application No. 23556/94, 8 July 1999, para 32; and, recently, *Perinçek v Switzerland*, supra note 38, para 196 (iii).

99 Weber, supra note 1, 33–46.

the Court in *Perinçek v Switzerland*, 'the interplay between the various factors rather than any one of them taken in isolation that determined the outcome of the case [in the cases discussed]. The Court's approach to that type of case can thus be described as highly context-specific'.[100] This does mean that it is difficult to predict the outcome of any case based on previous cases, although the above factors play a role in the Court's assessment. Each of these factors will be discussed in turn.

The purpose or aim pursued by the speaker or author

Weber writes that 'the objective that is pursued is crucial: is it to disseminate racist ideas and opinions through hate speech or to inform the public on a question of public interest'? The answer, according to this author, should make it possible to distinguish between expressions that attract the protection of article 10 and those that cannot be tolerated in a democratic society.[101] However, it is submitted that this might appear simpler than it is in practice in many cases. An example of a case where it was easy to make this distinction is *Jersild v Denmark*, where a journalist was convicted of aiding and abetting racist statements when he made a radio programme in which he interviewed three members of the so-called Greenjackets, who made abusive remarks about immigrants and ethnic groups in Denmark and showed a white supremacist attitude. The European Court of Human Rights considered that the programme was introduced with a reference to recent public discussions and press comments on racism in Denmark and with an announcement that the aim of the programme was to address aspects of this problem, by identifying certain racist individuals and by portraying their mentality and social background. The Court took into account that the programme meant, through an interview, to expose, analyse and explain this particular group of youths, who were limited and frustrated by their social situation, had criminal records and violent attitudes. The programme thus dealt with specific aspects of an issue that was of great public concern at the time.[102] Therefore, the journalist clearly did not pursue a racist motive and meant to contribute to the public debate and, thus, his conviction was held to be a violation of his right to freedom of expression.

In contrast, in both *Halis Doğan v Turkey*, where a publisher of a weekly journal was sentenced for spreading separatist propaganda, and in *Lindon, Otchakovsky-Laurens and July v France*, where the author, the chairman of the publishing company and the publications director of a book were convicted for defamation of Jean Marie le Pen, then leader of the far-right National Front party in France, the European Court of Human Rights looked at the intention of the applicant to stigmatise the other party in the conflict in its decision that article

100 *Perinçek v Switzerland*, supra note 38, para 208.
101 Weber, supra note 1, 33.
102 *Jersild v Denmark*, supra note 98, para 33.

10 had not been violated.[103] However, in both these cases and in *Sürek v. Turkey (No. 1)*, where the Court said the same, it wasn't just the intention to stigmatise the other party, the Court also looked at the contents, which it saw, in all three cases, as advocating violence and hatred.[104] This shows the difficulty in looking at the intention of the speaker or author: as they themselves will usually state that they intended to contribute to the public debate, how can it be established that they intended to stir up hatred and violence? In all three cases, the Court looked at other factors to determine the intention of the speaker or author and whether there was a violation of article 10 ECHR. So, the Court takes the objective, the intent of the speaker or author into account, but it appears to use the other factors, such as the content and the language used, to establish this intent.

The content of the expression

The content of the expression is thus also taken into account, including the language used and whether this language can be seen as encouraging violence against or hatred of certain groups. In *Leroy v France*, the creator of a cartoon representing the attack on the twin towers of the World Trade Centre on 11 September 2001, with a caption that parodied the advertising slogan of a famous brand: "We have all dreamt of it . . . Hamas did it", was convicted for complicity in condoning terrorism. The cartoon had been published in a newspaper on 13 September 2001, two days after the attack. The European Court of Human Rights considered that the drawing was not limited to criticising American imperialism, but supported and glorified its violent destruction. The Court based this on the caption accompanying the drawing as well as on the consideration that the applicant had expressed his moral support for those whom he presumed to be the perpetrators of the attacks. Through his choice of language, according to the Court, the applicant had commented approvingly on the violence perpetrated against thousands of civilians and diminished the dignity of the victims.[105] In *Balsyte-Lideikiene v Lithuania*, the Court considered that the words used by the applicant expressed aggressive nationalism and ethnocentrism and that this incited to hatred against Poles and Jews.[106]

On the other hand, the European Court of Human Rights has held in some cases that the words used, although they have a hostile tone or connote hostility, do not encourage or incite violence.[107] In establishing this, the Court will often

---

103 *Halis Doğan v Turkey*, Application No. 4119/02, 10 October 2006, para 34; *Lindon, Otchakovsky-Laurens and July v France*, Application Nos 21279/02 and 36448/02, 22 October 2007, para 57. See also: *Sürek v. Turkey (No. 1)*, Application No. 26682/95, 8 July 1999, para 62.

104 *Sürek v. Turkey (No. 1)*, supra note 103, para 62.

105 *Leroy v France*, supra note 36, para 43.

106 *Balsyte-Lideikiene v Lithuania*, Application No. 72596/01, 4 November 2008, para 79.

107 See, for example: *Polat v Turkey*, supra note 89, para 47; *Duzgoren v Turkey*, Application No. 56827/00, 9 November 2006, para 31; *GÜl and Others v. Turkey*, supra note 61, paras 41–42.

use the other factors given above and below as well. For example, in *Polat v Turkey*, the Court held that the narrative in question had a hostile tone, but it did not constitute an incitement to violence, armed resistance or an uprising and that this was an essential factor 'especially as the events related happened at a period which is already relatively distant in time'.[108] And, in *Karatas v Turkey*, the Court took into account that the applicant was a private individual and that he expressed his views through poetry, which by definition addressed a small audience. So, even though the poems were aggressive in tone, the fact 'that they were artistic in nature and of limited impact made them less a call to an uprising than an expression of deep distress in the face of a difficult political situation'.[109]

Context of the expression

From the above, it will be clear that the context in which the expression is made also plays a role in the assessment of the European Court of Human Rights. This context includes: the historical background and situation in the country where the statement is made and whether the statement contributes to the public debate; the means used to make the statement; and, the way it is distributed, including whether it is available to the public at large or just a small group who choose to hear, read or attend. The latter also affects the impact of the statement, as was clear from *Karatas v Turkey*, mentioned above.[110] The role of political discourse of public interest is very important here. An example of a case where the Court looked at the situation and at the contribution to the current public debate in the country involved was already given above when *Jersild v Denmark* was discussed.[111] In *Perinçek v Switzerland*, the Court said that one of the factors taken into account was 'whether the statements were made against a tense political or social background'.[112] This is also illustrated by *Leroy v France*, where the fact that the cartoon appeared two days after the 9/11 attacks played a role in the Court's considerations.[113] On the other hand, the Court also pointed out that a lapse of time might make it inappropriate to deal with issues in the same severe way as they were dealt with in the past and that the need for regulation is bound to recede with the passage of time.[114]

Zana v Turkey illustrates a number of these points.[115] The European Court of Human Rights considered that the expressions were made by a person with some political standing (the former mayor of the most important city in South-East Turkey), who, in an interview published in a major national newspaper, indicated

108 *Polat v Turkey*, supra note 89, para 47.
109 *Karatas v Turkey*, Application No. 23168/94, 8 July 1999, para 52.
110 Ibid. See also *Polat v Turkey*, supra note 107, para 47, as discussed above.
111 *Jersild v Denmark*, supra note 98, para 33.
112 *Perinçek v Switzerland*, supra note 38, para 205.
113 *Leroy v France*, supra note 36, para 43.
114 *Perinçek v Switzerland*, supra note 38, paras 249–250.
115 *Zana v Turkey*, supra note 84.

that he supported the PKK national liberation movement. The statements also coincided with the murders of civilians by PKK militants in South-East Turkey, where there was extreme tension at the material time. The statements were likely to exacerbate an already explosive situation in that region, according to the Court and, therefore, it concluded that the interference with the applicant's right by the Turkish authorities was justified.[116]

In *Zana v Turkey*, the fact that the statements were published in a major national newspaper was taken into account. This shows that the means used to make the statement and the way it is distributed are taken into account by the European Court of Human Rights as well. In *Handyside v the United Kingdom*, the Court stated that the scope of the duties and responsibilities that article 10(2) imposes on the person exercising their freedom of expression depends on 'the technical means he uses'.[117] And, in *Jersild v Denmark*, the Court pointed out that 'the audiovisual media have often a much more immediate and powerful effect than the print media. The audiovisual media have means of conveying through images meanings which the print media are not able to impart'.[118]

On the other hand, the European Court of Human Rights has considered that expressions made through poetry[119] or a literary work[120] rather than through the mass media, have a far more limited potential impact on national security, public order and territorial integrity. In *Okcuoglu v Turkey*, the Court observed that 'the applicant's comments, made during a round-table debate, were published in a periodical whose circulation was low' and thus would have limited impact.[121] So, the likely impact of the expression plays a role as well.

Related to this is the question whether the statement or expression is only available to a small group of people who choose to hear it, read it or attend. O'Reilly refers to Feinberg and his concept of 'reasonable avoidability' in this context.[122] In other words, in some cases, the offending expression can be avoided by not going to see or hear it and where this is the case, any restrictions should be held to violate the freedom of expression. This aspect does seem to have been somewhat overlooked by the European Court of Human Rights. In Chapter 2, we criticised the majority decision of the Court in *Otto-Preminger-Institut v Austria*[123] for holding that the right of the religious majority had been impaired by the film in question, which depicted the figures of Christ, God and Mary in a disparaging way. The three dissenting judges found that the seizure and the ban of the film were disproportionate and thus that there had been a violation

---

116 Ibid. paras 57–60.

117 *Handyside v United Kingdom*, supra note 50, para 49.

118 *Jersild v Denmark*, supra note 98, para 31.

119 *Karatas v Turkey*, supra note 109, para 52.

120 *Arslan v Turkey*, supra note 89, para 48; see also: *Polat v Turkey*, supra note 107, para 47.

121 *Okcuoglu v Turkey*, Application No. 24246/94, 8 July 1999, para 48.

122 O'Reilly, supra note 14, 253, referring to Feinberg, J., *The Moral Limits of the Criminal Law: Volume 2 Offense to Others* (Oxford, Oxford University Press, 1988) 48.

123 *Otto-Preminger-Institut v Austria*, Application No. 13470/87, 20 September 1994.

of the right to freedom of expression. The dissenters considered that the film was meant to be shown to a paying audience in a cinema that catered for a small public interested in experimental films; that the film makers had provided sufficient information so anyone had the opportunity of being warned about the content of the film; and, that the film was also restricted to anyone over 17 years. Therefore, according to the dissenters, there was 'little likelihood in the instant case of anyone being confronted with objectionable material unwittingly'.[124] The dissenters thus concluded that the filmmakers had acted responsibly to avoid possible harmful effects of the film and that their right to freedom of expression was violated.[125] Therefore, the dissenting judges appear to agree with the argument that, where an offending expression can be avoided by not going to see or hear it, there should be no restriction on the expression and if there is, this violates the right to freedom of expression. O'Reilly points out that 'it must be acknowledged that in *Otto-Preminger*,[126] *Wingrove*,[127] *IA*,[128] *Gay News*[129] and *Handyside*,[130] the impugned materials constituted optional viewing or reading', in contrast to the anti-homosexuality leaflets at issue in *Vejdeland and Others v Sweden*,[131] that were placed in students' lockers without their consent and that students could thus not avoid.[132] So, the fact that an offending expression can or cannot be avoided should be taken into account as part of the context of the expression.

Status and role of speaker or author

The status and role played in society by the speaker or author plays a role as well. Weber states, 'the States' margin of appreciation is significantly narrower when the applicant is a politician, because of the fundamental character of the free play of political debate in a democratic society'.[133] In *Castells v Spain*, the European Court of Human Rights held that

> While freedom of expression is important for everybody, it is especially so for an elected representative of the people. He represents his electorate, draws attention to their preoccupations and defends their interests. Accordingly, interferences with the freedom of expression of an opposition member of parliament, like the applicant, call for the closest scrutiny on the part of the Court.[134]

---

124 Ibid. para 9.
125 Ibid. para 11.
126 Ibid.
127 *Wingrove v the United Kingdom*, supra note 52.
128 *I.A. v Turkey*, Application No. 42571/98, 13 September 2005.
129 *Gay News and Lemon v the United Kingdom*, Application No. 8710/79, 7 May 1982.
130 *Handyside v the United Kingdom*, supra note 50.
131 *Vejdeland and Others v Sweden*, Application No. 1813/07, 9 February 2012.
132 O'Reilly, supra note 14, 253.
133 Weber, supra note 1, 37.
134 *Castells v Spain*, Application No. 11798/85, 23 April 1992, para 42.

In *Incal v Turkey*, the Court stated that 'an opponent of official ideas and positions must be able to find a place in the political arena' and then repeated what it had said in *Castells v Spain*.[135] So, the important role that politicians play in the public debate and the interests of a democratic society in a free and open public debate are stressed by the Court. In *Perinçek v Switzerland*, for example, the Court considered that the applicant spoke as a politician on an issue that it had already accepted as of public concern and as part of a heated debate in the international arena. The fact that the applicant expressed himself in strong terms did not detract from its public interest as it was in the nature of political speech to be controversial and often virulent. This did not diminish its public interest, provided of course that it did not cross the line and turn into a call for violence, hatred or intolerance.[136] From this, it is clear that the freedom of political debate is not absolute, as the Court confirmed in both *Castells v Spain* and *Incal v Turkey*.[137] For example, in *Zana v Turkey*, the Court considered that, at a time when serious disturbances were raging in south-east Turkey, a statement like the one in question made by a political figure well known in the region could have such an impact as to justify restrictions imposed to maintain national security and public safety.[138]

The European Court of Human Rights has also stressed the pre-eminent role of the press in furthering public debate in a democratic society. In *Castells v Spain*, for example, it stated that

> It is nevertheless incumbent on it [the press] to impart information and ideas on political questions and on other matters of public interest. Freedom of the press affords the public one of the best means of discovering and forming an opinion of the ideas and attitudes of their political leaders. In particular, it gives politicians the opportunity to reflect and comment on the preoccupations of public opinion; it thus enables everyone to participate in the free political debate which is at the very core of the concept of a democratic society.[139]

The important role played by the press in furthering public debate and thus the importance of free speech, of freedom of the press, has been stressed in many cases. For example, in *Jersild v Denmark*, the Court pointed out the vital role the press plays as public watchdog[140] and in *Sürek v Turkey No. 2*, the Court mentioned the 'essential role of the press in insuring the proper functioning of a political democracy' and that it is 'incumbent on the press to impart information

---

135 *Incal v Turkey*, supra note 128, paras 45 and 46.
136 *Perinçek v Switzerland*, supra note 38, para 231.
137 *Castells v Spain*, supra note 134, para 43; *Incal v Turkey*, supra note128, para 53.
138 *Zana v Turkey*, supra note 84, para 50.
139 *Castells v Spain*, supra note 134, para 43.
140 *Jersild v Denmark*, supra note 98, para 35.

and ideas on political issues, even divisive ones'.[141] In *Şener v Turkey*, the Court stressed that 'the "duties and responsibilities" which accompany the exercise of the right to freedom of expression by media professionals assume special significance in situations of conflict and tension'. The media should, on the one hand, not 'become a vehicle for the dissemination of hate speech and the promotion of violence', but, on the other hand, states:

> Cannot, with reference to the protection of territorial integrity or national security or the prevention of crime or disorder, restrict the right of the public to be informed of them by bringing the weight of the criminal law to bear on the media.[142]

Therefore, as with politicians, the freedom of expression of the press is not absolute and the press also has duties and responsibilities. As Buyse points out, the media are 'often used as a conduit for expression that might fuel violence. Mass and social media can reach large audiences and be key factors in violent escalation'.[143] The European Court of Human Rights has stressed that the duties and responsibilities of the media 'assume special significance in situations of conflict and tension' and that 'particular caution is called for when consideration is being given to the publication of the views of representatives of organisations that resort to violence against the State lest the media become a vehicle for the dissemination of hate speech and the promotion of violence'.[144] The Court continued that where this is not the case, states cannot restrict the right of the public to be informed by applying the criminal law to the media and by referring to the protection of territorial integrity or national security or the prevention of crime or disorder.[145] As Buyse points out, 'the key question then still remains how to determine whether a certain expression is indeed a call for violence?',[146] a question that was discussed in Chapter 3. So, both politicians and the press attract special protection of their right to freedom of expression because of their vital role in a democracy.

Status of persons targeted

The status of the person targeted by the remarks will also be taken into account. The European Court of Human Rights has, for example, held that the limits of acceptable criticism are wider for politicians than for private individuals, because politicians inevitably and knowingly lay themselves open to scrutiny of their words and deeds by the press and the general public. Politicians must therefore display

141 *Sürek v Turkey No. 2*, Application No. 24122/94, 8 July 1999, para 35.
142 *Şener v. Turkey*, Application No. 26680/95, 18 July 2000, para 42.
143 Buyse, supra note 7, 501.
144 *Sürek and Özdemir v. Turkey*, Application Nos 23927/94 and 24277/94, 8 July 1999, para 63.
145 Ibid. See also: *Şener v. Turkey*, supra note 142, para 42.
146 Buyse, supra note 7, 502.

a greater degree of tolerance, and, although the protection of the reputation of others under article 10(2) extends to politicians, 'in such cases the requirements of such protection have to be weighed in relation to the interests of open discussion of political issues'.[147] The same, and to an even greater extent, is true for the Government because, 'in a democratic system the actions or omissions of the Government must be subject to the close scrutiny not only of the legislative and judicial authorities but also of the press and public opinion'.[148] So, both politicians and the Government must expect to be criticised.

But does the European Court of Human Rights take the vulnerability of the group targeted by the speech into account? In *Vejdeland and Others v Sweden*, the European Court of Human Rights took into account that the homophobic leaflets were left in the school lockers of young people who were at an impressionable and sensitive age but this was not the only consideration leading to the finding that there was no violation of article 10 ECHR.[149] In *Vajnai v Hungary*, the applicant was convicted for wearing a red star, the symbol of the workers' movement, in public. The Court expressed its awareness that the systematic terror to consolidate communism in Hungary and other countries remains 'a serious scar in the mind and heart of Europe'. It also accepted that the display of a symbol that was worn everywhere during the communist era might make past victims and their relatives feel uneasy. However, this was, according to the Court, not enough to limit freedom of expression. The Court held that restrictions on human rights that are applied to satisfy the dictates of public feeling, do not meet a pressing social need and 'to hold otherwise would mean that freedom of speech and opinion is subjected to the heckler's veto'.[150] This suggests that the Court does consider the feelings of the targeted group, but will not accept the fact that members of this group feel uneasy and disrespected as sufficient justification for restrictions on the freedom of expression of the speaker or author.

This was confirmed in *Perinçek v Switzerland*, where a Turkish politician was convicted, in Switzerland, for expressing the view that the mass deportations and massacres of Armenians in 1915 and the years following did not amount to genocide.[151] The European Court of Human Rights expressed its awareness of the great importance the Armenian community attributed to the question whether these events were to be regarded as genocide. The Court found that the dignity of the victims and the dignity and identity of modern day Armenians were protected by article 8 ECHR and thus that it had to measure the extent to which the applicant's statements affected those rights.[152] The Court then stated that the statements in question could not be regarded as affecting the dignity of the members of the Armenian community to the point of requiring a criminal law

---

147 *Lingens v Austria*, Application No. 9815/82, 8 July 1986, para 42.
148 *Castells v Spain*, supra note 134, para 46.
149 *Vejdeland and Others v Sweden*, supra note 131, para 56.
150 *Vajnai v Hungary*, Application No. 33629/06, 8 July 2008, para 57.
151 *Perinçek v Switzerland*, supra note 38.
152 Ibid. para 251.

response in Switzerland, nor could the statements be considered to have a severe impact on the Armenians' identity as a group.[153] Therefore, the Court appears to take the feelings and vulnerability of the targeted group and the harm done to them into account, but always together with one or more of the other factors discussed here.

Nature and seriousness of the interference, including the severity of the penalty

The nature and seriousness of the interference with the speaker or author's freedom of expression is another factor the European Court of Human Rights takes into account. This includes the nature and severity of the penalty imposed and whether there were alternative means that had less impact on the speaker or author's freedom of expression. In *Perinçek v Switzerland,* the Court stated that the interference at issue here – a criminal conviction that could lead to imprisonment – was much more serious in terms of consequences for the applicant than, for example, regulatory schemes for radio or television broadcasts and thus should be scrutinised more strictly.[154] The Court also noted that a criminal conviction was 'a serious sanction, having regard to the existence of other means of intervention and rebuttal, particularly through civil remedies' and 'one of the most serious forms of interference with the right to freedom of expression'.[155]

This suggests that the nature and severity of the penalty plays a role and this is confirmed by a number of other cases. A severe penalty, especially a criminal conviction, is more likely to lead to a finding that the interference with freedom of expression is not justified. The European Court of Human Rights has pointed out that 'the dominant position which the government occupies makes it necessary for it to display restraint in resorting to criminal proceedings, particularly where other means are available for replying to the unjustified attacks and criticisms of its adversaries', although it remained open to the state to adopt criminal measures.[156] In a number of cases against Turkey, all heard on the same day, the European Court of Human Rights commented on the severity of the penalty and held that the interference was disproportionate and there was thus a violation of article 10 ECHR.[157] In *Ceylan v Turkey,* the Court also considered that the conviction led to the applicant's loss of office and loss of certain political and civil rights which compounded the severity of the conviction.[158] In other cases, the

---

153 Ibid. paras 252–253.
154 Ibid. para 272.
155 Ibid. para 273.
156 *Sürek v Turkey No. 2,* supra note 141, para 34.
157 *Arslan v Turkey,* supra note 89, para 49; *Ceylan v Turkey,* supra note 98, para 37; *Gerger v Turkey,* Application No. 24919/94, 8 July 1999, para 51; *Karatas v Turkey,* supra note 109, para 53; *Okcuoglu v Turkey,* supra note 109, para 49; *Polat v Turkey,* supra note 89, para 48.
158 *Ceylan v Turkey,* supra note 98, para 37.

Court mentioned the relatively modest or insignificant nature of the fine imposed and concluded that there was no violation.[159] Therefore, the severity of the penalty and the impact on the applicant are taken into account.

Moreover, the European Court of Human Rights is aware of the possible chilling effect of restrictions and severe penalties on freedom of expression. Especially when it concerns journalists or editors, the Court has stressed that a severe penalty imposed has 'the effect of censoring their profession, compelling them to refrain from publishing anything likely to be considered to be contrary to the interests of the State'.[160] And, in *Lingens v Austria*, the Court stated:

> In the context of political debate such a sentence [as the fine imposed on applicant] would be likely to deter journalists from contributing to public discussion of issues affecting the life of the community. By the same token, a sanction such as this is liable to hamper the press in performing its task as purveyor of information and public watchdog.[161]

The European Court of Human Rights is thus very aware that laws restricting free expression might stop the press doing their job as public watchdog. This chilling effect is also, in the context of political debate, applicable to politicians as was mentioned in Chapter 3.

Conclusion

This Chapter has analysed how the European Court of Human Rights determines whether laws against (religious) hate speech are justified restrictions on freedom of expression. The Court has employed two different approaches, using either article 17 or article 10(2) ECHR. Article 17 prohibits the abuse of ECHR rights to destroy or undermine the rights itself or to attack the Convention's underlying values. If the Court uses article 17, it does not apply any justification or balancing test. This could be open to abuse and allow states to arbitrarily impose restrictions on expressions. It was, therefore, submitted, based on the case law of the European Court of Human Rights that article 17 should only be used in exceptional and extreme cases where the fundamental democratic principles and values underlying the ECHR are threatened. Generally, where speech has been restricted because it incites to religious hatred, the use of article 10(2) and the application of the three part justification test is preferable because it allows the Court to take all aspects of the case into account, including the importance of free speech for the public debate and for a democratic society and the rights of

---

159 *Chauvy v France*, Application No. 64915/01, 29 June 2004, para 78; *I.A. v Turkey*, supra note 128, para 32; *Leroy v France*, supra note 36, para 47.
160 *Koc and Tambas v Turkey*, Application No. 50934/99, 21 March 2006, para 39.
161 *Lingens v Austria*, supra note 147, para 44. See also: *Giniewski v France*, Application No. 64016/00, 31 January 2006, para 54; *Sürek v Turkey No. 2*, supra note 141, para 41.

others to freely exercise their freedom of religion, not to be discriminated against because of their religion or belief or to be protected against violence.

Therefore, in most cases, restrictions on hate speech and incitement to hatred should be scrutinised by the European Court of Human Rights under the three part justification test of article 10(2) ECHR. It was submitted that accepting that mere fostering intolerance is enough to prohibit hate speech puts the threshold for justification under article 10(2) too low, especially in relation to speech about issues contributing to the public debate. Instead, it was argued that expressions should only be limited if there are very serious reasons to do so; laws against incitement to hatred or violence should only be held to be compatible with the ECHR if there is real impact, present risk and imminent danger of violence.

This Chapter finished with an examination of the factors the European Court of Human Rights takes into account when it has to decide whether an interference with a person's freedom of expression is justified. The following factors were deduced from the Court's case law: the aim pursued by the speaker or author; the content of the expression; the context in which it was disseminated and the potential impact of the remarks; the status and role in society of the speaker or author and of the individual or group targeted by the statement; and, the nature and seriousness of the interference with the freedom of expression of the speaker or author, including the severity of the penalty imposed. The next chapter will examine alternatives to hate speech laws.

5 Alternative approaches to (religious) hate speech

Introduction

In Chapter 4, restrictions on freedom of expression to spare religious feelings were analysed. First, the European Court of Human Rights has held that laws against hate speech can be compatible with the ECHR. Claims usually reach the Court when someone has been convicted for hate speech or for incitement to hatred or violence and then claims that this is a breach of their freedom of expression under article 10. However, the Court does not always examine such cases under article 10 but applies article 17 instead. Article 17 contains an abuse of rights clause: the Convention rights cannot be used to perform acts aimed at destroying any of the rights and freedoms laid down in the Convention. Which article is used by the Court is important, because if it uses article 10(2), it applies the three part justification test but it does not do so when article 17 is applied. In other words, if the Court uses article 17, it does not require the state to prove that the interference is justified. This has been criticised in the literature as was seen in Chapter 4. Therefore, article 17 should only be applied in very limited circumstances where the fundamental democratic principles and values of the state are at stake. Supervision by the Court and a balancing of all the interests involved under the three part justification test of article 10 is to be preferred to stop states from arbitrarily imposing restrictions on expressions, especially expressions of dissent. The factors taken into account when the Court applies the three part test were analysed in Chapter 4.

In Chapter 4, it was argued that laws against (religious) hate speech should not be held to be compatible with the ECHR merely because the speech 'fosters intolerance'. The reasons for this are that the term 'fostering intolerance' is too vague, brings legal uncertainty and is, therefore, open to abuse by states and that punishing expressions for the effect they might have in the future also presents huge problems from a criminal law point of view. Moreover, the European Court of Human Rights, as has been mentioned in previous chapters, has always held that freedom of speech, especially because of the very important role this right plays in a democratic society, includes expressions that offend, shock or disturb.[1] (Religious) hate speech should only be restricted when the expression incites to

---

1 *Handyside v the United Kingdom*, Application No. 5493/72, 7 December 1976, para 48.

hatred and violence and violence is likely to follow imminently. In the words of the Court, the expression must give rise to a 'present risk' and an 'imminent danger',[2] there has to be a 'clear and imminent danger'[3] or a 'real and present danger' and not a 'mere speculative danger'[4] which requires an interference with the right to freedom of expression of the applicant. This echoes the 'clear and present danger' and the 'imminent lawless action' tests as used in the United States to assess whether an interference with freedom of speech is justified. These tests will be examined in this chapter.

In Chapter 2, it was argued that speech that prevents religious believers exercising their right to freedom of religion or to manifest their religion should not attract the protection of article 10(2) either. This is linked to the point above because incitement to hatred and violence which is very likely to lead to violence can have such an effect. It is thus submitted that the freedom of expression of politicians and others who contribute to the public debate should only be limited in these two circumstances: where it constitutes hate speech and there is a real likelihood that violence will occur imminently; or, where it factually stops people from holding or manifesting their religious beliefs. And, even then, both restrictions are still subject to the three part justification test in article 10(2) ECHR and the European Court of Human Rights should scrutinise carefully whether the means used to restrict the right to freedom of expression are proportionate to the aim of protecting the rights of others. Outside these two circumstances, freedom of expression of politicians and others who contribute to the public debate should not be restricted by hate speech laws or laws against incitement to hatred and violence. Because the 'present risk' or 'imminent danger' test appears to be inspired by the 'clear and present danger' test used in the US and because the US treats freedom of expression as guaranteed by the First Amendment of the Constitution in a different way from most other countries, the US will be examined first.

As argued, criminal laws against (religious) hate speech, which go beyond the two circumstances mentioned, should be considered to violate the speaker or author's right to freedom of expression. But where does this leave the people targeted by the hate speech? Such speech can foster intolerance and lead to a hostile climate against them. The possible harms done by hate speech to the targeted group will be considered briefly in this Chapter and this is followed by an examination of alternative ways of dealing with expressions against religious people both by the people in the targeted groups and by others.

Free speech in the US

The US deals with restrictions on the freedom of speech in a different way to most other countries in the world and gives very strong protection to

---

2 *Erbakan v Turkey*, Application No. 59405/00, 6 July 2006, para 65.
3 *GÜl and Others v. Turkey*, Application No. 4870/02, 8 June 2010, para 42.
4 *Vajnai v Hungary*, Application No. 33629/06, 8 July 2008, paras 49 and 55.

this right, even affording protection to 'the most noxious forms of extreme speech imaginable'.[5] In the US, free speech interests prevail over hate speech regulation[6] or, as Weinstein puts it, 'hate speech bans, generally considered acceptable in virtually every democracy other than the United States, provide a good example of extreme speech regulation that would be summarily invalidated under contemporary American free speech jurisprudence'.[7] This appears to contrast with, for example, the way the European Court of Human Rights has dealt with hate speech laws, holding that these can be compatible with article 10 ECHR.

The First Amendment to the US Constitution determines that 'Congress shall make no law . . . abridging the freedom of speech or of the press'. However, even in the US, the right to free speech is not an absolute right and the US Supreme Court will balance free speech with other rights.[8] So, this could be seen as similar to what the European Court of Human Rights does under the three part justification test of article 10(2) ECHR. Moreover, the role of the public debate is stressed by both Courts. For the European Court of Human Rights this has become clear from the previous chapters. In the US, there is also an emphasis on the importance of free speech for the public discourse.[9] Barendt explains about the US that

> All expression contributing to the formation of public opinion on all political, social and cultural topics should be protected by the freedom of speech clause of the First Amendment, because open communication between individual citizens is essential for a fully participatory democracy. Freedom of political speech is constitutive of that democracy . . . Further, freedom of speech cannot be denied to cranks and extremists, even to people communicating hate messages, for all citizens enjoy the right to participate in public discourse. If their freedom is denied, the state loses its democratic legitimacy with respect of them.[10]

In other words, the strong protection afforded to speech in the US is based on the importance of freedom of speech for a participatory democracy. Although the importance of freedom of expression for a democratic society is stressed by the European Court of Human Rights as well, the second part of the quote suggests that this emphasis on the public discourse and especially on the participatory aspect

5 Weinstein, J. 'An Overview of American Free Speech Doctrine and its Application to Extreme Speech' in Hare, I. and Weinstein, J. (eds) *Extreme Speech and Democracy* (Oxford, Oxford University Press, 2009) 81.
6 Knechtle, J. 'When to Regulate Hate Speech', 110 (3) *Penn State Law Review* (2006) 539.
7 Weinstein, supra note 5, 84.
8 Knechtle, supra note 6, 564.
9 Weinstein, supra note 5, 85.
10 Barendt, E., 'Religious Hatred Laws: Protecting Groups or Belief?', 17 (1) *Res Publica* (2011) 44.

of this discourse plays a more important role in the US. As Dworkin writes, 'we might have the power to silence those we despise, but it would be at the cost of political legitimacy, which is more important than they are'.[11] The free marketplace of ideas and the moral autonomy and personal development arguments for guaranteeing freedom of expression, which were discussed in Chapter 1, thus appear to be more significant in the US than in the European Court of Human Rights' approach to this right.[12] As Leigh writes about the case law of the latter court, 'the notions of a marketplace of competing ideas and beliefs or the value of expression as an outworking of personal autonomy barely feature in the jurisprudence'.[13]

This emphasis on participation of everyone in the public discourse in the US leads to an 'intense hostility to the content-based regulation of public discourse'.[14] In the US, a clear distinction is made between content-based and content-neutral restrictions: the former are restrictions based on the message the expression conveys while the latter regulate speech for a reason unrelated to the message it conveys, for example because of the time, place or manner of the speech.[15] Content-based restrictions are suspect and thus subject to very strict scrutiny. They are presumed to be unconstitutional, while content-neutral restrictions are not considered in this way. The rationale for the distinction is 'that content-based restrictions are more likely to skew public debate for or against particular ideas and are more likely to be tainted by a constitutionally impermissible motivation'.[16] In contrast, the European Court of Human Rights does not make this distinction and takes both the content and the context of an expression into account when deciding on whether a restriction on someone's freedom of expression is justified under article 10(2), as was discussed in Chapter 4. Therefore, there is a distinct difference between the European Court of Human Rights and the US Courts here. It is argued, however, that, in relation to hate speech, this difference is not as big as it might seem.

It was pointed out that, even in the US, the freedom of expression is not absolute and that the US Supreme Court has accepted restrictions on free speech in certain circumstances. One of the restrictions accepted is in relation to hate speech, but only when there is a 'clear and present danger'. This test was first formulated in *Schenck v United States*, where Justice Holmes stated:

---

11 Dworkin, R., 'Foreword' in in Hare, I. and Weinstein, J. (eds) *Extreme Speech and Democracy* (Oxford, Oxford University Press, 2009) ix.

12 See further on this: Rosenfeld, M., 'Hate Speech in Constitutional Jurisprudence A Comparative Analysis', in Herz, M. and Molnar, P. (eds) *The Content and Context of Hate Speech Rethinking Regulation and Responses* (Cambridge, Cambridge University Press, 2012) 250–253.

13 Leigh, I., 'Damned if They Do, Damned if They Don't: the European Court of Human Rights and the Protection of Religion from Attack', 17 (1) *Res Publica* (2011) 70.

14 Weinstein, supra note 5, 81.

15 Ibid.

16 Stone, G., 'Free Speech in the Twenty-first Century: Ten Lessons from the Twentieth Century', in Koltay, A. (ed.) *Comparative Perspectives on the Fundamental Freedom of Expression* (Budapest, Wolters Kluwer, 2015) 124–125.

The question in every case is whether the words used are used in such circumstances and are of such a nature as to create *a clear and present danger* that they will bring about the substantive evils that Congress has a right to prevent [emphasis added].[17]

In *Brandenburg v Ohio*, the Supreme Court explained this test as meaning that speech that calls for violence or other illegal acts may only be restricted if it 'is directed to inciting or producing imminent lawless action and is likely to incite such action'.[18] Knechtle explains that this means that 'in the United States, a very high degree of correlation between hate speech and violence is required before the government may prohibit the speech: incitement to imminent violence'.[19] This is very similar to the argument made in this book that expressions that con-tribute to the public debate should attract the protection of article 10(2) ECHR unless they constitute incitement to hatred or violence and there is a real like-lihood, a clear and present danger, that violence or lawless action will occur. This 'clear and present danger' and 'imminent lawless action' tests appear to have influenced the European Court of Human Rights judgments where the Court uses the terms 'present risk' and 'imminent danger',[20] 'clear and imminent danger'[21] and 'real and present danger' and not a 'mere speculative danger'[22] to indicate what is required to hold restrictions on freedom of expression through hate speech laws to be justified. So, in this regard, the European Court of Human Rights appears to move towards a 'clear and present danger' test for hate speech and this is a welcome development as it means that restrictions on expressions by politicians and others contributing to the public debate will not often be held to be justified under article 10(2) ECHR. The US approach to freedom of expres-sion is thus not so much an alternative way to deal with restrictions on freedom of expression of politicians and others contributing to the public debate but an approach the European Court of Human Rights appears to be moving towards.

This confirms the main argument in this book that (criminal) laws against reli-gious hate speech should be held to violate the article 9 ECHR right to freedom of expression of the speaker or author except in the two exceptional circumstances: when there is incitement to hatred or violence and there is a clear and present danger that violence will occur; or, when the speech stops people from exercising their freedom of religion under article 9 ECHR. But if the speaker or author of such speech is not (criminally) liable and thus most of the time cannot be stopped from using offensive expressions by the use of criminal law, what does this mean for those targeted by the speech? Do they suffer harm and, if they do, can they do any-thing about this, do they have a remedy? This will be examined in the following.

17 *Schenck v United States*, 249 US 47 (1919).
18 *Brandenburg v Ohio*, 395 US 444 (1969).
19 Knechtle, supra note 6, 549.
20 *Erbakan v Turkey*, supra note 2, para 65.
21 *GÜl and Others v. Turkey*, supra note 3, para 42.
22 *Vajnai v Hungary*, supra note 4, paras 49 and 55.

Hate speech and harm

As mentioned, applying an 'imminent risk and present danger' test means that the European Court of Human Rights will scrutinise restrictions on the expressions of politicians and others contributing to the public debate very strictly and not easily find a violation of article 10 ECHR. But where does this leave the people targeted by the hate speech? The rhetoric of politicians all over Europe about immigration can, especially because it is often repeated, foster intolerance and create a climate that is hostile to the groups targeted. It can create stereotypical ideas about the group and stigmatise them. As Rorke points out, in relation to Roma people,

> That the torrent of disparaging, discriminatory and hateful speech targeting Roma fosters and sustains a broad consensus that 'Gypsies get what they deserve'; that beyond the hard core of haters, such speech contaminates the public sphere in a manner that inhibits any sense of solidarity or empathy; and the cumulative effect is that the majority populations fail (or feel emboldened to refuse) to recognize discriminatory treatment of Roma for what it is – unreconstructed racism.[23]

Rorke writes specifically about Roma people, but it is suggested that the effects of hate speech he describes can be applied to the rhetoric used by politicians in many European countries against immigrants, Muslims and other minorities. One dissenting judge in *Erbakan v Turkey* referred to a similar effect where she pointed out that the impact of Erbakan's words could only be measured over time but that his speech was, in her view, a harmful contribution to a climate of intolerance nourishing primitive prejudice and cleavages in society, as was mentioned in Chapter 4.[24] The rhetoric used often creates an 'us' versus 'them' atmosphere – the dissenting judge refers to 'cleavages' in society – that fosters a broader consensus that the targeted groups do not want to integrate and do not want to be part of 'us' and 'our society'. This kind of rhetoric against immigrants, Muslims and other minorities was originally used by far right politicians only, but it appears to have slowly invaded mainstream politics as well. The language appears to have been normalised and has become part of the main political discourse in many countries.[25]

23 Rorke, B., 'Free to Hate? Anti-Gypsyism in 21-Century Europe', in Molnar, P. (ed.) *Free Speech and Censorship around the Globe* (Budapest–New York, Central European University Press, 2015) 236.
24 *Erbakan v Turkey*, supra note 2, dissenting Opinion Judge Steiner, para 2.
25 See, for example, British Home Secretary Amber Rudd who said at the Conservative Party Conference in October 2016, that foreign workers should not be able to take the jobs that British people could do and that companies could be forced to publish the proportion of international staff on their books: Wilkinson, M., 'Amber Rudd vows to Stop Migrants "Taking Jobs British People could do" and Force Companies to Reveal the Number of Foreigners they Employ', *The Telegraph*, 4 October 2016 www.telegraph.co.uk/

The above suggests that hate speech has a harmful effect on the targeted group. In Chapter 3, this was discussed as one of the rationales for enacting hate speech laws: these laws are necessary to protect members of the targeted group from physical and mental harm. Such speech can be

> Highly wounding to members of the targeted group. In some cases it might inflict psychological injury or cause fear of isolation or physical attack. More generally, it lowers the self-esteem of those affected, particularly where the targeted group has historically been oppressed.[26]

But, the above also suggests a harmful effect on society at large. As Sottieaux writes:

> The fear is that the spread of hateful views may generate or reinforce hatred in the community and ultimately result in hateful attitudes, discrimination and violence. This, in turn, may damage the target group's position in the community or threaten social stability.[27]

This reflects another argument for enacting hate speech laws as discussed in Chapter 3: that such laws are necessary to prevent breaches of the peace and to protect public order. Both these arguments have been used by the European Court of Human Rights. For example, in *Féret v Belgium*, the Court held that attacks that injure and defame certain groups, violate the dignity and the security of the person, and that political speech that stirred hatred based on religious, ethnic or cultural prejudices was a threat to social peace and political stability in democratic States.[28] The Court actually pointed out that the electoral context in which racist or xenophobic comments were made helped to kindle hatred and intolerance and that the impact of this type of speech grew worse and more harmful. The interference with Féret's right to freedom of expression was held to be justified by the need to protect public order and the rights of others, namely the immigrant community.

In Chapter 4, it was concluded that the status of the person or group targeted by the hate speech is one of the factors taken into account by the European Court

news/2016/10/04/jeremy-hunt-nhs-doctors-theresa-may-conservative-conference-live/ ; and Dutch Prime Minister Mark Rutte, leader of the Party for Freedom and Democracy, has said that people should leave if they reject Dutch values: 'Rutte: Ga Weg als je Nederlandse Waarden Afwijst' (Rutte: Leave if you reject Dutch Values) 23 January 2017 http://nos.nl/artikel/2154459-rutte-ga-weg-als-je-nederlandse-waarden-afwijst.html. The full letter, in Dutch, can be found on the party website: *Lees Hier de Brief van Mark* (Read here the letter from Mark), https://vvd.nl/nieuws/lees-hier-de-brief-van-mark/. The letter accompanied a full page advert of the party in the major national newspapers with the slogan: 'Act Normal or Leave' (Doe Normaal of Ga Weg') (All material in Dutch is translated by author).

26 Barendt, E., *Freedom of Speech* (2nd edn, Oxford, Oxford University Press, 2005) 174.

27 Sottieaux, S., '"Bad Tendencies" in the ECtHR "Hate Speech" Jurisprudence', 7 (1) *European Constitutional Law Review* (2011) 47.

28 *Féret v Belgium*, Application No. 15615/07, 16 July 2009, para 73.

of Human Rights as part of the justification test under article 10(2) ECHR and that this includes the feelings and vulnerability of the targeted group and the harm done to them. On the other hand, the Court has also held that restrictions on human rights applied to satisfy the dictates of public feeling do not meet a pressing social need and, 'to hold otherwise would mean that freedom of speech and opinion is subjected to the heckler's veto'.[29] So, the fact that members of the targeted group feel uneasy and disrespected is not sufficient justification for restrictions on the freedom of expression of the speaker or author. In other words, there is, as was argued before, no right not to be offended present in the ECHR.

From the above, it can be concluded that hate speech can cause harm to the targeted group and can lead to tensions in society. But do either of these justify using the criminal law against hate speech? It is submitted that it does not for a number of reasons. First, it is very difficult to define hate speech and lay down a prohibition of hate speech in criminal law. Most national hate speech laws are overly broad and offer little legal clarity or certainty,[30] two characteristics a criminal law needs, as was mentioned in Chapter 3. Second, banning hate speech through criminal law leads to problems with proof, causation and culpability[31] and punishing expressions for the effect they might have in the future presents huge problems from a criminal law point of view, as concluded in Chapter 4. Third, in most countries there are a number of criminal offences that cover physical attacks, damage to property and disturbance of the public order and, therefore, there is no need for a separate hate speech offence. Many national laws also contain general provisions against incitement to a criminal offence and prohibitions of hate crime that provide for enhanced penalties in case of crimes committed with certain motives, for example, because of the religion of the victim. In the latter case, proving the motive of the speaker can be difficult, but if hate speech leads to immediate violence, the violence is prohibited by criminal law and the link between the hate speech and the violence might be used as proof of the motive. This argument can be expressed in another way: if hate speech calls on people to commit violence against people belonging to certain groups, it can usually be punished as such under normal criminal laws without the need for hate speech laws. Chan writes that, as opposed to hate speech laws, hate crime laws do not compromise free speech principles because they do not supress intolerant ideas or their expression but, instead, punish criminal acts committed in the execution of these bigoted ideas and attitudes.[32]

A fourth reason why the harm done by hate speech to the targeted group and to society does not justify criminal hate speech laws is that there is an 'absence

29 *Vajnai v Hungary*, Application No. 33629/06, 8 July 2008, para 57.
30 Callamard, A., 'Religion, Terrorism and Speech in a "Post-Charlie Hebdo" World', 10 (3) *Religion and Human Rights* (2015) 216.
31 Buyse, A., 'Dangerous Expressions: the ECHR, Violence and Free Speech', 63 (2) *International and Comparative Law Quarterly* (2014) 499.
32 Chan, S., 'Hate Speech Bans: An Intolerant Response to Intolerance', 14 *Trinity College Law Review* (2011) 94.

of statistically reliable evidence of direct causation from hate speech in public discourse to ascertainable harms', as Heinze writes.[33] There is also no evidence that bans reduce incidents of intolerance,[34] an argument also mentioned in Chapter 4. Not only is there no evidence that bans reduce intolerance, but, according to Heinze, there is evidence 'that bans far from curbing, actively provoke and "tutor" extremist groups' and that the 'ubiquitous whitewashing process in Western Europe' has largely been ignored.[35] Hate speech laws might have the effect of making politicians and others contributing to the public debate clean up their language or rephrase expressions so they do not break the law.[36] When Dutch Prime Minster Mark Rutte said 'leave if you reject Dutch values', he did not mention immigrants or foreigners explicitly, but referred to people who came to the Netherlands for the freedom 'our' country offers but who then abuse this freedom; people who do not want to adapt, mock 'our customs' and reject 'our values'; people who attack homosexuals, jeer at women in short skirts and who call 'normal Dutch people' racist.[37] This is a good example not only of the way the political rhetoric against immigrants has invaded mainstream politics but also of the way it tries to make a division between 'us' and 'them', tries to divide the 'us', in this case law-abiding, tolerant, liberal Dutch people from the 'them', incomers who abuse 'our' freedoms and reject 'our' values. It will be clear that this is also related to the argument in Chapter 3 about creating a wolf in sheep's clothing by banning hate speech.

One more argument against criminal hate speech laws is that the proportionality test that needs to be done under article 10(2) ECHR includes an examination of the question whether less restrictive means can be used to achieve the legitimate aim of a measure, as was mentioned in Chapter 2. This is supported by *Castells v Spain*, where the European Court of Human Rights considered that governments should 'display restraint in resorting to criminal proceedings, particularly where other means are available for replying to the unjustified attacks and criticisms of its adversaries or the media'.[38] In many situations, using the criminal law to restrict speech might well not be the least restrictive means of dealing with hate speech.

In conclusion, the harm done by hate speech does not justify enacting criminal law against such speech where it contributes to the public debate unless, as

---

33 Heinze, E., *Hate Speech and Democratic Citizenship* (Oxford, Oxford University Press, 2016) 137.
34 Chan, supra note 32, 93.
35 Heinze, supra note 33, 145.
36 For a good example of this see: Goodall, K., 'Incitement to Religious Hatred: All Talk and No Substance?' 70 (1) *Modern Law Review* 93–94, who points out the way the British National Party, a far-right party, exploited the fact that incitement to racial hatred was prohibited by law but religious hatred was not. This was changed by the Racial and Religious Hatred Act 2006, which made incitement to religious hatred an offence.
37 Translation by author. See: 'Rutte: Ga Weg als je Nederlandse Waarden Afwijst' (Rutte: Leave if you Reject Dutch Values) 23 January 2017 http://nos.nl/artikel/2154459-rutte-ga-weg-als-je-nederlandse-waarden-afwijst.html
38 *Castells v Spain*, Application No. 11798/85, 23 April 1992, para 46.

is argued throughout this book, it incites to violence and violence is likely to follow imminently or unless it stops people from holding or manifesting their religion or belief. If criminal prohibitions outside these circumstances should, as is argued here, be seen as an interference with the speaker or author's freedom of expression, are there any alternative ways the targeted groups can challenge hate speech? This will be discussed next.

Discrimination under the ECHR

Would the people targeted by hate speech be able to find a remedy in other laws? Civil laws against hate speech, providing for civil law remedies, might be available. The advantages of using civil law are that, first, the targeted individual or group has more input in and control over the procedure: they have to instigate a procedure by making a complaint to a tribunal or court and are not dependent on the public prosecutor to prosecute the speaker or author. On the other hand, this might make it more difficult as the person or group targeted might not be able or willing to take on this more active role. Second, civil law remedies might be more satisfactory for the targeted individual or group and are generally less severe and less intrusive for the speaker or author and thus such laws would be less likely to be seen as an interference with the freedom of expression. Some of these remedies will be discussed below. Third, the burden of proof is generally not as high in civil proceedings as it is in criminal proceedings.

Laws against discrimination, which often provide civil rather than, or sometimes as well as, criminal remedies, could fit the bill here. As discussed in Chapter 3, according to the Committee of Ministers of the Council of Europe, hate speech covers

> All forms of expression which spread, incite, promote or justify racial hatred, xenophobia, anti-Semitism or other forms of hatred based on intolerance, including intolerance expressed by aggressive nationalism and ethnocentrism, discrimination and hostility against minorities, migrants and people of immigrant origin.[39]

This suggests that hate speech can include intolerance expressed by discrimination. Moreover, hate speech can be seen as the denial of equality or equal treatment of the targeted individuals or group. This could thus amount to discrimination. As discussed in Chapter 2, article 14 ECHR prohibits discrimination by the state in the enjoyment of the rights and freedoms of the Convention on a large and open-ended number of grounds, including religion. Article 1, Protocol 12 to the ECHR prohibits discrimination on the same ground in the enjoyment of any right set forth by law. According to the European Court of Human Rights,

---

39 Committee of Ministers, Council of Europe, Recommendation No R(97)20 on 'Hate Speech'.

the latter should be interpreted in the same way as article 14.[40] The importance of the right to non-discrimination and equality was also stressed in Chapter 2, because 'equality and dignity of human beings regardless of their gender, race, religion, and similar classifications are themselves democratic values'.[41]

Neither article 14, nor Protocol 12, gives a definition of discrimination. The European Court of Human Rights has held that the right not to be discriminated against 'is violated when States treat differently persons in analogous situations without providing an objective and reasonable justification' or 'when States without an objective and reasonable justification fail to treat differently persons whose situations are significantly different'.[42] This indicates that discriminatory treatment is not against the law if there is an objective and reasonable justification for the treatment. To be justified, a difference in treatment must, according to the Court, pursue a legitimate aim and there must be a reasonable relationship of proportionality between the means employed and the aim sought to be realised.[43] Therefore, the ECHR prohibits religious discrimination, prohibits the state from treating people differently because of their religion, unless this is objectively and reasonably justified. The justification test is, as was mentioned in Chapter 2, similar to the tests for justification under articles 9 and 10 ECHR and here, too, the Court applies the margin of appreciation doctrine.[44] The margin of appreciation is narrower where a discrimination ground is considered to be 'suspect' because the European Court of Human Rights will scrutinise differences in treatment on 'suspect' grounds more carefully and it will require 'very weighty reasons' before it finds that the discrimination is justified.[45] And, as pointed out in Chapter 2, religion is a suspect ground,[46] as are nationality and race.[47]

But does religious hate speech fall under the above definition? Religious hate speech disparages certain religious groups and singles them out as different and of less value. Thus, hate speech against certain religious groups can be seen as treating these groups differently from other groups in society, as discrimination against these groups. From article 34 ECHR it is clear that, under the Convention, action can be taken by groups as well as by individuals. However, there is a different problem: Article 14 and Article 1, Protocol 12 protect against discrimination

40 *Sejdic and Finci v Bosnia and Herzogovina*, Application Nos 27996/06 and 34836/06, 22 December 2009, para 55.
41 Grimm, D., 'Freedom of Speech in a Globalized World', in Hare, I. and Weinstein, J. (eds) *Extreme Speech and Democracy* (Oxford, Oxford University Press, 2009) 13.
42 *Thlimmenos v Greece*, Application No. 34369/97, 6 April 2000, para 44.
43 *Case Relating to Certain Aspects of the Laws on the Use of Languages in Education in Belgium v Belgium*, Application Nos 1474/62; 1677/62; 1691/62; 1769/63; 1994/63; 2126/64, 23 July 1968, BI para 10 (Hereafter referred to as the *Belgian Linguistics* case).
44 *Willis v the United Kingdom*, Application No.36042/97, 11 June 2002, para 39.
45 See, for example, *Schuler-Zgraggen v Switzerland*, Application No. 14518/89, 24 June 1993, para 67; *Van Raalte v the Netherlands*, Application No. 20060/92, 21 February 1997, para 39.
46 *Vojnity v Hungary*, Application No. 29617/07, 12 February 2013, para 36.
47 Nationality: *Gaygusuz v Austria*, Application No. 17371/90, 16 September 1996, para 42; race: *Timishev v Russia*, Application Nos 55762/00 and 55974/00, 13 December 2005, para 58.

by the state and an individual or group targeted by religious hate speech could only challenge this as religious discrimination if there is a positive duty on the state under these articles to protect against discrimination. But does such a duty exist? In other words, could an individual or group targeted by religious hate speech claim that the state has not protected them against discrimination?

Article 1 ECHR imposes a duty on states to 'secure to everyone within their jurisdiction the rights and freedoms defined in Section 1 of this Convention'. This includes Article 14, which suggests that there is a positive duty on the states to protect a person against discrimination in the enjoyment of their Convention rights. Support for this can be found in the opinion of the European Commission of Human Rights in the Belgian Linguistics case, which stated that 'the word "secured" implies the placing of "an obligation which is not simply negative" on the Contracting States'.[48] Article 1 (1), Protocol 12 echoes article 14, except that it secures the enjoyment of any right set forth by law without discrimination. This can thus also be read as conferring a positive duty on the state. Article 1(2), Protocol 12 imposes a (negative) duty not to discriminate. So, there is a positive duty on the state to protect against discrimination under article 14 and article 1(1), Protocol 12, but what does this duty entail? For example, does it require that a state enacts legislation against discrimination? The Explanatory Report to Protocol 12 mentions possible positive obligations on the state parties to take measure to prevent discrimination even in relations between private persons, but that 'while such positive obligations cannot be excluded altogether, the prime objective of Article 1 is to embody a negative obligation for the Parties: the obligation not to discriminate against individuals'.[49] On the other hand, the Explanatory Report also considers that it cannot be totally excluded that the duty to 'secure' in article 1(1) 'might entail some positive obligations. For example, this question could arise where there is a clear lacuna in domestic law protection from discrimination'.[50] As most European states have enacted some form of anti-discrimination measures, this positive duty does not appear to be of use to individuals or groups targeted by hate speech.

Could these individuals or groups argue that the state has breached a duty to protect them against such speech or a duty under article 9 ECHR to protect their right to freedom of religion? Chapter 3 contains a brief analysis of the duty imposed on states by article 20(2) ICCPR to prohibit by law 'any advocacy of national, racial or religious hatred that constitutes incitement to discrimination, hostility or violence'. There is no such positive duty in the ECHR, which, as Temperman points out, 'does not speak of a prohibition of hate speech, let alone any right to be safeguarded against such speech'.[51]

---

48 *Belgian Linguistics* case, supra note 43, para 4.
49 Council of Europe, Explanatory Report, Protocol 12 to the Convention for the Protection of Human Rights and Fundamental Freedoms, ETS, 177, para 24, https://rm.coe.int/CoERM PublicCommonSearchServices/DisplayDCTMContent?documentId=09000016800cce48
50 Ibid.
51 Temperman, J., 'A Right to be Free from Religious Hatred? The Wilders Case in the Netherlands and Beyond' in Molnar, P. (ed.) *Free Speech and Censorship around the Globe* (Budapest/New York, Central European University Press, 2015) 527. See also: Bacquet, S.,

In relation to a positive duty on the state under article 9 ECHR, in *Begheluri and Others v Georgia*, the European Court of Human Rights referred to previous case law in holding that

> Where the acts complained of were carried out by individuals and were not therefore directly attributable to the respondent State, the Court must consider the issues in terms of the positive obligation on the State authorities to secure the rights under article 9 to those within their jurisdiction.[52]

This suggests that there is a positive duty on the state under article 9 as well. However, the Court, in *Begheluri and Others v Georgia*, not only referred to 'acts' and not to 'speech' or 'expressions', it also held that 'the responsibility of the State may be engaged where religious beliefs are opposed or denied in a manner which inhibits those who hold such beliefs from exercising their freedom to hold or express them' and that 'in such cases, the State may be called upon to ensure the peaceful enjoyment of the rights guaranteed under article 9 to the holders of the belief'.[53] This case concerned violent acts against Jehovah's Witnesses and the inadequate investigations of these acts by the police, both of which had stopped the Jehovah's Witnesses from being able to exercise their right to freedom of religion. The Court also considered that the attitude of the public authorities contributed to intensifying religious violence and came to the conclusion that 'the State's failures in connection with the circumstances concerning the Jehovah's Witnesses and the practice of their religion, seen as a whole, resulted in a violation of Article 9 of the Convention'.[54] This case thus concerned religious hate crimes, crimes motivated by the religion of the targeted group, rather than religious hate speech. Even so, this confirms what was argued in Chapter 2, that restrictions on religious hate speech would be justified when it stops people from holding or manifesting their religion or belief. Such speech could, it was argued, be restricted under article 10(2) ECHR without being an interference with the freedom of expression of the speaker or author, but as concluded above, there is no duty on the state to do so and to protect targeted individuals or groups from hate speech. Therefore, if the state does not enact such laws, the targeted group or individual will not be able to claim a breach by the state of an obligation under article 9 ECHR. Moreover, the state also has a positive duty to ensure the enjoyment of the right to freedom of expression.[55]

Freedom of Expression v Hate Speech: An Illustration of the Dilemma through and In-depth Analysis of Judicial Approaches in England and France (VDM Verlag, 2011) 16.

52 *Begheluri and Others v Georgia*, Application No 28490/02, 7 October 2014, para 160. See also, *Otto-Preminger-Institut v Austria*, Application No. 13470/87, 20 September 1994, para 47; *Eweida and Others v the United Kingdom*, Application Nos 48420/10, 59842/10, 51671/10 and 36516/10, 15 January 2013, para 84.

53 *Begheluri and Others v Georgia*, supra note 52, para 160. See also: *Öllinger v Austria*, Application No. 76900/01, 29 June 2006, para 39.

54 *Begheluri and Others v Georgia*, supra note 52, para 165.

55 See, for example: *Fuentes Bobo v Spain*, Application No. 39293/98, 29 February 2000, para 38; *Dink v Turkey*, Application Nos 2668/07, 6102/08, 30079/08, 7072/09 and

With Temperman we can conclude that 'there is not much in this treaty [ECHR] hate speech victims could complain about'.[56] The fact that article 14 ECHR can only be invoked together with another article of the Convention compounds the problem for people in states that have not signed and ratified Protocol 12. Therefore, it is very difficult for a group or individual targeted by religious hate speech to apply to the European Court of Human Rights and receive a remedy in this way. Moreover, most hate speech cases in the Court are brought by the speaker or author who seeks to challenge their conviction for hate speech.[57] And, as was analysed in Chapter 2, in a case brought by the speaker or author, the targeted group might face the difficulty that the right invoked by the applicant receives the most attention and that there might be a presumption in favour of the right of the applicant.[58]

Discrimination under other measures

It can thus be concluded that individuals or groups targeted by hate speech might find it very difficult to apply to the European Court of Human Rights alleging a violation of their right not to be discriminated against under the Convention. But could such a claim be made under national or other measures? In the following, the European Union (EU) provisions against religious discrimination will be analysed, because many Council of Europe member states are also members (or candidate members) of the EU and, as such, they are subject to a duty under EU law to provide against religious discrimination in their national law.

Directive 2000/78/EC[59] prohibits discrimination on the grounds of religion or belief and, of the conduct prohibited by this Directive, the provisions against direct discrimination and harassment could possibly be applicable to religious hate speech. According to article 2(2)(a) of the Directive, direct religion or belief discrimination shall be taken to occur where one person is treated less favourably than another is, has been or would be treated in a comparable situation, on the grounds of religion or belief. This is similar to the definition of discrimination under article 14 ECHR and, therefore, hate speech against certain religious individuals or groups can be seen as treating these groups less favourably from

---

7124/09, 14 September 2010, para 106; *Palomo Sanchez and Others v Spain*, Application Nos 28955/06, 28957/06, 28959/06 and 28964/06, 12 September 2011 (GC), para 59.

56 Temperman, supra note 51, 527.

57 Ibid.

58 Brems, E., 'Conflicting Human Rights: An Exploration in the Context of the Right to a Fair Trial in the European Convention for the Protection of Human Rights and Fundamental Freedoms', 27 *Human Rights Quarterly* (2005) 305; Tulkens, F., 'Conflicts between Fundamental Rights: Contrasting Views on Articles 9 and 10 of the European Convention on Human Rights', in Venice Commission, *Blasphemy, Insult and Hatred: Finding Answers in a Democratic Society*, (Strasbourg, Council of Europe, Science and Technique of Democracy No. 47) 124–125 www.venice.coe.int/webforms/documents/?pdf=CDL-STD(2010)047-e

59 Council Directive 2000/78/EC Establishing a General Framework for Equal Treatment in Employment and Occupation [2000] OJ L 303/16.

other individuals or groups in society, as discrimination against these groups. There is, however, an important difference between the prohibition of religious discrimination under the ECHR and in EU law: EU law does not allow for justification of direct religion or belief discrimination, unless in the circumstances specifically enumerated in the Directive which are not relevant for religious hate speech, while justification of (direct) discrimination under the ECHR is permitted, as discussed above. Therefore, religious hate speech could fall under the prohibition of direct discrimination in EU law and if it did, there would be no justification defence.

In *Centrum voor Gelijkheid van Kansen v Firma Ferijn NV*, the Director of a company that fitted security and garage doors, stated publicly that the company would not recruit immigrants because their customers would not want them in their homes. The Court of Justice of the European Union decided that this constituted direct (racial or ethnic origin) discrimination, because such statements were 'likely strongly to dissuade certain candidates from submitting their candidature and, accordingly, to hinder their access to the labour market'.[60] This suggests that mere speech can be (direct) discrimination and thus that those targeted by hate speech might have a remedy under EU law. Belavusau appears to view the expressions in this case as hate speech constituting direct discrimination as he writes that 'since there is no other evidence of direct discrimination, the discriminatory utterances, suggesting the racial, national or religious inferiority of the identifiable groups, is the only proof of labour discrimination at stake'.[61] However, it must be noted that Belavusau mentions 'labour discrimination'. Whether the provision against direct (religious) discrimination does provide a remedy for those targeted by hate speech will be discussed further below.

Directive 2000/78/EC also prohibits harassment on the grounds of religion or belief. This is defined in article 2(3) of the Directive as a form of discrimination that occurs when unwanted conduct related to religion or belief takes place with the purpose or effect of violating the dignity of a person and of creating an intimidating, hostile, degrading, humiliating or offensive environment. Could religious hate speech fall under this? This question raises a number of issues. The first is that harassment might be seen as targeting individuals and as falling outside the public discourse, as Heinze does.[62] This is based on the fact that expressions addressed to individuals are considered unlikely to have any significant impact on the public debate. If harassment is seen as such, then the anti-immigration and anti-Muslim rhetoric by politicians would not be covered by harassment, as it was

---

60 Case C-54/07, *Centrum voor Gelijkheid van Kansen v Firma Ferijn NV*, ECLI:EU: C:2008:397. The Court of Justice of the EU found direct discrimination under Council Directive 2000/43/EC Council Directive 2000/43/EC of 29 June. 2000 Implementing the Principle of Equal Treatment between Persons Irrespective of Racial or Ethnic Origin [2000] OJ L 180/22, which contains the same definition of direct discrimination as Directive 2000/78/EC.

61 Belavusau, U., *Fighting Hate Speech through EU Law*, Amsterdam Law Forum, Winter Issue, 2012, 30 http://amsterdamlawforum.org/article/view/253/441

62 See, for example, Heinze, supra note 33, 28 and 84.

argued throughout this book that such speech contributes to the public debate; and, because such speech is targeted at groups rather than individuals.

Another possible problem is that the definition of harassment in Directive 2000/78/EC mentions 'conduct' and this raises the question whether speech falls under 'conduct'. Directive 2006/54/EC, which concerns equal treatment between men and women, defines 'harassment' in the same way as Directive 2000/78/EC, but it defines 'sexual harassment' as taking place where any form of unwanted verbal, non-verbal or physical conduct of a sexual nature occurs, with the same purpose or effect as harassment.[63] So, for sexual harassment, it is made clear that conduct can be verbal and thus that words can amount to sexual harassment. The omission of the words 'verbal, non-verbal or physical' in the definition of harassment other than sexual harassment might mean that words cannot amount to harassment in general. However, it could also be argued that 'harassment' in both situations must be interpreted in the same way and thus that in all definitions of harassment the term 'conduct' must be interpreted as including verbal, non-verbal or physical conduct. In addition, harassment is defined as a form of discrimination and, as discussed above, *Ferijn* suggests that mere speech can be discrimination.[64] There is no case law of the Court of Justice of the European Union on this but words are certainly included in the definition of harassment in national anti-discrimination laws in some member states.[65] In their Guidance on Freedom of Expression, the British Equality and Human Rights Commission points out that 'offensive or insulting language may also constitute harassment, either under the Equality Act 2010, or if directed against an individual under the Protection from Harassment Act'.[66] The British Equality Act 2010, the anti-discrimination law in Britain, prohibits harassment because of, among other grounds, religion or belief, while the Protection from Harassment Act 1997 prohibits harassment as such, without specifying any grounds for this. Under the latter Act, both criminal and civil remedies are available for victims of harassment. However, a single incident cannot give rise to a claim because the Act requires a 'course of conduct' which means that at least two incidents are needed. This shows that there might

---

63 Council Directive 2006/54/EC on the Implementation of the Principle of Equal Opportunities and Equal Treatment of Men and Women in Matters of Employment and Occupation (Recast) [2006] OJ L 204/23.

64 Case C-54/07, supra note 60.

65 For example, in Austria, Malta and the UK harassment covers words as well: see Chopin, I. and Germaine, C., *A Comparative Analysis of Non-discrimination Law in Europe 2016*, European Network of Legal Experts in Gender Equality and Non-Discrimination (Luxembourg: Publications Office of the European Union, 2016) 52–53; Hungary also covers words (in this case in an open letter by a town major): see Decision EBH/549/2016, Equal Treatment Authority, 8 November 2016, www.equalitylaw.eu/downloads/4005-hungary-mayor-found-to-have-committed-harassment-when-calling-on-local-residents-not-to-sell-real-estates-to-roma-people-pdf-136-kb

66 Equality and Human Rights Commission, *Guidance – Legal Framework: Freedom of Expression*, 2015, www.equalityhumanrights.com/en/publication-download/freedom-expression-legal-framework

also be other laws at national level that can provide a (civil) remedy for those targeted by (religious) hate speech.

Based on the above, religious hate speech could amount to discrimination and, possibly, to harassment under EU law. However, Directive 2000/78/EC is only applicable in the area of employment and occupation, and this would thus not cover politicians using anti-immigration or anti-Muslim rhetoric in their speeches. Directive 2000/43/EC, covering discrimination and harassment on the grounds of racial and ethnic origin, is applicable beyond the area of employment and occupation and also covers social protection, including social security and healthcare; social advantages; education; and, access to and supply of goods and services that are available to the public, including housing. Many EU member states have extended the protection against discrimination on the grounds covered by Directive 2000/78/EC to these and other areas, but whether this covers anti-immigration or anti-Muslim speeches by politicians in the public arena depends on which areas are covered by the national anti-discrimination law. Therefore, it is dependent on the national law whether anti-discrimination legislation or other legislation provides a remedy for individuals and groups targeted by hate speech. A claim under anti-discrimination law would be preferable to a criminal hate speech law if the law provided for civil law remedies as such remedies are less likely to be held to interfere with the speaker or author's freedom of expression.

Therefore, it is certainly arguable that religious hate speech in certain circumstances amounts to discrimination or harassment. Australia can be used as an example of a country that generally treats offensive speech against religious groups and individuals as part of its anti-discrimination law and, although some criminal laws against hate speech or 'vilification' do exist there as well, they are seldom used.[67] According to Gelber, 'the federal statute makes it unlawful to do an act if the act is reasonably likely to "offend, insult, humiliate or intimidate another person or group of people" on a specified ground'.[68] There are also similar state level provisions. Under these laws, a person can usually lodge a complaint with a relevant authority, for example, an anti-discrimination commission. Although the number of claims is modest, it is significant in comparison with the lack of use of the criminal law.[69] The body dealing with the claim will mediate a remedy, which might include an apology, education in a workplace, publication of a retraction, or a commitment not to reoffend. Recalcitrant cases are referred to a Tribunal or, to the Federal Court, where possible remedies include an order to apologise or retract and/or a fine.[70]

---

67 See on this: Kapai, P. and Cheung, A., 'Hanging in the Balance: Freedom of Expression and Religion', 15 *Buffalo Human Rights Law Review* (2009) 71; Gelber, K., 'Reconceptualizing Counterspeech in Hate Speech Policy (with a Focus on Australia)', in Herz, M. and Molnar, P. (eds) *The Content and Context of Hate Speech: Rethinking Regulation and Responses* (Cambridge, Cambridge University Press, 2012) 199–202.

68 Gelber, supra note 67, 201.

69 Ibid.

70 Ibid. 202.

Codes of conduct

It has been argued so far, in relation to religious hate speech, that the freedom of speech of politicians should only be restricted by criminal laws if such speech incites to violence and there is a real likelihood, a clear and present danger, that violence will follow; or, if it stops people from holding or practising their belief. Other legal remedies have been explored and it was submitted that civil law and civil law remedies are preferable and that these might be available through a claim under anti-discrimination law, but that such a claim is unlikely to be successful under the ECHR. If it is possible to claim direct discrimination or harassment under national anti-discrimination law, very much depends on the areas covered by the national anti-discrimination law. All this raises the question whether there are other, possibly more effective ways of dealing with (religious) hate speech.

Article 10(2) ECHR determines, as was pointed out in Chapter 1, that the exercise of freedom of expression brings with it duties and responsibilities and this also applies to politicians. It will be clear that politicians have a duty to point out problems and issues of concern in society and speak out about these but do they also have a duty to exercise their freedom of expression responsibly because of their position as politicians? Some authors suggest that politicians have greater responsibilities here, because they have more power to speak and more access to the media and thus broader opportunities for spreading prejudice against certain groups.[71] Malik, for example, writes that 'what is needed is the exercise of responsible speech by those who have power, especially politicians and the media'.[72] As has been argued throughout this book, there is no right not to be offended present in the ECHR and, according to the European Court of Human Rights, politicians can use offensive, shocking or disturbing language,[73] they can use a degree of exaggeration and provocation,[74] and immoderation[75] and they can be controversial and virulent.[76] On the other hand, there is also no duty on politicians to be offensive or use such language, but the above mentioned authors appear to suggest that not only is there no duty to do so, there is a responsibility to avoid such language. These authors find support for this in the cases of

71 See, for example, Lawson, R., 'WILD, WILDER, WILDST Over de Ruimte die het EVRM laat voor de Vervolging van Kwetsende Politici' (WILD, WILDER, WILDEST About the Room given by the ECHR for the Prosecution of Offending Politicians), 33 (4) *NJCM-Bulletin* (2008) 472–473; Malik, M. 'Extreme Speech and Liberalism', in Hare, I. and Weinstein, J. (eds) *Extreme Speech and Democracy* (Oxford, Oxford University Press, 2009) 105; Poole, E., 'The Case of Geert Wilders: Multiculturalism, Islam and Identity in the UK', 5 *Journal of Religion in Europe* (2012) 173; Tulkens, F., *The Hate Factor in Political Speech Where do Responsibilities Lie?* (2013) point 16, https://rm.coe.int/CoERMPublicCommonSearchServices/DisplayDCTMContent?documentId=09000016800c170e

72 Malik, supra note 71, 105.

73 *Handyside v the United Kingdom*, supra note 1, para 49; *Féret v Belgium*, supra note 28, para 77.

74 *Le Pen v France*, Application No. 18788/09, 20 April 2010.

75 *Otegi Mondragon v Spain*, Application No. 2034/07, 15 March 2011, para 54.

76 *Perinçek v Switzerland*, Application No. 27510/08, 15 October 2015, para 231.

the European Court of Human Rights discussed in previous chapters where the Court held that politicians have a duty not to foster intolerance.[77] Leigh, on the other hand, writes that allowing restrictions on expressions that convey a political message because they could be rephrased in less offensive terms 'would interfere with the autonomy of the speaker to choose their own means of expressing his or her message'.[78] The suggestion that politicians have a duty to avoid language that fosters intolerance also ignores the fact that 'provocation and mockery have important roles in the competition of ideologies'[79] and that 'offensive language may in reality be the best communicative style available'.[80] As was argued before, mere 'fostering intolerance' is not enough to restrict the freedom of expression of politicians, especially because politicians play such an important role in the public debate.

The Action Programme adopted at the 2001 World Conference against Racism, Racial Discrimination, Xenophobia and Related Intolerance pointed to the key role of politicians and political parties in combating the targeted forms of intolerance, and it encouraged political parties

> To take concrete steps to promote equality, solidarity and non-discrimination in society, inter alia by developing *voluntary codes of conduct* which include internal disciplinary measures for violations thereof, so their members refrain from public statements and actions that encourage or incite racism, racial discrimination, xenophobia and related intolerance [emphasis added].[81]

It is submitted that these forms of intolerance should include religious intolerance. An example of a voluntary code of conduct is the Charter of European Political Parties for a Non-Racist Society, which was adopted in 1998 and 'appeals to the democratic political parties in the European Union to act responsibly concerning discrimination on the basis of race, ethnic or national origin, and religion'.[82] So, here discrimination on the ground of religion is explicitly mentioned. This Charter, according to the EU website, 'applies both with respect to the parties'

---

77 *Erbakan v Turkey*, supra note 2, para 64; *Féret v Belgium*, supra note 28, para 75.
78 Leigh, supra note 13, 71.
79 Nathwani, N., 'Religious Cartoons and Human Rights – a Critical Legal Analysis of the Case Law of the European Court of Human Rights on the Protection of Religious Feelings and its Implications in the Danish Affair Concerning Cartoons of the Prophet Muhammad', 4 *European Human Rights Law Review* (2008) 499.
80 O'Reilly, A., 'In Defence of Offence: Freedom of Expression, Offensive Speech, and the Approach of the European Court of Human Rights', 19 *Trinity College Law Review* (2016), 241–242.
81 Programme of Action, World Conference against Racism, Racial Discrimination, Xenophobia and Related Intolerance, 2001, Durban, South Africa, para 115 www.un.org/WCAR/durban.pdf
82 EU website on Charter: https://ec.europa.eu/migrant-integration/librarydoc/charter-of-political-parties-for-a-non-racist-society. The Charter of European Political Parties for a Non-Racist Society itself can be found here, www.coe.int/t/dghl/monitoring/ecri/activities/38-seminar_ankara_2011/Charter.asp

own organisation and to their interaction with the outside world'.[83] This EU website has a link to the Charter on the website of the European Commission against Racism and Intolerance (ECRI), a Council of Europe body.[84] This suggests that the Charter can be applied to all Council of Europe member states and not just the EU member states.

In this Charter, the democratic political parties of Europe commit themselves to adhere to a number of principles of good practice. The first principle is 'to defend basic human rights and democratic principles and to reject all forms of racist violence, incitement to racial hatred and harassment and any form of racial discrimination'. This is followed by the commitment:

> To refuse to display, to publish or to have published, to distribute or to endorse in any way views and positions which stir up or invite, or may reasonable be expected to stir up or to invite prejudices, hostility or division between people of different ethnic or national origins or religious beliefs, and to deal firmly with any racist sentiments and behaviour within its own ranks.

This explicitly includes prejudices and hostility based on religious beliefs and it is suggested that this would cover the anti-immigration and anti-Muslim speeches made by some European politicians. Another commitment is 'to refrain from any form of political alliance or cooperation at all levels with any political party which incites or attempts to stir up racial or ethnic prejudices and racial hatred'. The latter refers to what is sometimes called a 'cordon sanitaire': where political parties declare that that they will not work together or form a coalition with a party they consider to be racist. The Charter also contains commitments to avoid stigmatisation of certain groups in society and to strive for fair participation of these groups at all levels of the party.[85]

Niessen, writing in 2001, looked at the results of a survey done among political parties at the end of 1999 and concluded from this that 'the Charter is not very well known, or does not play an important role in the life of the party'.[86] Niessen also concluded that most parties had general principles about human rights, equality and non-discrimination, but only a few mentioned measures to implement these principles in the areas of immigrants and minorities.[87] However, the Charter has been referred to in relation to racist, xenophobic and intolerant discourse a number of times since then. In September 2003, the President of the Council of Europe's Parliamentary Assembly and the President of the European

---

83 See: https://ec.europa.eu/migrant-integration/librarydoc/charter-of-political-parties-for-a-non-racist-society

84 See: Charter of European Political Parties for a Non-Racist Society, supra note 82.

85 Ibid.

86 Niessen, J., 'The Charter for Political Parties for a Non-Racist Society', 3 *European Journal of Migration and Law* (2001) 83.

87 Ibid.

Parliament both signed the Charter.[88] In the same year, the Parliamentary Assembly of the Council of Europe also adopted a resolution on 'racist, xenophobic and intolerant discourse in politics' in which it strongly encouraged extension of the application of the Charter throughout Europe and recommended that all political parties in all member states of the Council of Europe sign the Charter.[89] The Parliamentary Assembly expresses its full support for 'the establishment of a permanent body representative of political parties from all Europe to monitor implementation of the charter and considers that co-operation with the European Parliament is highly desirable in this respect'.[90] The Resolution refers to politicians and political parties whose 'elevated public profile, influential role and privileged status indicate both that greater responsibility and awareness are expected of them'.[91] This does show interest in the Charter within the Council of Europe and a desire for cooperation with the EU on this issue. Although religion is not mentioned explicitly in this Resolution, 'xenophobic and intolerant discourse' would cover anti-immigration and anti-Muslim rhetoric as both are linked and speeches by politicians are often against immigrants because they are foreign and/or Muslim. Moreover, xenophobia is generally defined as a hatred or fear of foreigners and all things foreign, so this would include hatred or fear of Muslims.

In 2005, ECRI issued a declaration in which it condemned the use of anti-Semitic and xenophobic elements in political discourse.[92] The Commission expressed its alarm over the consequences of this type of discourse on the general climate of public opinion in Europe and its deep concern that 'the use of racist, antisemitic and xenophobic political discourse is no longer confined to extremist political parties, but is increasingly infecting mainstream political parties' and that this risks 'legitimising and trivialising this type of discourse'. According to ECRI, this type of discourse 'conveys prejudices and stereotypes in respect of non-citizens and minority groups and strengthens the racist and xenophobic content of debates on immigration and asylum'. ECRI actually explicitly mentions Islam as it 'notes with serious concern that this type of discourse often conveys a distorted image of Islam, intended to portray this religion as a threat'. ECRI points to the 'essential role political parties can play in combating racism, by shaping and guiding public opinion in a positive fashion' and makes a number of suggestions, including

---

88 See: Council of Europe, Information Documents SG/inf (2008) 20 rev, Contribution of the Council of Europe to the Implementation of the Durban Declaration and Programme of Action, Council of Europe Action to Combat Racism and Intolerance (2001–2008) para 64.

89 Parliamentary Assembly, Council of Europe, Resolution 1345 (2003) *Racist, Xenophobic and Intolerant Discourse in Politics*, paras 9 and 11 www.assembly.coe.int/nw/xml/XRef/Xref-XML2HTML-en.asp?fileid=17143&lang=en

90 Ibid. para 9.

91 Ibid. para 12.3.

92 European Commission against Racism and Intolerance, *Declaration on the Use of Racist, Anti-Semitic and Xenophobic Elements in Political Discourse* (2005) www.coe.int/t/dghl/monitoring/ecri/activities/14-Public_Presentation_Paris_2005/Presentation2005_Paris_Declaration_en.asp

self-regulatory measures for political parties or national parliaments; the signature and implementation by political parties of the Charter of Political Parties for a Non-Racist Society; and, 'the establishment of an obligation to suppress financing of organisations which promote racism, including public financing of political parties'.[93] So here ECRI suggests a possible remedy in the form of refusing or withdrawing public money from parties who do not comply with the Charter.

In 2010, the Party of European Socialists, which is an alliance of Socialist, Social Democratic and Labour Parties within the EU, adopted a resolution in which it pledged not to have any relations with a party threatening fundamental rights, human dignity, equality and non-discrimination.[94] The resolution urges all European Political parties to sign up to the Charter 'in order to confront the rise of the extreme-right by isolating those parties from the political scene'. It also urges them to adopt a code of conduct that includes: to condemn all racist, xenophobic, discriminatory or nationalist statements and action; not to get into a ruling coalition or electoral alliance with a party that incites or attempts to stir up racial and ethnic prejudices and racial hatred and to refuse implicit support from such a party; to fight 'the legitimization of the discourses of such parties by refusing to engage into their terms of the debate, by not taking up their ideas into its political platforms nor in the policies it implements when in government'; and, to isolate its members when they are not respecting those principles.

In its 2015 General Policy Recommendation on combating hate speech, ECRI recommends that governments 'provide support for self-regulation by public and private institutions (including elected bodies, political parties, educational institutions and cultural and sports organisations)' through encouraging the adoption of such codes; through encouraging political parties to sign the Charter and through encouraging the unambiguous condemnation of breaches of these codes.[95] ECRI also recommends withdrawing all financial and other forms of support by public bodies from political parties that use hate speech or do not sanction their members if they do so and even dissolving such organisations, while respecting the right to freedom of association in article 11 ECHR.[96] ECRI points out that, although the recommendation is particularly concerned with the use of hate speech that falls within the Commission's work, its provisions are envisaged as being applicable to all forms of such speech on a number of grounds, including religion. Moreover, the recommendation defines racism as including religion and it defines Islamophobia as meaning prejudice against, hatred towards or fear of the religion of Islam or Muslims.[97]

93 All: ibid.
94 Party of European Socialists, *Confronting the Extreme-Right in Europe: our Way*, Resolution adopted by the PES Presidency on 14th of October 2010, www.pes.eu/export/sites/default/Downloads/Policy-Documents/Democracy/adopted_resolution_extreme_right_141010_en.pdf_551059009.pdf
95 European Commission against Racism and Intolerance, General Policy Recommendation No. 15, on Combating Hate Speech, CRI (2016) 15, 2015, recommendation 6.
96 Ibid. recommendation 9.
97 Ibid. paras 6, 7w and 7r.

Therefore, the Charter of European Political Parties for a Non-Racist Society appears to play a role in Europe and has been signed by both the EU Parliament and the Parliamentary Assembly of the Council of Europe. However, it is difficult to assess its influence. The Charter ends with a pledge 'to take appropriate action to ensure that all persons who work for or associate themselves in any way with any of our election campaigns or other activities will be aware of and at all times act in accordance with the above principles'.[98] However, the Charter itself does not provide any sanctions in case signatories do not follow the principles enumerated in the Charter. There is also no monitoring body as suggested by the Parliamentary Assembly of the Council of Europe. The only suggestions for sanctions, in the form of suppressing public finances, are made by ECRI, but this assumes that political parties get funded out of the public purse, which is not the case in all European states. Moreover, who decides on withholding public funding? If this is decided by the state, the current government, similar objections can be brought forward to such sanctions as were raised against hate speech laws in Chapter 3: they are open to abuse by the state and can be used to stifle opposition parties; and, they could create an extra platform for the speaker or author and allow them to portray themselves as free speech martyrs. Therefore, the Charter is important because it lays down principles to be followed by the European political parties, but sanctions against politicians might be more effectively taken within individual party regulations. However, as Niessen reports, 'there were only a few parties that explicitly mentioned sanctions against members, elected official or party employees on the basis of racism and discrimination'.[99] Therefore, voluntary codes of conduct such as the Charter provide an alternative to criminal law, but it is difficult to assess how effective these codes are in practice.

Other ways of dealing with hate speech

It can be argued that:

> The strategic response to hate speech is more speech: more speech that educates about cultural differences; more speech that promotes diversity; more speech to empower and give voice to minorities, ... More speech can be the best strategy to reach out to individuals, changing what they think and not merely what they do.[100]

ECRI's General Policy Recommendation on Hate Speech defines 'counter-speech' as speech that reaffirms the values threatened by hate speech and that

---

98 Charter of European Political Parties for a Non-Racist Society, supra note 82.

99 Niessen, supra note 86, 83.

100 Joint Statement by the Special Rapporteurs on Freedom of Expression, Freedom of Religion or Belief and on Racism, Racial Discrimination, Xenophobia and Related Intolerance to the 2011 Expert Workshop on the Prohibition of National, Racial and Religious Hatred, Vienna 9–10 February 2011, 12 www.ohchr.org/Documents/Issues/Religion/CRP3Joint_SRSubmission_for_Vienna.pdf

challenges the assumptions on which hate speech relies.[101] And, Barendt points out that the defenders of free speech argue that hate speech is best met by more speech, advocating the moral and cultural superiority of a multiracial society.[102] This suggests that hate speech should be challenged and countered by everyone and in all fields of life. According to ECRI, public figures, such as politicians, religious leaders, community leaders and personalities from arts, business and sport, can make an extra contribution here because their voices have considerable influence.[103] ECRI also points out that non-governmental organisations, equality bodies and National Human Rights Institutions have been and are playing an important role in this regard.[104] Counter-speech should include not only condemnation of the speech but also the promotion of the values of pluralism, equality, diversity and tolerance. Just condemning the hate speech is not enough. Mainstream political parties are sometimes quick to condemn and reject statements made by far-right politicians, but then take on some of the rhetoric used by those politicians in their election manifestos.

Counter speech can also come from those targeted by the hate speech and they can make use of their right to freedom of expression to criticise and challenge negative images of their community. However, this is not always easy for minority groups and this is why intercultural dialogue and cultural policies that encourage participation of minorities in public debate are proposed.[105] But minorities can also be empowered by 'support of community media and their representation in the mainstream media'.[106]

However, in relation to counter speech the question can be raised whether this is not out-of-date in today's social media dominated world. Counter speech assumes that you can reach the majority of people with the same message but many people's access to 'news' is now highly (self) filtered. Whereas in the past, many people would watch or listen to the same main evening news programme, nowadays people exchange information with other people from a like-minded group via social media and this tends to reinforce their views. Therefore, the ability for counter speech to reach those that have been persuaded by hate speech appears to be reducing all the time.

From the quote from the Joint Statement given above it is clear that education plays an important role in tackling hate speech. Education on the values of tolerance, human rights and equality, on cultural differences is often mentioned as another alternative to hate speech laws.[107] These values should be taught at

101 European Commission against Racism and Intolerance, supra note 95, para 88.
102 Barendt, supra note 26, 171–172.
103 Ibid. para 98.
104 Ibid. para 100.
105 See, for example, Joint Statement, supra note 100, 12; Malik, M., 'Religious Freedom, Free Speech and Equality: Conflict or Cohesion?' 17 *Res Publica* (2011) 39; European Commission against Racism and Intolerance, supra note 95, recommendation 4c.
106 Joint Statement, supra note 100, 12.
107 Ibid. See also: Chan, supra note 32, 93; European Commission against Racism and Intolerance, supra note 95, recommendation 4e and para 93.

all levels, from primary school to professional education, including education of public officials such as police officers and judges. But education should also contribute towards empowering and giving voice to minorities by building their capacity to respond to hate speech and is thus linked to the issue of counter-speech by targeted groups.

Awareness raising campaigns could also help towards creating more awareness of and tolerance between groups in society. As ECRI points out, this could take the form of 'art and film festivals, concerts, culinary events, drama and role plays, exhibitions, lectures and seminars and special projects involving schools as well as broadcasts and publications'.[108] Media campaigns are another way of dealing with hate speech and of raising awareness. A good example of such a campaign is the 'kick it out' campaign that is tackling racism and discrimination in football and that works throughout the football, educational and community sectors to encourage inclusive practices and campaigns for positive change.[109]

But, Chan raises a good question about media campaigns and educational initiatives, where he writes:

> It is not clear, however, that these long-term, soft measures meet the needs of society today. It is not clear whether they would provide an adequate deterrent to or a sufficient denunciation of a rising tide of prejudice, discrimination and intolerance within society.

Chan suggests as an alternative the adoption of hate crime laws that 'may better address this predicament'.[110] Above it was argued that such laws are indeed better than laws prohibiting hate speech.

Conclusion

This chapter started with an examination of the way hate speech is dealt with in the US, because the approach there is often seen as contrasting with most other countries. The US gives very strong protection to freedom of speech although, even in the US, the right is not an absolute right. This freedom and the role it has in public discourse, with an emphasis on the participatory aspect of this discourse, plays an important role in the US. This has led to a rejection of any content-based regulation of public discourse and restrictions on speech because of the message it conveys are subject to very strict scrutiny. The distinction between content-based and content-neutral restrictions is not made by the European Court of Human Rights which takes both into account when deciding on whether a restriction on someone's freedom of expression is justified under article 10(2) ECHR. However, it was argued that, in relation to hate speech, the difference

108 European Commission against Racism and Intolerance, supra note 95, para 94.
109 See: www.kickitout.org
110 Chan, supra note 32, 94.

between the European Court of Human Rights' approach and the US approach is not as big as it seems. In the US, restrictions on the freedom of expression are accepted in relation to hate speech when there is a 'clear and present danger' or a risk of 'imminent lawless action'.[111] This is very similar to the terms used by the European Court of Human Rights, which has held that restrictions on hate speech are only justified if there is a 'present risk' and 'imminent danger', a 'clear and imminent danger' and a 'real and present danger' and not a 'mere speculative danger' of violence following the speech. It was argued that the European Court of Human Rights is thus moving towards a test that is similar to the 'clear and present danger' test used in the US and that this is a welcome development.

The harmful effect of hate speech not only to the individuals or groups targeted but also to wider society was discussed. Hate speech can foster intolerance, create a hostile climate and generate an 'us' versus 'them' feeling. However, it was argued that this does not justify having criminal laws against hate speech for a number of reasons, including problems inherent in criminal law, such as the definition of hate speech, proof, causation and culpability, and punishment based on future effects; the presence of other criminal offences that could deal with the issues raised; the absence of evidence that there is a direct link between hate speech and harm; and, the fact that criminal law might very well not be the least restrictive means of dealing with hate speech.

Next, measures against discrimination were considered as an alternative to criminal hate speech laws. It was argued that civil laws against hate speech are preferable to criminal laws and that anti-discrimination laws, which often provide for civil law remedies, might be used by those targeted by hate speech. However, it was concluded that it might be difficult to use article 14 or article 1 of Protocol 12 ECHR, which both prohibit discrimination, because a state that has enacted anti-discrimination law has fulfilled its positive obligations under these articles.

The EU measures against religion or belief discrimination were analysed and it was concluded that a possible claim may be made for direct discrimination. If religious hate speech falls under the prohibition of direct discrimination in EU law, there would be no justification defence available. Hate speech might also be held to fall under the prohibition of harassment. However, the EU prohibitions of direct discrimination and harassment on the ground of religion or belief do not extend beyond the field of employment and occupation. Many national laws go beyond these areas, but whether the national anti-discrimination legislation provides a remedy for individuals and groups targeted by hate speech depends on the areas covered by this legislation.

The Charter of European Political Parties for a Non-Racist Society, which was adopted in 1998 and has been endorsed by both the EU and the Council of Europe, was analysed as a good example of a voluntary code of conduct for politicians. Although the Charter is important because it lays down principles to be followed by the European political parties and because it has been

---

111 *Schenck v United States*, 249 US 47 (1919); *Brandenburg v Ohio*, 395 US 444 (1969).

referred to both within the Council of Europe and the EU, it is difficult to assess its effectiveness. It also does not provide for sanctions in case of breach, nor is there a supervisory body to oversee compliance.

The last part of this chapter discussed other ways of dealing with hate speech. It was suggested that counter-speech condemning and challenging hate speech and promoting values of pluralism, equality, diversity and tolerance is needed from everyone and in all fields of life, including politicians and those targeted by hate speech. However, it was pointed out that, in a world where social media are playing a big role in the way people access news, effective counter speech has become more difficult. Education on the values of tolerance, human rights and equality, on cultural differences also plays an important part in countering hate speech. Awareness raising campaigns and media campaigns can also contribute to countering hate speech.

In the following chapter, the expressions of Dutch politician Geert Wilders, who has been prosecuted twice for his many remarks against Islam and Muslims and against Moroccans in the Netherlands, will be analysed using the arguments examined in this and the previous chapters.

6 Case in point
The prosecutions of Geert Wilders

Introduction

In Chapter 5, possible alternatives to criminal laws against hate speech were examined. The approach to hate speech in the US was analysed and compared to the approach of the European Court of Human Rights and it was concluded that a similar test appears to be used by the Court as the one used in the US: a clear and present danger test, which means that hate speech can be restricted without violating the right to freedom of expression of the speaker or author if there is a clear and present danger of violence occurring.

Throughout the previous chapters, it has been argued that the freedom of expression of politicians should only be limited in two circumstances: where it constitutes hate speech and there is a real likelihood, a clear and present danger, that violence will occur, or where it factually stops people from holding, manifesting or practising their religious beliefs. And, even then, both restrictions are still subject to the three part justification test in Article 10(2) ECHR. Outside these two circumstances, freedom of expression of politicians should not be restricted by criminal hate speech laws or laws against incitement to hatred and violence.

Chapter 5 also examined the harm done by hate speech to the individuals and groups targeted and to wider society and concluded that this does not justify criminal measures against hate speech. Because this leaves those targeted by hate speech without a remedy, it was suggested that civil laws might be used to challenge hate speech. Anti-discrimination laws often provide civil procedures and civil remedies and, therefore, these laws were analysed. The conclusion was that challenges under Article 14 or Article 1, Protocol 12 would have little chance of success but that EU or national anti-discrimination law might provide a remedy. Hate speech could be argued to be direct discrimination or harassment on the ground of religion or belief under Directive 2000/78/EC. The problem with this Directive is its limited scope, as it only applies in the areas of employment and occupation. This means that member states do not have to enact legislation against religion or belief discrimination outside that area, although many have done so. Therefore, whether the national anti-discrimination legislation provides a remedy for individuals and groups targeted by hate speech depends on where the hate speech takes place and whether that area is covered by the national anti-discrimination law.

Voluntary codes of conduct were discussed, with a special focus on the 1998 Charter of European Political Parties for a Non-Racist Society, which has been endorsed by both the EU and the Council of Europe and which can be seen as covering religious intolerance as well as racial intolerance. The Charter lays down a number of good practice principles to be followed by European political parties but it does not contain any sanctions for non-compliance, nor is there any supervision on its implementation. The conclusion was that its effectiveness is uncertain. The same conclusion was drawn about the other alternatives discussed.

This chapter contains a case study about the prosecutions of Dutch politician Geert Wilders which are assessed using the arguments put forward in the previous chapters. This case study was chosen because it illustrates clearly a number of arguments put forward in the previous chapters. Geert Wilders, the leader of the Dutch Party for Freedom (PVV), has, over the years, made many comments about Islam and Muslims. In this chapter, the expressions that have led to him being prosecuted on two occasions are assessed using the content of the previous chapters as a yardstick. The first prosecution of Wilders led to an acquittal, but the second prosecution led, in December 2016, to a conviction without the imposition of any punishment. Both Wilders and the Dutch Public Prosecutor have appealed against this conviction.[1] Wilders has appealed because he sees his conviction as a clear violation of his right to free speech,[2] while the Dutch Public Prosecutor has appealed because they want to make sure that the full case is presented to the Court of Appeal.[3] If the conviction is upheld, Wilders will, no doubt, appeal again and once all domestic procedures are exhausted he is likely to apply to the European Court of Human Rights alleging that his conviction is a violation of his right to freedom of expression under Article 10 ECHR, a right that he is quick to invoke whenever any of his expressions are challenged. The Chapter also contains an assessment of the way the Court should deal with the case, based on the content of the previous chapters and the Court's own case law set out in these chapters.[4]

1 See: *Dutch Politician Wilders Convicted of Discrimination Against Moroccans* www. reuters.com/article/us-netherlands-wilders-trial-idUSKBN13Y0OX ; and: *Ook OM Gaat in Beroep in Zaak-Wilders* (Public Prosecutor also Appeals Wilders Case): http://nos.nl/artikel/2149910-ook-om-gaat-in-beroep-in-zaak-wilders.html (in Dutch; all references to Dutch cases or articles have been translated by author).

2 See: *Video: Nederland is een Ziek Land Geworden (Video: the Netherlands has become a Sick Country)* http://nos.nl/artikel/2147381-video-wilders-nederland-is-een-ziek-land-geworden.html

3 See: *Ook OM Gaat in Beroep in Zaak-Wilders* (Public Prosecutor also Appeals Wilders Case), supra note 1.

4 See also on this: Howard, E., 'Freedom of Speech versus Freedom of Religion? The Case of Dutch Politician Geert Wilders', 17 (2) *Human Rights Law Review* (2017) 313–337.

The first prosecution of Geert Wilders

Geert Wilders is the leader of the Dutch right wing Party for Freedom (PVV) which he founded himself. He is the only member of his party as he does not allow anyone else to become a member, not even those people who are elected members of parliament for the PVV. He has, time and again, voiced strong opinions against Islam and what he calls the islamisation of the Netherlands. Islam is, in his view, a totalitarian and violent ideology with extreme views that wants to destroy Western civilisation and convert and subjugate non-believers. He has likened the Quran to Hitler's Mein Kampf and has often linked Islam with criminality. Wilders proposes the closure of all mosques, a ban on the Quran, the closure of the Dutch borders to Muslims and the loss of Dutch nationality for all Muslim criminals. Wilders links Islam to Dutch Moroccans and has often stated that Moroccan (young) people are criminal and violent and that this behaviour is inspired by their Muslim religion and culture. Many Moroccans came to the Netherlands in the 1970s to work and then stayed on and made the Netherlands their home. They are one of the larger minority groups in the Netherlands. Wilders has aired his views frequently and through all kinds of media and is an avid twitter user. In 2008, Wilders made a short film called *Fitna*, in which very negative views about Islam and about the adverse influence of Islam in the Netherlands were expressed. After the film was released, a number of organisations and individuals reported what was said by Wilders to the authorities. The Public Prosecutor declined to prosecute because they did not think this would lead to a conviction. They considered that the expressions were part of the political debate in the Netherlands and were directed against Islam rather than against Muslims. The Public Prosecutor thus followed established case law from the European Court of Human Rights about expressions that are part of the political debate and about the distinction between criticising a religion and insulting that religion's believers.

The Amsterdam Court of Appeal

Under Dutch law, a complaint can be made to the Court of Appeal against the decision by the Public Prosecutor not to prosecute. This happened in this case and the Amsterdam Court of Appeal, in January 2009, ordered the Public Prosecutor to prosecute Wilders for intentionally insulting a group of people based on their race or religion (article 137c Sr (Dutch Penal Code)) and incitement to hatred, discrimination or violence on the grounds of race and religion (article 137d Sr).[5] No distinction is made in these articles between racial or religious insult or between incitement on racial or on religious grounds. The Court

---

5 See: *Gerechtshof Amsterdam* (Amsterdam Court of Appeal), 21 January 2009, ECLI:NL: GHAMS:2009:BH0496, https://uitspraken.rechtspraak.nl/inziendocument?id=ECLI:NL: GHAMS:2009:BH0496 .

pointed out that, if it decided to order a prosecution, it expected that a conviction would follow, but that it was up to the criminal court to decide on this.[6]

The Amsterdam Court of Appeal brought forward a number of arguments for its decision. It considered, first, that Wilders' expressions were radical in scope and were being repeated with increasing vehemence, which showed incitement to hatred. These expressions were also considered insulting because they harmed the religious dignity of Muslims. Moreover, by insulting the symbols of the Muslim religion, Wilders had also insulted the Muslim believers. The content and the way of presenting the expressions were aimed at inciting the Dutch population to discrimination, intolerance, contempt and hostility towards this group of believers.[7] Both the content and context of the expressions were thus clearly taken into account. The Court of Appeal saw the expressions, contrary to the view of the Public Prosecutor, as insulting Muslims and as going beyond mere criticism of Islam as a religion. The Court thus appears to suggest that there is a right not to be offended in one's religious feelings. It was argued, throughout this book, that such a right is not present in the ECHR and that the fact that expressions are offensive to religious believers is, on its own, not enough to justify restrictions on the right to freedom of expression. The argument also seems to run counter to case law of the Dutch Supreme Court that hurtful expressions about a religion might insult or offend the believers in that religion, but that this was not enough to consider the expressions to be insulting of the religious group.[8] The Amsterdam Court of Appeal did consider that the political context and the importance of expressions for the public debate can take away the criminal nature of the expressions, but that this was not applicable to Wilders' expressions, as these should not be seen in isolation from each other but should be taken together. Seen in this way, the criminal nature of the expressions was enhanced rather than diminished.[9]

Although a politician must have the widest possible freedom of expression to bring forward his political views and contribute to the public debate, this did not mean, according to the Amsterdam Court of Appeal, that he did not have a responsibility to do so in an acceptable way.[10] This seems to suggest that the Court saw Wilders expressions as contributing to the public debate but, despite that, they were not protected under article 10(2) because they were not presented in an acceptable way. This argument was based on the consideration that, in the past, people, including politicians, have been convicted for lesser expressions than

---

6 Ibid. para 11.

7 Ibid. para 12.1.2.

8 *Hoge Raad* (Supreme Court), 10 March 2009, ECLI:NL:PHR:BF0655, https:// uitspraken.rechtspraak.nl/inziendocument?id=ECLI:NL:PHR:2009:BF0655 This case concerned a poster with the text: *stop het gezwel that Islam heet* (stop the tumour that is Islam).

9 Amsterdam Court of Appeal, supra note 5, para 12.1.3.

10 Ibid. para 12.1.4.

those of Wilders.[11] It is submitted that denying protection to expressions because they are not presented in an acceptable way is very dangerous because what is acceptable and who determines this? Is this determined by the majority? What is acceptable is also a very subjective notion: what is acceptable to some is unacceptable to others. Moreover, this would require politicians and others contributing to the public debate to use 'acceptable language', which does not fit in with the case law of the European Court of Human Rights that politicians who contribute to the public debate can use offensive, shocking or disturbing language,[12] they can exaggerate and provoke[13] and be immoderate,[14] controversial and virulent.[15]

The Amsterdam Court of Appeal's next argument was that the prosecution was compatible with the ECHR because, under the Convention case law (the Court referred to *Zana v Turkey, Erbakan v Turkey* and *Gündüz v Turkey*[16]), expressions that incite to hatred were not protected under article 10(2) ECHR.[17] This reasoning is compatible with the case law of the European Court of Human Rights in so far as it has held that restrictions on incitement to hatred can be compatible with article 10(2), but it ignores that only in *Zana v Turkey* was a conviction for incitement to hatred held not to violate the speaker's right to freedom of expression.[18] In *Erbakan v Turkey,* it was held that there needed to be a present risk or an imminent danger of violence following the expression and that, in the absence of this, the conviction of the applicant for his expression was held to constitute an interference with article 10(2).[19] As was pointed out in Chapters 4 and 5, the European Court of Human Rights has confirmed the requirement of a 'present risk' and 'imminent danger' of violence in *GÜl and Others v Turkey*, where it mentioned a 'clear and imminent danger',[20] and in *Vajnai v Hungary,* where it used the terms 'real and present danger' and 'not mere speculative danger'.[21] However, the Amsterdam Court of Appeal did not consider whether there was a clear and imminent danger of violence following Wilders' expressions. Moreover, in *Gündüz v Turkey,* the European Court of Human Rights held that the expressions at issue in that case were contributing to the public discourse and were not

---

11 Ibid. The Amsterdam Court of Appeal refers to a case of the Dutch Supreme Court in which a politician was convicted for stating that he would abolish multicultural society if he came to power, see: Hoge Raad (Supreme Court) 18 May 1999, ECLI:NL:HR:1999:ZD1538, NJ 1999,634.
12 *Féret v Belgium,* Application No. 15615/07, 16 July 2009, paras 76 and 77.
13 *Le Pen v France,* Application No. 18788/09, 20 April 2010.
14 *Otegi Mondragon v Spain,* Application No. 2034/07, 15 March 2011, para 54.
15 *Perinçek v Switzerland,* Application No. 27510/08, 15 October 2015, para 231.
16 *Zana v Turkey,* Application No. 18954/91, 25 November 1997; *Erbakan v Turkey,* Application No. 59405/00, 6 July 2006; *Gündüz v Turkey,* Application No. 35071/97, 4 December 2003.
17 Amsterdam Court of Appeal, supra note 5, para 12.2.2.
18 *Zana v Turkey,* supra note 16.
19 *Erbakan v Turkey,* supra note 16.
20 *GÜl and Others v. Turkey,* Application No. 4870/02, 8 June 2010, para 42.
21 *Vajnai v Hungary,* Application No. 33629/06, 8 July 2008, paras 49 and 55.

gratuitously offensive and thus that there was a violation of article 10(2).[22] The view of the Amsterdam Court of Appeal on the contribution of Wilders' expressions to the public debate were discussed above. There was no discussion of the question whether Wilders' expressions were 'gratuitously offensive' or not.

The Amsterdam Court of Appeal also mentioned that immigration and integration were an important but controversial issue in the public debate at that time and that participants in this debate enjoyed a very wide right to freedom of expression, although this did not mean that they had a 'right to insult'.[23] From all of the above it is clear that both the content and the context of Wilders' expressions are taken into account and that the Court saw Wilders' expressions as contributing to the public debate. However, it is submitted that the Court was wrong in stating that there is no 'right to insult'. There is no right not to be offended or insulted, and, as was mentioned in Chapter 5, there is no duty to offend, but the case law of the European Court of Human Rights shows, as mentioned above, that politicians who contribute to the public debate can offend shock, disturb, exaggerate, provoke, and be immoderate, controversial and virulent.[24] This would suggest, contrary to what the Court stated, that there is a 'right to offend' or a 'right to insult'.

The Amsterdam Court of Appeal continued that, traditionally, public debate in the Netherlands was based on tolerance for different opinions and that one could expect Muslim immigrants to understand the feelings of others about their religion which, in some parts, might clash with Dutch and European values. Controversial expressions within the public debate should be countered, first and foremost, in that public debate. Civil law could also be used to counter such speech as this encourages participation in the public debate. However, according to the Court of Appeal, exceptions to this should be made for offending expressions that make comparisons with Nazism (Wilders comparison between Hitler's *Mein Kampf* and the Quran) and that, therefore, fall within the criminal law. Moreover, according to the Court of Appeal, Wilders expressions, that Muslims who want to take part in the public debate must distance themselves from the Quran, that the Quran and mosques must be banned and that the Dutch borders should be closed to Muslims, were excluding Muslims from this public debate and this was against the fundamental values of a democracy. Destroying the rights of others based on an ideology such as Islamophobia was not compatible with the values of the ECHR.[25] This seems to suggest that the Court saw Wilders' expressions as contrary to article 17 ECHR. This is confirmed by the consideration, with a footnote reference to *Gündüz v Turkey*,[26] that a politician who incites to discrimination and hate abuses their right to freedom of expression and thus

22 *Gündüz v Turkey*, supra note 16.
23 Amsterdam Court of Appeal, supra note 5, para 13.1.
24 *Féret v Belgium*, supra note 12, *Le Pen v France*, supra note 13, *Otegi Mondragon v Spain*, supra note 14, *Perinçek v Switzerland*, supra note 15.
25 Amsterdam Court of Appeal, supra note 5, para 13.2.
26 *Gündüz v Turkey*, supra note 16.

they cannot invoke the protection of article 10 ECHR.[27] However, this appears to run counter to what was concluded from the case law of the European Court of Human Rights, in Chapter 4, that article 17 ECHR should only be applied in exceptional and extreme cases where the fundamental democratic principles and values of the state are at stake and, if this is not the case, restrictions on the freedom of expression should be scrutinised under the three part test of article 10(2).

Based on the arguments discussed, the Amsterdam Court of Appeal ordered the Public Prosecutor to prosecute Wilders.[28] Thereby, it allowed for a much wider justification of restrictions to the freedom of expression of politicians than has been argued for in this book: that such restrictions should only be held to be justified if there is an imminent danger of violence occurring or if this stops people from holding or manifesting their religion or belief. It is submitted that neither applied to the expressions of Wilders which led to this first prosecution and, thus, that the Amsterdam Court of Appeal was wrong in its decision to order the prosecution of Wilders. The judgment and the arguments on which it was based 'gave many people the idea that he [Wilders] had already been convicted'.[29] It also put the Public Prosecutor in an awkward position: they had to prosecute, despite having decided earlier that a prosecution would have little chance of success.

The Amsterdam District Court

Following the decision of the Amsterdam Court of Appeal, Wilders was prosecuted in the Amsterdam District Court for insulting a group of people based on race (non-Western immigrants and/or Moroccans) or religion (Muslims) and incitement to hatred and discrimination on racial and religious grounds (the same groups). Wilders did not deny having made any of the expressions at issue, but argued that he had made these as a politician and in the context of the public debate. At the end of the trial, the Public Prosecutor used the same reasons they had given for their earlier decision not to prosecute Wilders, to argue for a full acquittal. The Amsterdam District Court followed many of these arguments and acquitted Wilders on all counts.[30] The Court referred to the parliamentary history of article 137c Sr and the case law of the Dutch Supreme Court, already mentioned above, that hurtful expressions about a religion might insult or offend the believers in that religion, but that this was not enough to consider the expressions to be insulting of the religious group.[31] Therefore, Wilders' expressions

27 Amsterdam Court of Appeal, supra note 5, para 12.2.2.
28 Ibid. para 14.
29 Noorloos, M. van, 'The Politicisation of Hate Speech Bans in the Twenty First Century Netherlands: Law in a Changing Context', 40 (2) *Journal of Ethnic and Migration Studies* (2014) 257.
30 See: *Rechtbank Amsterdam* (Amsterdam District Court), 23 June 2011, ECLI:NL: RBAMS:2011:BQ9001, https://uitspraken.rechtspraak.nl/inziendocument?id=ECLI:NL: RBAMS:2011:BQ9001
31 See: Supreme Court, supra note 8.

did not breach article 137c Sr on group insult because criticism, even strong criticism, of a group's opinions or behaviour fell outside the ambit of this article.[32] It also referred to the fact that the legislative history showed that the legislator had specifically intended to make incitement to hatred or discrimination a criminal offence, but that it had wanted to keep expressions about religion outside the scope of article 137d Sr.[33] So, neither article 137c nor 137d Sr were meant to protect religious believers against criticism of their religion even if this offended their religious feelings. The Dutch Supreme Court and the Amsterdam District Court thus appear to follow the case law of the European Court of Human Rights, and the argument made throughout this book, that criticism of a religion is protected by the right to freedom of expression and that mere offence of religious believers is not enough to justify an interference with this right.

The Amsterdam District Court considered the case law of the European Court of Human Rights on restrictions on speech by politicians and mentioned that article 10(2) leaves little room for restrictions on expressions of politicians because of the importance of the political debate for a democratic society and, that this was especially true for an elected politician who represents his voters.[34] The Court noted that a 'pressing social need' and proportionality was required for restrictions on the freedom of expression; that, in *Erbakan v Turkey*,[35] the European Court of Human Rights had held that it was crucially important that, in their speeches, politicians should avoid making comments likely to foster intolerance; and, that, in *Féret v Belgium*,[36] it was held that fostering the exclusion of foreigners was a fundamental attack on their rights, and everyone – including politicians – should exercise particular caution.[37] The Court came to the conclusion that most of the expressions at issue here were aimed at the religion of Islam rather than at Muslims and that the remarks which were aimed at people, targeted politicians who Wilders criticised for not recognising the problematic aspects of Islam. Neither could be seen as incitement to hatred on the ground of religion.[38] In relation to incitement to discrimination, the Court considered that, although the expressions might be discriminatory, there must be room for a politician to voice his ideas which he hopes to realise when he comes to power in a democratic manner. These expressions were political proposals that Wilders hoped to bring into force when he was democratically elected and that were part of the public debate or criticism on government and other parties' policies and thus they did not constitute incitement to discrimination. According to the Court, they were, as Wilders himself stated, necessary in a democratic society to flag up what he

32 Amsterdam District Court, supra note 30, para 4.2.
33 Ibid. para 4.3.1.
34 Ibid. The Amsterdam District Court refers here to *Féret v Belgium*, supra note 12, paras 63 and 65.
35 *Erbakan v Turkey*, supra note 16, para 64.
36 *Féret v Belgium*, supra note 12, para 75.
37 Amsterdam District Court, supra note 30, para 4.3.1.
38 Ibid. para 4.3.2.

saw as a major problem.[39] Therefore, the significance of the public and political debate and the important role politicians play in this debate were stressed. It will be clear that the Court took account of the purpose of the speaker or author (to flag up problems in society within the public debate), the content and the context of the expressions and the status of the speaker or author.

The Amsterdam District Court then examined the film *Fitna* and found that the main message was to point out the dangers of Islam and its negative influence on Dutch society.[40] The Court considered that the film was made at a time when multicultural society and immigration played a big role in the public debate and that, as a politician, Wilders made a contribution to this debate. Although the film contained images and expressions that were shocking, offensive and disturbing, taken as a whole and within this context, the Court held that the film did not incite to hatred or discrimination.[41] Wilders was, therefore, acquitted on all counts against him. The importance of the public debate and the contribution of all politicians, including those opposing or criticising the government in this debate, clearly played a role in the Court's deliberations. However, the Court did consider that some of Wilders' expressions almost crossed the line of what is prohibited by criminal law,[42] or, as Temperman observes, the Court 'did not shy away from observing that Wilders did get dangerously close to that fine line between legal and illegal speech'.[43]

The Human Rights Committee

After the acquittal, three of the victims of the alleged hate speech incidents brought a case against the Netherlands to the UN Human Rights Committee under article 20(2) of the International Covenant on Civil and Political Rights (ICCPR). This article was briefly discussed in Chapter 3 and, as was explained there, it imposes a duty on states to prohibit by law 'any advocacy of national, racial or religious hatred that constitutes incitement to discrimination, hostility or violence'. The three authors of the application were all Muslims with dual Dutch–Moroccan nationality who felt personally and directly affected by Wilders' hate speech and who suffered the effects of it in their daily lives because they had been either personally attacked or threatened and humiliated via the internet. They argued that the failure to convict Wilders had sent out a signal that his conduct was not criminal and that this signal made them anxious about their future.[44] They also contended that, by not convicting Wilders, the

39 Ibid.
40 Ibid.
41 Ibid.
42 Ibid.
43 Temperman, J., 'A Right to be Free from Religious Hatred? The *Wilders* Case in the Netherlands and Beyond' in Molnar, P. (ed.) *Free Speech and Censorship around the Globe* (Budapest/New York, Central European University Press, 2015) 510. In the same vein, van Noorloos, supra note 29, 258.
44 *M.R., A.B.S. and N.A. v The Netherlands* (2124/11), Views, CCPR/C/117/D/2124/2011, para 2.11.

Netherlands had breached the duty imposed by article 20(2) ICCPR because it had not protected them enough against increasing racism and hatred; and, that the judgment of the Amsterdam District Court did not balance their interests against the interests of the freedom of expression of Wilders.[45] It is submitted that these three victims applied to the Human Rights Committee under article 20(2) ICCPR because, as was discussed in Chapter 5, the ECHR does not impose a duty on states to protect against hate speech and thus there is little that victims of hate speech can complain about under the ECHR.

In July 2016, the Human Rights Committee first considered the admissibility of the communication and held that the authors were members of the particular group targeted by Wilders' statements and thus that they were persons whom article 20(2) ICCPR was intended to protect. Wilders' expressions had specific consequences for them, including creating discriminatory social attitudes against their group and against them as members of the group. Article 20(2) provided protection for people as individuals and as members of groups against such discrimination.[46] Therefore, the communication was held to be admissible.[47] In its considerations on the Merits, the Human Rights Committee stressed that freedom of expression under article 19 ICCPR (which guarantees the freedom of expression) embraces even expressions that may be regarded as deeply offensive. It also emphasised that the free communication of information and ideas about public and political issues between citizens, candidates and elected representatives is essential to the promotion and protection of free expression.[48] Therefore, the right to freedom of expression in the ICCPR also covers offensive language and the importance of the political and public debate is stressed as it is under article 10 ECHR. The Human Rights Committee came to the conclusion that the Netherlands had not breached any of the provisions of the ICCPR. The state had taken the necessary and proportionate measures to prohibit statements made in violation of article 20(2) ICCPR and had guaranteed an effective remedy for persons targeted by such statements. The Committee mentioned that article 20(2) ICCPR does not impose an obligation on states to ensure a conviction.[49] As Seetulsingh writes in his individual opinion, 'the Committee cannot compel the State Party to punish the alleged wrongdoer in spite of an acquittal'.[50]

The second prosecution of Geert Wilders

The second prosecution of Wilders concerned remarks made during an interview at a market in The Hague and during a post-vote meeting with supporters at the time of the local elections in March 2014, also in The Hague. At this meeting, Wilders asked the crowd 'and do you want more or fewer Moroccans in your

45 Ibid. paras 3.1–3.3.
46 Ibid. paras 9.6 and 9.7.
47 Ibid. para 9.10.
48 Ibid. para 10.4.
49 Ibid. paras 10.7 and 11.
50 Ibid. Annex 1 Individual opinion of Committee Member Mr Dheerujlall Seetulsingh.

city and in the Netherlands?' To which the crowd chanted: 'fewer, fewer, fewer'. 'We'll arrange that,' Wilders said, smiling, when the chanting died down.[51] Wilders had made similar comments in the interview at the market the week before the post-vote meeting. The chanting at the meeting and the earlier comments led to nearly 6,500 complaints to the Public Prosecutor's office. Action groups, local politicians and Mosques encouraged people to make a complaint, often via pre-printed forms. Such forms were also used by the police because they could not take every person's statement personally.[52] Some PVV Members of Parliament, Members of the European Parliament and local and provincial councillors also broke their ties with the party.[53] The Public Prosecutor considered that 'freedom of speech means that politicians should not feel limited in saying what they want, but this freedom has its boundaries, especially when it comes to discrimination',[54] and decided to prosecute Wilders on similar charges as in the first prosecution for insulting a population group based on race against article 137c Sr and inciting hatred and discrimination against a group of people based on race against article 137d Sr. Both charges were made for the remarks made at the market and for those made at the post-election meeting. None of the charges mentioned religion. This will be discussed below.

On this occasion, the case was dealt with by the District Court of The Hague, which, on 9 December 2016, convicted Wilders, in relation to the remarks made at the post-election meeting, of insulting a group based on race and incitement to discrimination on the ground of race, but he was acquitted of incitement to hatred. Wilders was acquitted of all charges in relation to the remarks made in the interview at the market place. Despite convicting Wilders, the Court did not impose any penalty.[55] It started its judgment by stressing the importance of freedom of expression and by pointing out that this right could be restricted for the protection of the rights and freedom of others, among other reasons. It also stated clearly that this was not a political process, an allegation Wilders had made repeatedly on twitter and in interviews,[56] because even a democratically elected politician is not above the law and that, even for him, the freedom of expression is not unlimited. This is clearly in line with what the European Court of Human Rights has always held. Wilders' point of view that a conviction

---

51 See on this: *PVV Leader Geert Wilders will be Prosecuted for Inciting Hatred (update)* www. dutchnews.nl/news/archives/2014/12/pvv-leader-geert-wilders-will-be-prosecuted-for-inciting-hatred-and-discrimination/

52 See: Pieters, J., *Nearly 6,500 People Pressed Hate-Speech Charges against Wilders*, 31 October 2016, http://nltimes.nl/2016/10/31/nearly-6500-people-pressed-hate-speech-charges

53 *PVV Leader Geert Wilders will be Prosecuted for Inciting Hatred (update)*, supra note 51.

54 See: *OM to Prosecute Geert Wilders on Charges of Discrimination*, 18 December 2014, www. om.nl/onderwerpen/zaak-wilders/@90740/to-prosecute-geert/

55 See: *Rechtbank Den Haag* (The Hague District Court), 9 December 2016 https:// uitspraken.rechtspraak.nl/inziendocument?id=ECLI:NL:RBDHA:2016:15014

56 See, for example, *Wilders won't Attend 'Fewer Moroccans' Trial; says it is a Political Process* www.dutchnews.nl/news/archives/2016/10/wilders-wont-attend-fewer-moroccans-trial-says-it-is-a-political-process/

would be restricting his ability as a politician to talk about problems in society was evidently untrue, according to the District Court of The Hague, because a conviction meant nothing more and nothing less than that his criminal expressions were not protected by the freedom of expression.[57]

Wilders did not attend the trial (under Dutch law, it is not compulsory to do so), but he did attend to make use of his right to have the last word. However, he tweeted often during the trial, calling the court a fake court, saying that the verdict had already been written and showing photos of the judges alleging their links with another political party without giving any evidence in support of his allegations. He was also rather immoderate in his closing words. The District Court of The Hague mentioned that they had cautioned Wilders every time he tweeted during the trial and expressed that it saw Wilders' reactions as unworthy of a Member of Parliament.[58]

Wilders' defence team argued that the Public Prosecutor's case should be declared inadmissible, because, first, the Public Prosecutor had endangered the rule of law and had misused the criminal law to further its own political agenda. The District Court of The Hague rejected this argument with the consideration that, aside from the lack of evidence of a political agenda, the Public Prosecutor's job is to prosecute if there is any suspicion of a criminal offence.[59]

The second argument brought forward by the defence team was based on what it called 'the Castells exception' (from the European Court of Human Rights case of *Castells v Spain*[60]), that criminal law will only be applied when other ways of stopping the unwanted expressions have been explored. The defence team suggested that the government could have reacted by stating that the expressions were undesirable and by distancing itself from the expressions or that they could have used an official reprimand under the rules of order of the Second House of Parliament. This was not considered and, thus, the Public Prosecutor had reacted too strongly and without considering the interests of a politician or the use of alternative ways of dealing with these kinds of expressions.[61] As was explained in Chapter 2, one of the issues in the balancing test that needs to take place under article 10(2) to establish whether the interference is justified is whether the aim of the restriction could be achieved in another, less restrictive way. So, Wilders defence team was right in raising this defence. The District Court of The Hague rejected this argument with the consideration that *Castells v Spain* concerned an elected Member of Parliament expressing criticism of the government, while Wilders expressions did not criticise the government or its actions.[62] Wilders will, no doubt, strongly reject this and argue that he is

---

57 The Hague District Court, supra note 55, para 1.
58 Ibid. para 3.3.
59 Ibid. para 4.2.
60 *Castells v Spain*, Application No. 11798/85, 23 April 1992.
61 The Hague District Court, supra note 55, para 4.3.
62 Ibid.

criticising the government's policies on multiculturalism and immigration, that he is suggesting alternatives that he will implement when he is elected and that he is contributing to the current public debate on these issues. It is submitted that Wilders' argument here is more in line with what the European Court of Human Rights held in *Castells v Spain* and that his expressions did point out what Wilders saw as a problem in Dutch society which the government failed to see or deal with. His remarks can thus clearly be seen as part of the political debate. The District Court of The Hague's argument here also seems to go against the Amsterdam District Court in the first case against Wilders which held that the remarks at issue there and the film *Fitna* were both part of the political debate and criticism of the government.[63] By rejecting this argument on these grounds, the District Court of The Hague did not really address the question whether there were alternatives to a criminal prosecution available. Whether there are alternatives will be discussed below.

Wilders' defence team also argued that the case should be declared inadmissible because the Public Prosecutor had breached the *lex certa* principle laid down in article 7 ECHR: the principle that no-one should be held guilty of a criminal offence when the act was not a criminal offence at the time it was committed. According to the defence, Wilders' expressions were made before the decision of the Dutch Supreme Court that articles 137c and 137d Sr included not only expressions that incited to violence or discrimination, but also those that incited to intolerance.[64] This appears to go against what was argued throughout this book on the basis of the case law of the European Court of Human Rights that mere fostering intolerance is not enough to justify restrictions on hate speech. Be that as it may, the judgment of the Supreme Court meant, according to the defence team, that Wilders could not be held guilty of incitement to intolerance. The District Court of The Hague replied that both article 10 and the term 'intolerance' as used by the Supreme Court would be part of the examination of the merits of the case but that this did not mean that the case should be declared inadmissible. Moreover, the Public Prosecutor had given, as its opinion, that the term 'intolerance' should not be applied in the case against Wilders so the judgment of the Supreme Court did not play a role in the allegations.[65] This argument from the defence that the case was inadmissible was thus also rejected. But it is clear that the ECHR played a role even at the admissibility stage of the case.

The District Court of The Hague concluded from witness statements that the expressions at the post-election meeting had been made after considerable thought, that the chanting had been carefully orchestrated (the public was clearly

---

63 Amsterdam District Court, supra note 30, para 4.3.2.
64 The Hague District Court, supra note 55, para 4.4. For the Supreme Court case see: *Hoge Raad* (Supreme Court), 16 December 2014, ECLI:NL:HR:2014:3583 https://uitspraken.rechtspraak.nl/inziendocument?id=ECLI:NL:HR:2014:3583.
65 The Hague District Court, supra note 55, para 4.4.

told beforehand what to do)[66] and that it was meant to have as much impact as possible: Wilders made his remarks at a time when he was certain that the questions and the chanting would be reported widely on the main news bulletins on television and radio and in all national newspapers.[67] Here, the Court referred to the case law of the European Court of Human Rights which has, in a number of cases, mentioned the impact of the audio-visual media.[68] The questions were also carefully chosen and worded provocatively. Moreover, it was clear from witness statements that there had been a discussion between Wilders and some of his aides on whether to ask about 'criminal Moroccans' or 'Moroccans' and that Wilders had clearly chosen to ask about 'Moroccans'.[69]

Wilders' defence team argued that the expressions at the post-election meeting were consistent with the viewpoints he had stated for years and were also clearly set out in the PVV party and election manifestos. Therefore, a judgment about these expressions would be a political judgment about the ideas of the PVV. However, the Court rejected this because this was not the case: if the manifestos or earlier expressions by Wilders mentioned the 'Moroccan problem' it referred to criminal Moroccans only, a limitation that Wilders had consciously rejected in his speech at the post-election meeting. He referred to all Moroccans, to the whole group without any nuance, which was not in line with earlier expressions. This was supported by the fact that some of the witnesses were surprised at the expressions and that other witnesses had left the party after the post-election meeting speech.[70] The Court also considered it irrelevant that Wilders had, after he had left the podium, given further explanation of his remark, without retracting his words.[71]

So, the District Court of The Hague clearly looked at both content and context of the expressions. It concluded that Wilders remarks were aimed at the whole group of Moroccans living in the Netherlands and labelled them as of less value than other people and this amounted to insulting a group based on race as they were aimed at a group of people because of their national or ethnic origin. The Court considered that the Explanatory Memorandum to articles 137c and 137d showed that the term 'racial or ethnic origin' must be interpreted in the light of article 1 of the International Convention on the Elimination of all Forms of Racial Discrimination to include race, colour, descent and national or ethnic origin and that the term 'Moroccans' referred to descent, national origin and ethnic origin.[72] This was also supported by the case law of the Dutch Supreme Court that the term 'Moroccans', like the term 'Turks', meant to refer to

---

66 Ibid. para 5.4.1.
67 Ibid. para 5.4.3.1.
68 Ibid. The District Court of The Hague referred to *Jersild v Denmark*, Application No. 15890/89, 23 September 1994 (Grand Chamber).
69 The Hague District Court, supra note 55, paras 5.1.2 and 5.4.3.1.
70 Ibid. para 5.4.3.1.
71 Ibid.
72 Ibid. para 5.4.2.

ethnic or national origin.[73] The expressions about 'Moroccans' were thus based on race.[74] The defence had contested whether Moroccans could be considered a race and saw the term as indicating nationality rather than race, a question that might well come back on appeal, although it appears that the District Court of The Hague was right in accepting that the term 'Moroccans' indicated ethnic or national origin and thus fell under the term 'race' in articles 137c and 137d Sr.

The District Court of The Hague also considered, albeit rather briefly and without much explanation, that this conviction was compatible with article 10(2) ECHR. It discussed the requirements for justification and concluded that the restriction was prescribed by law and necessary in a democratic society to protect the rights of others, in this case to stop people from expressions that painted a minority group as inferior. Therefore, the expressions made at the post-election meeting were not protected by article 10 ECHR.[75]

The District Court of The Hague then considered the charge of incitement to hatred and discrimination and held that, for incitement to hatred, it was necessary to establish an aggravating element that rouses others to take (illegal) action. The content of the expression was the deciding factor to establish this and it was not necessary that the action had indeed been taken or that it was reasonably likely that it would be taken. It is submitted that this is not in line with the case law of the European Court of Human Rights, which, as has been argued in this book, requires a present risk or imminent danger.[76] But, Wilders was acquitted of this charge anyway, because there was no evidence of any aggravating element in his 'fewer Moroccans' remarks.[77] However, he was found guilty of incitement to discrimination as this did not require any aggravating element, nor did it require that discrimination had actually followed. According to the District Court of The Hague, the expressions were discriminatory because they clearly aimed at making a distinction between Moroccans and other population groups in the Netherlands. Taking this, together with the circumstances under which they were made and the inflammatory character of the expressions into account, the remarks were held to be incitement to discrimination.[78] So, again, the content and context of the expressions and the aim of the speaker or author are clearly taken into account. Therefore, Wilders was convicted of insulting a group and of incitement to discrimination for the speech at the post-election meeting.

---

73   *Hoge Raad* (Supreme Court), 14 March 1989, ECLI:NL:HR:1989:AC3487, NJ 1990, 29; *Hoge Raad*, 1 march 1990, ECLI:NL:HR:1990:AB7604, https://uitspraken.rechtspraak. nl/inziendocument?id=ECLI:NL:HR:1990:AD1017; *Hoge Raad*, 29 March 2016, ECLI: NL:HR:2016:511, www.recht.nl/rechtspraak/uitspraak?ecli=ECLI:NL:PHR:2016:511.
74   The Hague District Court, supra note 55, para 5.4.2.
75   Ibid. para 5.4.3.1.
76   *Erbakan v Turkey*, supra note 16, para 65.
77   The Hague District Court, supra note 55, para 5.4.3.2.
78   Ibid.

Wilders was acquitted of all charges regarding the remarks at the market in The Hague, as these had been less well thought out and planned as was clear from the witness statements.

Wilders defence team argued: that Wilders had been sworn in as Member of Parliament and his oath imposed a special duty to act for those who could not do so themselves; that his expressions were done as a representative of the people and were based on his duty to flag up problems in society; that the sentiment behind the expressions were shared by many people in the Netherlands, as opinion polls showed and as the objective statistics of the Dutch Central Bureau for Statistics supported; and, that this duty to speak out also played a role under the justification test of article 10 ECHR. According to the defence, all this supported a finding that Wilders expressions were justified and thus that he should not be convicted.[79] The District Court of The Hague rejected this by stating that Wilders could have used different means to raise the problems he saw in Dutch society.[80]

In relation to sanctions, the Public Prosecutor had demanded the imposition of a fine of 5,000 euros. The District Court of The Hague considered that this was an extraordinary case because of the defendant's position as a democratically elected Member of Parliament, founder of the PVV and leader of the PPV party in Parliament, and thus that it would not be guided by the sanctions imposed in other cases, as the Public Prosecutor had done. Therefore, it did not impose any penalty on Wilders because it considered that the determination that the accused, as *politician* [italics in original Dutch], was found guilty of insulting a group and of incitement to discrimination was sufficient penalty. It also considered that the conviction confirmed that a person, even a politician and democratically elected representative of the people, cannot invoke their right to freedom of expression to insult groups or incite to discrimination.[81] As already mentioned, Wilders announced immediately after the verdict that he would appeal the judgment and the Public Prosecutor did so a few days later.[82]

The acquittal in the first case and the conviction in the second raise the question whether there was a difference between the expressions at stake in the two cases. It is submitted that there was indeed a difference: the first prosecution concerned expressions mainly against Islam and the threat it poses to the Netherlands and not against Muslims, against a group of people distinguished on the ground of their religion, as the Amsterdam District Court concluded. The Amsterdam Court of Appeal came, as mentioned, to another conclusion. On the other hand, the 'fewer Moroccans' remarks, which were central in the second prosecution, were aimed at a group of people because of their national or ethnic origin, as

79 Ibid. para 7.1.
80 Ibid. para 7.2.
81 Ibid. para 8.3.
82 See: *Dutch Politician Wilders Convicted of Discrimination against Moroccans,* supra note 1; *Ook OM Gaat in Beroep in Zaak-Wilders* (Public Prosecutor also Appeals Wilders Case), supra note 1.

the District Court of The Hague stated. The outcomes of both prosecutions appear to be supported by the text of articles 137c and 137d Sr, the Explanatory Memorandum and the Dutch case law mentioned in the two judgments.

Assessment *Wilders* cases

European Court of Human Rights

If Wilders conviction is upheld and he exhausts all domestic appeal avenues, he might well challenge his conviction in the European Court of Human Rights as a violation of his freedom of expression under article 10 ECHR. Based on the Court's case law, as examined in previous Chapters, the Court will, very likely, hold that articles 137c and 137d Sr are compatible with freedom of expression and that Wilders claim should not be rejected under article 17 ECHR. As was concluded in Chapter 4, article 17 should only be applied in exceptional and extreme cases where the fundamental democratic principles and values of the state are at stake and, if this is not the case, restrictions on the freedom of expression should be scrutinised under the three part justification test of article 10(2). As Wilders expressions in both cases cannot be said to be so exceptional or extreme that they threaten the democratic principles of the state, the Court should assess Wilders' conviction under this three part test.

The argument throughout this book, backed up by the case law of the European Court of Human Rights, has been that the freedom of expression of politicians and others who contribute to the public debate should not be restricted unless their expressions either incite to hatred and violence and there is a present risk or imminent danger that violence is going to follow; or, unless they stop people from holding, practising or manifesting their religion or belief. It is submitted that there was no evidence that Wilders 'fewer Moroccans' expression did either and, therefore, the European Court of Human Rights should find that Wilders' conviction violates his right to freedom of expression. The expressions and the film *Fitna* subject to the first prosecution would not be considered by the Court as Wilders was acquitted but, if they were, the same conclusion should be drawn regarding these expressions. Furthermore, these expressions and the 'fewer Moroccans' remark cannot be said to be gratuitously offensive, as they all contributed to the political and public debate at the time they were made. In the following, the Wilders cases are analysed using the arguments from the previous chapters.

Arguments for freedom of expression

In Chapter 1, four arguments for having a right to freedom of expression were advanced, all linked together and connected to the fact that the right includes not only a right to impart information and ideas but also to receive these. These arguments were: the role the right plays in the discovery of truth; in the self-development and self-fulfilment of the individual; in the maintenance of a democratic society through open and public debate; and, in its ability to show suspicion of the government. It is submitted that all four arguments can be applied to the expressions of Wilders that were the subject of the two prosecutions against him. People must be able to discover the truth, to find things out for themselves and to develop their own ideas and opinions about, for example, who to vote for, and this is best done through open and public debate. Wilders' expressions, which did and do raise issues that many people in the Netherlands are worried about, can be seen as contributions to this debate. The European Court of Human Rights has always particularly emphasised the importance of an open, public debate for a democratic society and the role of (opposition) politicians in this debate. The last argument, that the right to freedom of expression allows an individual to show suspicion of the government in supressing speech that criticises or opposes their policies is also applicable here, because Wilders is an opposition politician who criticises the government's policies on multiculturalism and immigration. Wilders himself, when challenged, invokes his right to free speech and the fact that he contributes to the public debate on matters of concern in the Netherlands.

The right not to be offended

In relation to the existence of a right not to be offended in one's religious feelings, as was discussed above, the Amsterdam Court of Appeal appeared to have accepted that such a right does exist. It was submitted that it was mistaken in this as it is contrary to the parliamentary history of S 137c Sr and the case law of the Dutch Supreme Court.[83] Both showed that criticism, even strong criticism, of a group's opinions or behaviour falls outside the ambit of article 137c Sr on group insult, as the Amsterdam District Court in the first *Wilders* Case pointed out.[84] It would also be contrary to the case law of the European Court of Human Rights as has been argued in earlier chapters. On the other hand, the District Court of The Hague, in the second *Wilders* case, convicted Wilders of intentionally insulting a group based on race, which would suggest that mere insult is enough to restrict freedom of expression. However, this was based on the opinion that Wilders had done more than criticising the opinions and behaviour of Moroccans by his 'fewer Moroccans' remarks, that he had intentionally and purposefully painted a whole minority group within the Dutch population as being inferior to others within that society. It is argued that article 137c Sr can be interpreted to cover such expressions, but that, in this case, the District Court of The Hague should not have convicted Wilders because even his 'fewer Moroccans' remarks, although they can be said to be provocative, exaggerated, immoderate and virulent, could be seen as part of the public debate, did not lead to violence and did not stop anyone from holding or manifesting their religion or belief.

83 Supreme Court, supra note 8.
84 Amsterdam District Court, supra note 30, para 4.2.

Gratuitously offensive and fostering intolerance

Whether Wilders' expressions at issue in both cases could be seen as 'gratuitously offensive' was not discussed by any of the Dutch Courts but, as argued above, these expressions can and should be seen as contributing to the public and political debate on current issues and thus they cannot be said to be gratuitously offensive. In Chapter 1, it was also argued that the case law of the European Court of Human Rights suggests that expressions that merely foster intolerance should not be restricted and if they are this should be considered to be an interference with the speaker's or author's freedom of expression. However, the Dutch Supreme Court has held that article 137d includes not only incitement to hatred, violence and discrimination, but also incitement to intolerance.[85] The case concerned a politician who had made remarks about aggressive homosexuals taking over a number of institutions and that these 'deviant' people should be expelled, because 'we' want a country of heterosexual people.[86] The Supreme Court considered: that article 10 ECHR does not preclude prosecutions under articles 137c and 137d Sr; that it must be examined whether the expressions contribute to the public debate; and, that they should not be gratuitously offensive. The Supreme Court continued that, to establish whether an expression that is made by a politician as part of the public and political debate is gratuitously offensive, a balancing needs to take place. On the one hand, the politician must be able to raise issues of general concern even if his expressions offend, shock or disturb. On the other hand, there is the responsibility of the politician to prevent his expressions from being against the law or against the fundamental principles of a democratic state. These expressions not only include expressions that incite to hatred, violence or discrimination, but also those that incite to intolerance.[87] Based on what was argued in Chapter 1, this appears to be a mistaken interpretation of the case law of the European Court of Human Rights. That case law suggests that expressions that contribute to the public and political debate are not gratuitously offensive and that mere fostering intolerance is not sufficient to justify restrictions on the freedom of expression. As mentioned, in the first *Wilders* case, the Amsterdam District Court referred to the duty on politicians not to foster intolerance with a reference to *Erbakan v Turkey*[88] without acknowledging that this case also required a present risk or imminent danger.[89] The Public Prosecutor in the second *Wilders* case declared that incitement to intolerance was not part of the charges so this did not play a role in the case, although the District Court of The Hague did remark that Wilders expressions had contributed to a further polarisation of the Netherlands.[90]

85 Supreme Court, supra note 64, para 4.4.4.
86 Ibid. para 2.1.
87 Ibid. para 4.4.4.
88 *Erbakan v Turkey*, supra note 16.
89 Amsterdam District Court, supra note 30, para 12.2.2.
90 The Hague District Court, supra note 55, para 8.3.

Clashing rights

In Chapter 2, it was argued that there is no conflict between the rights to freedom of expression and freedom of religion in cases where a person uses expressions that are offensive to religious believers, unless the expressions factually prevent any religious believers from holding or manifesting that belief. There is no evidence that Wilders remarks in either case have done so, therefore there is no clash between freedom of expression and freedom of religion in these cases. However, can it be said that there was a clash between freedom of expression and the right to be free from discrimination on religious grounds? The Amsterdam Court of Appeal was the only court in the *Wilders* case to point out that there was a clash between fundamental rights: between freedom of expression, freedom from religious discrimination and freedom of religion.[91] This Court considered the case law of the Dutch Supreme Court: that no hierarchy existed between fundamental rights; that a balancing of all interests involved needed to take place, taking into account the nature and scope of the rights involved and the seriousness and the consequences of the interference; and, that the European Court of Human Rights left a wide margin of appreciation to the state when it comes to striking a balance between conflicting rights.[92] All this follows the case law of the European Court of Human Rights as explained in Chapter 2. The Amsterdam Court of Appeal then considered the circumstances under which an interference with freedom of expression could be justified and concluded that the right not to be hurt or discriminated against on the ground of religion, which can be derived from the right to freedom of religion, was central in the case and that this could be a reason to restrict the freedom of expression.[93] It has been argued that the Amsterdam Court of Appeal was mistaken in accepting that a right not to be offended can be derived from article 9 ECHR. The Court did not mention a possible clash with article 14. The possible conflict between Wilders' freedom of expression and the right not to be discriminated against on religious grounds will be discussed below.

Religious hate speech and racist hate speech

In Chapter 3, the question whether there is a distinction between religious hate speech and racial hate speech was analysed and it was concluded that, if these forms of hate speech should be treated differently from a free speech perspective, then restrictions on racial hate speech should be held to be justified more easily than restrictions on religious hate speech. From the two *Wilders* cases, it is not clear whether the fact that the first one concerned a religious group, while the second one concerned a racial or ethnic group, played a role in the decisions. Articles 137c and 137d Sr do not, as was already mentioned, make any

91 Amsterdam Court of Appeal, supra note 5, para 10.
92 Ibid.
93 Ibid. para 12.2.3.

distinction between race and religion in relation to the criminal offences in these articles. While religion was an important element in the first *Wilders* case, the only reference to religion in the second case was in relation to article 137c and religion did not play a role in that case at all. Therefore, the difference between the two cases appears to rest more on the fact that the second case targeted a specific group while the first targeted a religion rather than a religious group. The difference between criticising a religion and offending the believers of that religion was mentioned by the Amsterdam District Court, which pointed out that the legislative history showed that the legislator had wanted to keep expressions about religion outside the scope of article 137d Sr and thus that Wilders' expressions, which were aimed at criticising Islam, were not covered by that article.[94]

Arguments for and against hate speech laws

The arguments for and against enacting hate speech laws were also analysed in Chapter 3. Did these play a role in the *Wilders* cases? Do they support the prosecutions and the conviction of Wilders? The first argument for enacting laws against hate speech was that these were necessary to protect public order and prevent breaches of the peace, while the second argument was that these laws were necessary to protect the targeted group. The third argument was that hate speech laws have an important declaratory and symbolic function. Although the Amsterdam Court of Appeal accepted the protection of the rights of others not to be offended in their religious feelings as a legitimate aim for the restrictions that articles 137c and 137d Sr impose on hate speech, it pointed out that the protection of the public order is also a legitimate aim in article 10(2) ECHR and that articles 137c and 137d Sr are placed in the Dutch Criminal Code under the title 'Offences against the public order'.[95]

The District Court of The Hague mentioned the protection of the public order only in its considerations of the admissibility of the claims by victims of Wilders' expressions. Under Dutch law, victims of a criminal offence can claim compensation in the criminal case against the offender and this happened in both *Wilders* cases. The Amsterdam District Court acquitted Wilders and thus the claim by the victims was rejected. The District Court of The Hague also rejected the claims for compensation with a reference to the legislative history which showed that the protection of the public order was the first and foremost aim of articles 137c and 137d Sr and that the protection of the honour and good name of the groups targeted came after that, with the protection of individuals in a, not very important, third place.[96] As both articles 137c and 137d Sr concern offences against groups, there was no direct damage to the individuals.[97] This suggests that the protection

---

94 Ibid. para 4.3.1.
95 Amsterdam Court of Appeal, supra note 5 , para 12.2.3.
96 The Hague District Court, supra note 55 , para 9.2.
97 Ibid. The rejection of the claim for compensation was also discussed by the Human Rights Committee, for more information on this see *M.R., A.B.S. and N.A. v The Netherlands,* supra note 44.

of the public order was the first and foremost aim of the relevant articles and that the protection of victims was of secondary importance. However, as there was no indication that Wilders' expressions had led to disturbances of the public order or to infringement of the rights of others in either case, these arguments cannot be said to support either of Wilders' prosecutions.

The third argument for enacting legislation against hate speech was that such laws have an important declaratory and symbolic function by reflecting what society deems inappropriate. The Amsterdam Court of Appeal considered whether prosecution of Wilders would serve a general purpose and concluded that Wilders should be prosecuted because a clear boundary should be drawn for incitement to hatred in public debate in a democratic society.[98] The District Court of The Hague also appeared to refer to the declaratory function where it considered that the judgment confirmed that the Dutch legal norm, that one cannot invoke freedom of expression to insult groups or incite to discrimination, applied to everyone, including politicians.[99] The question whether Wilders should be prosecuted for his 'fewer Moroccans' expression and whether this had any benefits for society, was subject to discussion in the Netherlands, and the following arguments were brought forward, which can all more or less be seen as part of the declaratory and symbolic function of articles 137c and 137d Sr. First, the state must guarantee the equal status of Dutch Moroccans; second, the law must be upheld to avoid this type of insult in future; and, third, it is important to make clear where the boundaries of the incitement offence are.[100] However, it was also pointed out that it can be argued that it is up to parliament, not judges, to draw these boundaries.[101]

The arguments against hate speech laws analysed in Chapter 3, were: that such laws can be used arbitrarily and against anyone who opposes a government's viewpoints; that they have a chilling effect on speech; that they provide the speaker with an extra platform to speak and spread their views; that hate speech laws lack legal clarity and certainty; and, that they are counterproductive. When it was announced in 2014 that he was going to be prosecuted for his 'fewer Moroccans' remarks, Wilders commented that 'the PPV is currently the biggest party in the polls. That obviously does not please the elite'.[102] And, after the end of the second prosecution and before the verdict was announced, Wilders and his defence painted him as the victim of a political process and as a free speech martyr and he, himself, said that the government and other politicians wanted to silence him through a judge because they could not do so in parliament, but that they would

98 Amsterdam Court of Appeal, supra note 5, para 13.2.

99 The Hague District Court, supra note 55, para 8.3.

100 Heck, W., *Drie Argumenten Voor and Drie Tegen Vervolging van Wilders* (Three Arguments For and Three Against Prosecuting Wilders) 3 April 2014, www.nrc.nl/nieuws/2014/04/03/drie-argumenten-voor-en-drie-tegen-vervolging-van-wilders-a1426036

101 Ibid.

102 *PVV Leader Geert Wilders will be Prosecuted for Inciting Hatred (update)*, supra note 51.

not succeed and that he would always speak out about terrorism, immigration from Muslim countries and the 'mega-Moroccan problem'.[103] So Wilders accused the Dutch government of trying to silence him as an opposition politician, but promised that this would not have a chilling effect on his speech. That Wilders sees himself as a 'free speech martyr' is also clear from his reaction to the conviction, where he said that the Netherlands had become a sick country and that the judges of the District Court of The Hague had violated his and millions of Dutch people's right to freedom of speech.[104] The argument that a trial provides the speaker with an extra platform to promote and publicise his message is very much applicable to the *Wilders* cases: both cases led to a lot of media attention and interviews for national news programmes and national newspapers and every time Wilders got a chance to push forward his political views.[105] For example, after the first *Wilders* case, it was said that there were only losers in the trial but, if there was a winner, it would be Wilders because the trial had given him a stage and had strengthened his political position.[106] And, according to one newspaper, Wilders exploited the second trial to the maximum. By tweeting throughout the trial at carefully selected times and by not turning up, except to have the last word, he made sure that the latter got extensive media coverage.[107] In this sense, it can be argued that the prosecution for hate speech was counterproductive: rather than stopping Wilders from expressing his ideas, it has given them more public exposure. For example, at the time of the second trial, Wilders' party was riding high in opinion polls, most of which showed the PVV as the biggest party in the Netherlands. Whether the conviction has made Wilders moderate his language is doubtful: Wilders launched his 2017 election campaign 'with a stinging attack on the country's Moroccan population. The anti-immigration MP called them "scum" and said he wanted to make the Netherlands "ours again"'.[108] However, he did add that 'not all are scum' which might have been influenced by the verdict of the District Court in The Hague which did consider that he targeted the whole group of Moroccans living in the Netherlands.

In relation to the argument that hate speech laws lack clarity and legal certainty, the fact that the Amsterdam Court of Appeal mentioned the need for

103 Niemandsverdriet, T., *Wilders heeft er Alles aan Gedaan om zijn Process Politiek te Maken* (Wilders has done everything to make his Process a Political One) 24 November 2016, www.nrc.nl/nieuws/2016/11/24/pvv-leider-heeft-er-zelf-alles-aan-gedaan-om-zijn-proces-politiek-te-maken-5469305-a1533445

104 Hotse Smit, P., Stoker, E. and de Vires, J., *Reacties op Wilders Vonnis: Nederland is een Ziek Land Geworden* (Reactions to the Wilders Conviction: The Netherlands has become a Sick Country) 9 December 2016, www.volkskrant.nl/binnenland/reacties-op-wilders-vonnis-nederland-is-een-ziek-land-geworden~a4431076/

105 Heck, supra note 100.

106 Boomsma, K. and Rigter, N., *Process Wilders: Enkel Verliezers* (Trial Wilders: Only Losers), 23 June 2011, www.metronieuws.nl/binnenland/2011/06/proces-wilders-enkel-verliezers

107 Niemandsverdriet, supra note 103.

108 McKie, R., *Far-right Leader Geert Wilders calls Moroccan Migrants 'Scum'*, 18 February 2017, www.theguardian.com/world/2017/feb/18/geert-wilders-netherlands-describes-immigrants-scum-holland

the setting of boundaries might indicate that the scope of these articles is not clear. However, the District Courts in both *Wilders* cases did not appear to have a problem in relation to the interpretation of articles 137c and 137d Sr. The different decisions in the cases do not appear to be based on different interpretations of these articles but rather on the difference in the expressions subject to the prosecutions.

Article 10(2) ECHR

Above it was argued that Wilders expressions at issue in his prosecutions were not such that they would fall under the abuse of rights clause in article 17 ECHR because they are not so exceptional or extreme that they threaten the democratic principles and values of the state. Therefore, they have to pass the three part justification test of article 10(2): they must be prescribed by law; necessary in a democratic society; and, the means used to achieve one of the legitimate aims mentioned in article 10(2) must be proportionate. Six factors that are taken into account in this test were identified in Chapter 4: the aim pursued by the speaker or author; the content of the expression; the context in which it was disseminated; the potential impact of the remarks; the status and role in society of the maker and of the target of the statement; and, the nature and seriousness of the interference, including the severity of the penalty. Some of the factors taken into account by the different courts involved in the *Wilders* cases have already been pointed out. For example, all three Dutch courts took account of the contents, the context and the status of Wilders as a politician and representative of the people. Here the factors will be briefly examined in relation to the expressions of Wilders.

The aim of Wilders' expressions and his film in the first case, as he alleged and the Amsterdam District Court accepted, was to highlight the dangers of Islam and the associated threat this posed to Dutch society at a time when the multicultural character of that society was being questioned. It can certainly be argued that the 'fewer Moroccans' remark also aimed to express a concern about immigration and integration of many people in the Netherlands, as Wilders himself argued. The District Court of The Hague did consider that the European Court of Human Rights gave more room to freedom of expression during a public debate – which it described as a discussion between two or more participants – but that Wilders' 'fewer Moroccans' remarks were not made during such a debate but during a speech aimed at his supporters and everyone he hoped to reach via the media.[109] It is submitted that the District Court of The Hague interpreted the term 'debate' in a much narrower sense than the European Court of Human Rights does, and that the 'fewer Moroccans' remark were part of what that Court sees as the public and political debate on matters of public interest which is so important for a democratic society.[110] This could, therefore, be open to challenge on appeal.

109 The Hague District Court, supra note 55, para 5.4.3.1.
110 See, for example, *Ceylan v Turkey*, Application No. 23556/94, 8 July 1999, para 34.

In Chapter 4, it was briefly discussed that the European Court of Human Rights also considers the intention to stigmatise the other party but that this factor is seldom looked at in isolation.[111] The District Court of The Hague held that Wilders' remarks labelling the whole group of Moroccans living in the Netherlands as of less value amounted to insulting a group based on race.[112] It also held that the expressions were discriminatory because they clearly aimed at making a distinction between Moroccans and other population groups in the Netherlands. Taking this, together with the circumstances under which they were made and the inflammatory character of the expressions into account, the remarks were held to be incitement to discrimination.[113] So the fact that the 'fewer Moroccans' remark stigmatises a whole group of the Dutch population played a role in the decision of the District Court of The Hague but this was taken together with other considerations about the context and content.

As mentioned already, both the content and the context of Wilders' expressions were taken into account by all three Dutch courts. For example, the fact that the 'fewer Moroccans' remarks were planned carefully to have maximum media impact played a role in the decision of the District Court of The Hague. The expressions by Wilders at issue in both prosecutions were seen in the context of a political climate where immigration, integration and multiculturalism were and are very much issues of public debate, not only in the Netherlands but across many European countries. All three Dutch courts also remarked on the fact that Wilders was an elected politician who enjoyed a very wide freedom of expression but that this freedom was not absolute. This would mean that, if the second *Wilders* case ever reaches the European Court of Human Rights, the Court will – and should – scrutinise the interference with his freedom of expression very closely.

The status of the group targeted and their specific vulnerability did not appear to play a big role in the *Wilders* cases. The Amsterdam Court of Appeal held that Wilders' expressions were offending to the Muslim population group because of their disparaging tone, but it did not mention that this group was in any way more vulnerable than other groups. The same can be said for the District Court of The Hague, which held that Wilders had insulted the whole group of (Dutch) Moroccans and had incited to discrimination against them.

A last factor taken into account in the assessment of the European Court of Human Rights whether a restriction on freedom of expression is justified under article 10(2) ECHR, is the nature and the severity of the penalty imposed and, a severe penalty is more likely to lead to a finding that the interference is not justified. As mentioned above, the District Court of The Hague did not impose

---

111 *Halis Doğan v Turkey*, Application No. 4119/02, 10 October 2006, para 34; *Lindon, Otchakovsky-Laurens and July v France*, Application Nos 21279/02 and 36448/02, 22 October 2007, para 57.

112 The Hague District Court, supra note 55, para 5.4.2.

113 Ibid.

any penalty at all on Wilders and this could play a role if the case ends up in the European Court of Human Rights.

Alternative approaches to hate speech

Some of the issues examined in Chapter 5 find resonance in relation to Wilders' expressions: for example, the rhetoric on immigration and integration that creates an 'us' versus 'them' atmosphere, with 'them', the Moroccan, Muslim immigrants, not wanting to be part of 'our' Dutch society. As referred to above, the District Court of The Hague pointed out that Wilders' expressions had contributed to a further polarisation of the Netherlands.[114] There are also signs that this has invaded mainstream politics, as is clear from the Dutch Prime Minister's 2017 election message about 'Leave if you reject Dutch values'.[115]

The use of the least restrictive means to suppress hate speech, or 'the Castells exception', which the defence in the second Wilders case invoked, means that criminal law will only be applied as a last resort and that other ways of stopping the unwanted expressions should be explored first. The Amsterdam Court of Appeal stated that controversial expressions within the public debate should be countered, first and foremost, in that debate and that civil law could also be used to counter such speech as this encourages participation in the public debate. But it then pointed out that Wilders' expressions aimed to exclude Muslims from the public debate altogether, suggesting that other than criminal law measures were thus not enough to stop Wilders' expression.[116] The District Court of The Hague rejected 'the Castells exception' based on an argument that was already criticised above and that could well be challenged on appeal.

In Chapter 5, it was also suggested that alternative remedies might be found in anti-discrimination law but that there appears little chance of doing this under either article 14 ECHR or under article 1, Protocol 12 (although the Netherlands have signed and ratified the Protocol), as these articles protect against discrimination by the state. The state does have a duty to protect people in the Netherlands against discrimination, but as the General Equal Treatment Act does this, it might be difficult to claim that the Dutch state has not done enough in this area. This Act prohibits both direct discrimination and harassment (in Dutch the term 'intimidatie' (intimidation) is used) but it does not cover this in the public arena which is covered by criminal law only. The Netherlands Institute for Human Rights had indicated that the 'fewer Moroccans' expressions were discriminating because they distinguished a group of Dutch people purely on the ground of their descent, but it also said that it was up to a court to judge whether these

---

114 The Hague District Court, supra note 55, para 8.3.
115 Rutte: Ga Weg als je Nederlandse Waarden Afwijst' (Rutte: Leave if you reject Dutch Values) 23 January 2017 http://nos.nl/artikel/2154459-rutte-ga-weg-als-je-nederlandse-waarden-afwijst.html
116 Amsterdam Court of Appeal, supra note 5, para 13.2.

expressions fell under criminal law. With the conviction, they have done so and they have made clear where the boundaries of the freedom of expression lie, according to the Institute.[117]

In relation to codes of conduct and the Charter for Political Parties for a Non-Racist Society, there is no information on anything re certain codes of conduct or the Charter on the Website of the PVV party, but it appears very unlikely that Wilders would sign up to the Charter. There is, in general and not only in relation to the PVV, little information on which parties have signed the Charter. One more point from Chapter 5 should be mentioned here: the 'cordon sanitaire', where political parties declare that they will not work together or form a coalition with a party they consider to be racist. In the run-up to the Dutch elections on 15 March 2017, the VVD, the party of Dutch prime Minster Mark Rutte, has repeatedly excluded any cooperation with Wilders PPV party after the elections.[118]

Conclusion

In this Chapter, the prosecutions of Dutch politician Geert Wilders were used as a case study to assess the arguments made in the previous chapters. Wilders has been prosecuted twice, with an acquittal at the end of the first prosecution but a conviction for insulting a racial group and for incitement to discrimination of a racial group resulting from the second case. Wilders will appeal against his conviction and, if the conviction is upheld on appeal and once all domestic procedures are exhausted, he is likely to apply to the European Court of Human Rights alleging that his conviction is a violation of his right to freedom of expression under article 10 ECHR.

The first prosecution of Wilders concerned a number of expressions, made in interviews, against Islam and a film about the dangers of Islam. The Public Prosecutor did not prosecute because they did not think that it would lead to a conviction, but the Amsterdam Court of Appeal then ordered them to prosecute Wilders on charges of insulting a group based on race or religion and of incitement to hatred, violence and discrimination against a racial or religious group. Wilders was acquitted of all charges with the main argument that he had criticised Islam and pointed out the dangers of the Islamisation of the Netherlands, but that he did not insult Muslims.

After Wilders' acquittal, three of the victims of the alleged hate speech incidents brought a case against the Netherlands to the UN Human Rights Committee

---

117 Netherlands Institute for Human Rights, *Rechter veroordeelt Geert Wilders voor Discriminatie* (Judge convicts Geert Wilders for Discrimination) 9 December 2016, https://www.mensenrechten.nl/berichten/rechter-veroordeelt-geert-wilders-voor-discriminatie

118 See: *Zijlstra: 'VVD Gaat Niet Samenwerken met PVV'* (Zijlstra [party leader of the VVD] VVD is Not Going To Work Together With PPV), 26 December 2016, https://fd.nl/economie-politiek/1180964/zijlstra-vvd-gaat-niet-samenwerken-met-pvv; *Rutte: Kans dat VVD Gaat Regeren met PVV is Nul* (Chances of VVD governing with PVV is zero) www.rtlnieuws.nl/nederland/politiek/rutte-kans-dat-vvd-gaat-regeren-met-pvv-is-nul

under article 20(2) of the International Covenant on Civil and Political Rights (ICCPR). In July 2016, the Human Rights Committee concluded that the Netherlands had not breached any of the provisions of the ICCPR.

Wilders' 'fewer Moroccans' remarks made in an interview at a market and at a post-election meeting with supporters, led to a second prosecution, this time for insulting a population group based on race against article 137c Sr and inciting hatred and discrimination against a group of people based on race against article 137d Sr. On 9 December 2016, the District Court of The Hague convicted Wilders, in relation to the remarks made at the post-election meeting, of insulting a group based on race and incitement to discrimination on the ground of race, but it did not impose any penalty. The District Court of The Hague mentioned that they had cautioned Wilders every time he tweeted during the trial and expressed that it saw Wilders' reactions as unworthy of a Member of Parliament.

It was submitted that the difference between the expressions subject of the two prosecutions was that the first prosecution concerned expressions mainly against Islam and the threat it poses to the Netherlands and not against Muslims, while the 'fewer Moroccans' remarks were aimed at a group of people because of their national or ethnic origin.

Wilders' conviction could well end up being challenged in the European Court of Human Rights as a violation of Wilders' freedom of expression under article 10 ECHR. It was concluded from the Court's case law as examined in previous Chapters, that the Court will, very likely, hold that articles 137c and 137d Sr are compatible with freedom of expression and that Wilders claim should not be rejected under article 17 ECHR. The Court should then examine Wilders' conviction under the three part justification test of article 10 (2) ECHR. Following its own case law, it should consider the fact that Wilders is an opposition politician who is raising issues of concern in Dutch society and who is suggesting his own solutions to these issues. He is, therefore, contributing to the current public and political debate in the Netherlands and his expressions cannot be said to be gratuitously offensive. The Court should thus scrutinise Wilders' conviction very strictly. The argument throughout this book, backed up by the case law of the European Court of Human Rights, has been that the freedom of expression of politicians and others who contribute to the public debate should not be restricted unless their expressions either incite to hatred and violence and there is a present risk or imminent danger that violence will follow; or, unless they stop people from holding or manifesting their religion or belief. It was submitted that there was no evidence that Wilders' 'fewer Moroccans' expression did either and, therefore, the European Court of Human Rights should find that Wilders' conviction violates his right to freedom of expression.

Conclusion

Introduction

In this book, the central question has been whether legal prohibitions of religious hate speech violate the speaker's or author's right to freedom of expression as guaranteed by article 10 of the ECHR. In examining this question, a number of premises were made: first, freedom of expression, freedom of speech and free speech were used interchangeably; second, the same is true for the terms 'hate speech' and 'incitement to hatred' which have also been used interchangeably; third, the analysis was confined to religious hate speech that targets people because of their religion or belief, and speech motivated by the religion of the speaker or author against other than religious groups was not addressed; and, fourth, the focus was on the use of anti-Muslim rhetoric by politicians and others contributing to the public debate all over Europe, which meant that the freedom of expression as guaranteed by the ECHR and the case law of the European Court of Human Rights was examined rather than the free speech guarantees under global human rights instruments. Because the focus was on religious hate speech, the right to freedom of religion as guaranteed by article 9 ECHR was also analysed.

The main argument throughout this book has been that the freedom of expression of politicians and others who contribute to the public debate should not be restricted by the state through laws against religious hate speech or against incitement to religious hatred unless such expressions either incite to hatred, violence or discrimination and violence is likely to follow imminently; or, where such expressions prevent someone from holding, practising or manifesting their religion or belief. It was argued that outside these two situations, restrictions on expressions by politicians and others contributing to the public debate should be held to violate the right to free speech of the speaker or author. In the last part of this conclusion, the reasons behind this argument will be discussed. This concluding chapter starts with a summary of the previous chapters and the conclusions drawn from those chapters.

Concluding chapter summaries

Freedom of expression and freedom of religion under the European Convention on Human Rights

In Chapter 1, the fundamental human right to freedom of expression in article 10 ECHR was examined first because this right forms the focal point of the entire book. The right to freedom of religion was also analysed because it can play a role in relation to expressions against religious believers: the freedom of expression of the speaker or author of the religious hate speech is engaged and the freedom of religion of the individuals or groups targeted by the speech might also come into play.

In relation to Article 10 ECHR, it was pointed out that the freedom of expression includes both the right to express one's own views and the right to receive information. Four arguments for the existence of the right were discussed. It is an important right for individuals because it plays a role in both the discovery of truth and in the self-development and self-fulfilment of the individual. It is also crucial in the maintenance of a democratic society and the open and public debate such a society depends upon. And, it allows individuals to show suspicion of the government, something that is also essential in a democratic society. The European Court of Human Rights mostly uses the argument of the vital role free speech plays for political and public discourse in a democratic society.

Article 9 ECHR guarantees the freedom of thought, conscience and religion and the freedom to manifest one's religion. Both articles 9 and 10 ECHR permit restrictions on the right under certain prescribed circumstances. However, article 9(2) only allows restrictions on the right to manifest one's religion, while the right to freedom of thought, conscience and religion cannot be limited by the state at all. A restriction or limitation of the freedom of expression and the freedom to manifest one's religion can be justified if it is prescribed by law and necessary in a democratic society for one of the legitimate aims laid down in the second paragraph of articles 10 and 9 respectively. The term 'necessary in a democratic society' means, according to the European Court of Human Rights, that there must be a 'pressing social need' and this, in turn, means that the restriction must be proportionate to the legitimate aim pursued. It can be said that this is a three part test of legality (prescribed by law); necessity (necessary in a democratic society); and proportionality (the means used to achieve the legitimate aim must be proportionate to that aim).

States have a certain margin of appreciation when it comes to assessing what is necessary in a democratic society, but this margin is not unlimited and the European Court of Human Rights will have the final say in this. The width of the margin of appreciation is, however, not always the same and, if the margin of appreciation is narrow, the Court will scrutinise restrictions very strictly. Restrictions on the freedom of expression will generally be scrutinised more closely by the Court than restrictions on the freedom to manifest one's religion because the margin of appreciation afforded to states is wider under article 9 than it is under article 10. However, even under article 10, the margin of appreciation is narrower for expressions by politicians and others contributing to the public debate than for expressions on moral or religious matters.

It was argued that there is no right not to be offended in one's religious feelings present in article 9 ECHR. This is an important thread that has run through many of the discussions in the other chapters. The European Court of Human Rights has held that the right to freedom of expression also applies to expressions that offend, shock and disturb; and, that people who exercise their right to freely manifest their religion cannot expect to be exempt from criticism. Article 10 imposes 'duties and responsibilities' on those who exercise their free speech right and, according to the Court, this includes an obligation to avoid expressions that are gratuitously offensive in the context of religious opinions and beliefs. It was concluded that 'gratuitously offensive' expressions are expressions that do not contribute to the public debate and/or are not capable of furthering progress in human affairs.

Another issue addressed was whether politicians who contribute to the public debate have a duty to avoid fostering intolerance when they exercise their right to free speech. It was concluded from the case law of the European Court of Human Rights that restrictions on speech merely because it fosters intolerance should be considered to violate the freedom of speech of the speaker or author. Real, and not potential, impact, in the shape of an imminent danger of violence occurring, needs to be demonstrated. And even if this is established, the restriction is still subject to the justification test in article 10(2) ECHR.

Conflicts of rights?

In Chapter 2, conflicts that could arise between the rights to freedom of expression, freedom of religion and freedom from discrimination were analysed. It was argued that, in cases where a person uses expressions that criticise religions or beliefs or that offend religious believers, there is no conflict between these two rights unless the expressions prevent or deter any religious believers from believing what they wish, or from practising or manifesting their beliefs. If this is not the case, then the right to freely manifest one's religion is not engaged at all and thus there is no clash between these rights. In the rare circumstances where these two rights do clash, a balancing of all interests involved needs to take place at the domestic level and the role of the European Court of Human Rights is to verify whether the national authorities have struck a fair balance. In deciding cases of conflicting rights, the national authorities are afforded a wide margin of appreciation.

In cases of conflicting ECHR rights, there is no hierarchy between the different rights and all rights deserve equal respect, as is clear from the European Court of Human Rights case law. All interests need to be taken into account. However, the test is not always easy to apply because: there are no common scales to measure the rights against; the judge's view on which right deserves more protection could influence the decision; and, the different rights involved might not be compared on the same plane and the importance of each right might be based on the view of the majority in society. In their supervisory role, the European Court of Human Rights should be very aware of these issues. Moreover, the balancing test is very much dependent on the facts of each particular case, so it is not very easy to make abstract and general determinations about the outcome of cases based on previous judgments of the Court.

In cases of religious hate speech, another right that could clash with the freedoms of expression or religion is the right to be free from religious discrimination as laid down in article 14 and article 1, Protocol 12 of the ECHR. Both rights and the differences between them were explained as was the fact that the latter needs to be interpreted in the same way as the former. Under both articles, the discrimination is not unlawful if it is justified and this means that the difference in treatment must pursue a legitimate aim and there must be a reasonable relationship of proportionality between the means employed and the aim sought to be realised. Again, the states enjoy a certain margin of appreciation in determining this. The same rules as set out above for conflicts between fundamental rights apply in cases where the right to be free from religious discrimination clashes with the freedoms of expression or religion.

Religious hate speech and religious hate speech laws

Chapter 3 started with an analysis of the concept of hate speech and the conclusion was reached that, although there is a lack of consensus on the meaning of the term, this did not present a problem because the specific focus of the book is on the question whether and under what circumstances religious hate speech or expressions inciting to religious hatred attract the protection given by article 10 ECHR. The European Court of Human Rights has held that some forms of hate speech are protected by freedom of expression. On the other hand, laws against hate speech can be compatible with article 10(2) as long as they satisfy the justification test in that article.

Whether religious hate speech deserves different, either more or less, protection than other forms of hate speech was briefly examined, as was the difference between speech criticising religions or beliefs and speech offending religious believers. Most authors, who see religious hate speech as different from race hate speech, use this difference to argue for less protection of religious hate speech. It was argued that the right to freedom of religion does not protect religions or beliefs as such and thus criticism of religions or beliefs is protected by the right to freedom of speech. However, expressions criticising or offending religious people can be restricted if this is justified under the three part justification test of article 10(2) ECHR, although this does not mean that there is a right not to be offended in one's religious feelings included in article 9 ECHR, because, as concluded in Chapter 1, such a right does not exist. In relation to blasphemy laws, it was concluded that the European Court of Human Rights should revisit the case law in this area and hold that blasphemy laws are not compatible with article 10 ECHR. The conclusion was reached that there are only two situations where restrictions on expressions would be justified. The first situation, as examined in Chapter 2, is when it stops people from holding or manifesting their religion or belief. The second situation is when the expression incites to hatred and violence and violence is likely to follow imminently, which was analysed in Chapter 4.

The arguments brought forward for and against enacting hate speech laws were examined. In favour of enacting such laws were: that they protect the public order and prevent breaches of the peace; that they protect the group(s) targeted; and, that they have a symbolic function by declaring what society finds inappropriate. Against the enactment of hate speech laws, the following objections were raised: such laws are open to abuse and states can easily use them to stifle opposition; they have a chilling effect and lead to self-censorship; they give speakers, authors or publishers an extra platform for spreading their ideas; they might make people moderate their speech but this does not change their views so they might create a 'wolf in sheep's clothing'; and, there might be other, more efficient ways of dealing with hate speech. Criminal laws against hate speech were described as particularly problematic, because they lack clarity and certainty, two important requirements of criminal law.

Restrictions on freedom of expression to spare religious feelings

Chapter 4 contained an examination of the issues that play a role in the decision of the European Court of Human Rights on the question whether and when laws against (religious) hate speech are justified restrictions on freedom of expression. The Court sometimes employs Article 17, which contains an 'abuse of rights' clause and prohibits the abuse of ECHR rights to destroy or undermine these rights or to attack the ECHR's underlying values. If the Court decides that article 17 is applicable, it does not perform any justification or balancing test and this means that states do not have to justify any interference with the right to freedom of expression. Because this allows states to arbitrarily impose restrictions on freedom of speech, article 17 should only be used in extreme and exceptional cases where the fundamental democratic principles and values underlying the ECHR are threatened. This follows the case law of the European Court of Human Rights, although the Court itself has not always been consistent in using article 17 only in exceptional cases and it has been criticised for this. Generally, where speech has been restricted because it incites to (religious) hatred, it is preferable that the Court uses article 10(2) and applies the three part justification test in that paragraph because this requires states to justify the restriction and allows the Court to balance all issues at stake.

It was also submitted, in Chapter 4, that restrictions on expressions just because they foster intolerance should be held to violate the right to freedom of expression of the speaker or author because the mere fostering of intolerance should never be enough to satisfy the three part justification test in Article 10(2) ECHR. It was concluded that expressions should only be limited if there are very serious reasons to do so and laws against incitement to hatred or violence should only be held to be compatible with the ECHR if there is real impact, present risk and imminent danger of violence occurring.

The factors that the European Court of Human Rights takes into account when deciding whether an interference with a person's freedom of expression is justified were examined. These factors can be deducted from the Court's case law and include: the aim pursued by the speaker or author; the content of the expression; the context in which it was disseminated and the potential impact of the remarks; the status and role in society of the speaker or author and of the targeted persons or groups; and, the nature and seriousness of the interference, including the severity of the penalty imposed on the speaker or author.

Alternative approaches to (religious) hate speech

The approach to freedom of expression and the way of dealing with hate speech in the US is often said to be different from the rest of the world and this is why the US approach was discussed in Chapter 5. Although, even in the US, the protection of freedom of expression is not absolute, the right and the important role it plays in public discourse, especially because it allows everyone to take part in this discourse, is stressed. Because of this, any content-based regulation of public discourse is strongly rejected and, therefore, restrictions on speech because of the message it conveys are subject to very strict scrutiny by the courts. The European Court of Human Rights does not make this distinction between content-based and content-neutral restrictions and, as was discussed in Chapter 4, it takes both into account when deciding on whether the justification test of article 10(2) ECHR has been satisfied. However, in Chapter 5, it was argued that the difference between the European Court of Human Rights approach and the US approach in relation to hate speech is not as big as the above would suggest. This is because, in the US, restrictions on the freedom of expression are accepted in relation to hate speech when there is a 'clear and present danger' of violence or a risk of 'imminent lawless action'.[1] It was argued that this is very similar to the terms used by the European Court of Human Rights, which has held that restrictions on hate speech are only justified if there is a 'present risk' and 'imminent danger',[2] a 'clear and imminent danger'[3] and a 'real and present danger' and not a 'mere speculative danger'[4] of violence following the speech. It was therefore concluded that the European Court of Human Rights appears to be moving towards a test that is similar to the 'clear and present danger' test used in the US and that this is a welcome development.

Because it has been argued throughout the book that speech criticising or offending religious believers should only be restricted in two very limited

1 *Schenck v United States*, 249 US 47 (1919); *Brandenburg v Ohio*, 395 US 444 (1969).
2 *Erbakan v Turkey*, Application No. 59405/00, 6 July 2006, para 65.
3 *GÜl and Others v. Turkey*, Application No. 4870/02, 8 June 2010, para 42.
4 *Vajnai v Hungary*, Application No. 33629/06, 8 July 2008, paras 49 and 55.

circumstances and thus that politicians and others contributing to the public debate have a very wide freedom of speech, the question arose as to what this means for those targeted by such speech. It was concluded that (religious) hate speech can have a harmful effect not only on the individuals or groups targeted but also on wider society. Such speech can foster intolerance, can create a hostile climate and can generate an 'us' versus 'them' feeling. But, because of the absence of evidence that there is a direct link between hate speech and harm, it was argued that the harm suffered by victims of hate speech does not justify having laws against hate speech, especially not criminal laws. This was supported by a number of other reasons, including: problems inherent in criminal law such as the definition of hate speech, proof, causation and culpability, and punishment based on future effects; the presence of other criminal offences that could deal (in a more efficient way) with the issues raised; and, the fact that criminal law might very well not be the least restrictive means of dealing with hate speech.

Measures against discrimination were considered as an alternative to criminal hate speech laws. It was argued that civil laws against hate speech are preferable to criminal laws and that anti-discrimination laws, which often provide for civil law remedies, might be used by those targeted by hate speech. However, it was concluded that it might be difficult to use article 14 or article 1, Protocol 12 of the ECHR, which both prohibit discrimination, because a state that has enacted anti-discrimination law has fulfilled its positive obligations under these articles. A claim for discrimination by the individuals or groups targeted by religious hate speech might possibly be made for direct religious discrimination or harassment on religious grounds under EU law and under laws that have implemented the EU anti-discrimination Directives, but whether this can be done with speech that takes place outside the employment sphere depends on the national anti-discrimination legislation.

The 1998 Charter of European Political Parties for a Non-Racist Society, which has been endorsed by both the EU and the Council of Europe, was discussed as a good example of a voluntary code of conduct for politicians. But it was found that it is very difficult to discover which parties have subscribed to the Charter and to assess its effectiveness, because the Charter lacks sanctions or a supervisory mechanism. It also seems unlikely that those far right politicians, who particularly use anti-Muslim rhetoric, have signed up to the Charter. Other ways of dealing with hate speech were suggested, like counter speech, although it was recognised that effective counter speech has been made more difficult in a world of social media. Education, awareness raising and media campaigns were also mentioned.

Case in point: the prosecutions of Geert Wilders

The prosecutions of Dutch politician Geert Wilders, leader of the PVV, the Party for Freedom, were used as a case study to assess the arguments made in the five previous chapters. Wilders' first prosecution led to an acquittal, but the second prosecution led, in December 2016, to a conviction for insulting a racial group and for incitement to discrimination of a racial group. Both Wilders and the Public Prosecutor are appealing the conviction. If it is upheld on appeal and once all domestic procedures are exhausted, Wilders might well apply to the European Court of Human Rights, claiming that his conviction violates his right to freedom of expression under article 10 ECHR.

The first Wilders case related to a number of expressions, made in interviews, against Islam and a film about the dangers of Islam. The Public Prosecutor originally made a decision not to prosecute as they were of the opinion that there was little chance of securing a conviction. However, they were then ordered, by the Amsterdam Court of Appeal, to prosecute Wilders on charges of insulting a group based on race or religion and of incitement to hatred, violence and discrimination against a racial or religious group. The Amsterdam District Court held that Wilders had criticised Islam and pointed out the dangers of the Islamisation of the Netherlands, but that he did not insult Muslims and thus the Court acquitted him of all charges. When three of the victims of the alleged hate speech incidents brought a case against the Netherlands to the UN Human Rights Committee, it held that the Netherlands had not breached article 20(2) of the International Covenant on Civil and Political Rights.

The second *Wilders* case concerned remarks made in an interview at a market and at a post-election meeting with supporters. At the meeting, Wilders had asked the crowd 'and do you want more or fewer Moroccans in your city and in the Netherlands?' To which the crowd chanted: 'fewer, fewer, fewer'. 'We'll arrange that,' Wilders said, smiling, when the chanting died down. This time, Wilders was prosecuted for the same criminal acts, insulting a group and inciting hatred and discrimination against a group of people, but this time it was a group based on race. However, the relevant articles of the Dutch Criminal Code (articles 137c and 137d Sr) do not make any distinction between groups based on race and groups based on religion. On 9 December 2016, the District Court of The Hague convicted Wilders without imposing a penalty, but only in relation to the remarks made at the post-election meeting, of insulting a group based on race and incitement to discrimination on the ground of race. The fact that the 'fewer Moroccans' remarks were carefully orchestrated played a role in the Court's decision. The Court acquitted Wilders of the other charges.

If the second *Wilders* case is ever challenged in the European Court of Human Rights as a violation of article 10 ECHR, the Court will, very likely, hold that articles 137c and 137d Sr are compatible with freedom of expression and that Wilders' claim should not be rejected under article 17 ECHR. This submission is based on the Court's case law as examined in previous Chapters. The Court should then examine Wilders' conviction under the three part justification test of article 10 (2) ECHR. It should, following its own case law, take account of the fact that Wilders is a (opposition) politician who is raising issues of concern in Dutch society and who is, thus, clearly contributing to the current public and political debate. In this sense, Wilders' expressions cannot be said to be gratuitously offensive. The Court should thus scrutinise Wilders' conviction very strictly. It was suggested that the European Court of Human Rights should find that Wilders' conviction violates his article 10 ECHR right to freedom of expression. The next part of the conclusion will analyse why this suggestion is made.

Freedom of expression and religious hate speech

Based on the case law of the European Court of Human Rights, the argument throughout this book has been that the freedom of expression of politicians and others who contribute to the public debate should not be restricted unless their expressions either incite to hatred and violence and there is a present risk or imminent danger that violence will follow, or, unless they stop people from holding or manifesting their religion or belief. This argument was grounded in the crucial role freedom of expression plays in a democratic society, in both its active and its passive side: freedom to impart ideas and freedom to receive information. Without this right, a democratic society could not exist. As was discussed in Chapter 1, democracy is a fundamental feature in the European public order and is the only political model compatible with the ECHR.[5] And, in a democracy, people should be able to take part in the public debate and be able to express their views on issues of concern. To fully take part in this public and political debate, they should also be able to receive all the information they need to make decisions, including decisions on who to vote for. As Barendt points out, 'freedom of expression plays a crucial role in the formation of public opinion on political questions'.[6] Therefore, free and open debate on matters of public interest is of vital importance in a democracy.

Because politicians play an important role in the public and political debate, the European Court of Human Rights has always afforded political speech a very high level of protection and has subjected restrictions on such speech to a strict level of scrutiny.[7] Moreover, according to the Court, to get their message across, politicians can use offensive, shocking or disturbing language,[8] they can use a degree of exaggeration and provocation,[9] and immoderation[10] and they can be controversial and virulent in their expressions.[11] Therefore, even expressions couched in such language attract the protection provided by article 10 ECHR.

The term 'political speech' has been defined widely, following Barendt, and refers to 'all speech relevant to the development of public opinion on the whole

---

5 *United Communist Party of Turkey and Others v Turkey*, Application No. 19392/92, 30 January 1998, para 45.

6 Barendt, E., *Freedom of Speech* (2nd edn, Oxford, Oxford University Press, 2005) 18.

7 See, for example, *Lingens v Austria*, Application No. 9815/82, 8 July 1986, para 42; *Erbakan v Turkey*, Application No. 59405/00, 6 July 2006, para 55.

8 *Handyside v the United Kingdom*, Application No. 5493/72 (1979–1980), 7 December 1976, para 49.

9 *Le Pen v France*, Application No. 18788/09, 20 April 2010.

10 *Otegi Mondragon v Spain*, Application No. 2034/07, 15 March 2011, para 54.

11 *Perinçek v Switzerland*, Application No. 27510/08, 15 October 2015, para 231.

range of public issues which an intelligent citizen should think about'.[12] This means that the expressions not only of politicians but also of anyone contributing to the public debate attract strong protection under article 10 ECHR. The open and public discussion of matters of public interest includes issues of religion and belief. The right to freedom of religion is, according to the European Court of Human Rights, also one of the foundations of a democratic society.[13] This right includes, as article 9(1) clearly states, the right to change one's religion. This freedom to change one's religion would be meaningless if one could not receive or impart views that criticise or deny the tenets of one's religion or support those of another religion. The Court has held that:

> The concepts of pluralism, tolerance and broadmindedness on which any democratic society is based . . . mean that Article 10 does not, as such, envisage that an individual is to be protected from exposure to a religious view simply because it is not his or her own.[14]

In a democratic society, there should thus be room to strongly criticise and deny religious beliefs even if this might be offensive or insulting to believers. As has been stressed throughout the book, there is no right not to be offended in one's religious feelings present in article 9 ECHR.

It should also be noted that 'often the speech we find most offensive will be made in relation to issues of public concern', as O'Reilly writes.[15] Moreover, the public debate is the arena for the exchange of all kinds of opposing (political) ideas and views. Some of these, especially those one does not agree with, might be offensive but 'offensive language may in reality be the best communicative style available' for political and other views.[16] Indeed, much political speech might, by its very nature, be offensive to opponents. O'Reilly also writes that 'comments about Islam or immigration may appear xenophobic and tantamount to hate speech, but such speech undoubtedly touches on issues of public interest, as well as being representative of the views of certain members of society'.[17] This is an argument regularly used by Wilders himself: whenever his expressions are challenged he points out that he is only raising an issue of public interest and saying what many people in the Netherlands are thinking.

The District Court of The Hague in the second *Wilders* case rejected the argument of the defence that 'the Castells exception' (from the European Court

---

12 Barendt, supra note 6, 162.
13 *Kokkinakis v Greece*, Application No. 14307/88, 25 May 1993, para 31.
14 *Murphy v Ireland*, Application No. 44179/98, 10 July 2003, para 72.
15 O'Reilly, A., 'In Defence of Offence: Freedom of Expression, Offensive Speech, and the Approach of the European Court of Human Rights', 19 *Trinity College Law Review* (2016) 239.
16 Ibid. 241–242
17 Ibid. 239.

of Human Rights case of *Castells v Spain*[18]), applied with the consideration that *Castells v Spain* concerned an elected Member of Parliament expressing criticism of the government, while Wilders' expressions did not criticise the government or its actions.[19] It was submitted, in Chapter 6, that the District Court was mistaken in this. Wilders is highlighting an issue that is of concern to many people in Dutch society and, by doing so, he is not only criticising the government's policies on multiculturalism and immigration, but he is also proposing ways to deal with these issues which he would try to implement if he is elected. He is doing what an elected representative of the people should do: raising concerns that are living among the people he is representing. Wilders' remarks can thus clearly be seen as part of the current public and political debate. All this is supported by what the European Court of Human Rights held in *Castells v Spain*, that 'while freedom of expression is important for everybody, it is especially so for an elected representative of the people. He represents his electorate, draws attention to their preoccupations and defends their interests'.[20] The Court continued that, 'interferences with the freedom of expression of an opposition member of parliament, like the applicant, call for the closest scrutiny on the part of the Court'.[21] Therefore, Wilders is, as an opposition Member of Parliament, in the same position as Castells.

Restrictions on the freedom of expression of politicians and others who contribute to the public debate should, therefore, only be held to be justified in the two very limited circumstances set out in this book. One of these is where the speech stops people from exercising their right to freedom of religion, but, as was mentioned in Chapter 2, speech will hardly ever have this effect. The other of these circumstances is when expressions are inciting to hatred and to violence and violence is likely to follow imminently; or, in the words of the European Court of Human Rights, the expression must give rise to a 'present risk' and an 'imminent danger', there has to be a 'clear and imminent danger' or a 'real and present danger' and not a 'mere speculative danger' which requires an interference with the right to freedom of expression of the applicant. These expressions clearly echo the 'clear and present danger' and the 'imminent lawless action' tests as used in the United States to assess whether an interference with freedom of speech is justified. It was submitted that there was no evidence that Wilders' 'fewer Moroccans' expression did either and, therefore, the European Court of Human Rights should, if the case ever reaches this Court, find that Wilders' conviction violates his right to freedom of expression under article 10. The same

---

18 *Castells v Spain*, Application No. 11798/85, 23 April 1992. The exception means that that criminal law will only be applied when other ways of stopping the unwanted expressions have been explored.

19 See: *Rechtbank Den Haag* (The Hague District Court), 9 December 2016, para 4.3, https://uitspraken.rechtspraak.nl/inziendocument?id=ECLI:NL:RBDHA:2016:15014

20 *Castells v Spain*, supra note 18, para 42.

21 Ibid.

can be said about the expressions subject to the first Wilders case, although they would not be subject to scrutiny in the European Court of Human Rights.

One more point to note is that Wilders has frequently invoked his right to freedom of expression and has argued that his expressions are protected because they contribute to the public debate on current concerns in Dutch society. He said after his conviction that the judgment restricts the freedom of expression of millions of Dutch people.[22] Therefore, he clearly uses the language of human rights. However, Wilders himself does not see the right to freedom of expression as absolute and does not appear to extend this right to Muslims as he 'has proposed banning the Quran with the argument that it incites to violence and thus transgresses freedom of expression'.[23]

A caveat is in order: throughout this book free and open public debate has been placed at the heart of allowing for very strong protection of expressions on matters of public interest that contribute to this debate. However, does this free and open debate still exist in reality? This is linked to the problems raised in relation to counter speech in Chapter 5. In an open and public debate, there should be room for speech and counter speech, room for everyone to impart their views and hear about others' views. This assumes that the majority of people do take part in this free and open debate. But, in today's world, which is dominated by social media, many people's access to 'news' is highly (self) filtered and, whereas in the past, many people would watch or listen to the same main evening news programme, nowadays people exchange information with other people from a like-minded group via social media and this tends to reinforce their views. Therefore, it can be asked whether this free and open debate in which a number of different views are exchanged still exists or is in danger of disappearing.

Despite this question, it is still submitted that the freedom of expressions of politicians and others who contribute to the public debate should not be restricted unless the expressions stop people from holding or manifesting their religion or belief or unless they incite to hatred and violence and there is an imminent danger of violence. Wilders expressions, irrespective of whether you agree or disagree with them, did not do either and thus his conviction should be held to violate his right to freedom of expression under article 10 ECHR.

---

22 See: *Video: Nederland is een Ziek Land Geworden (Video: the Netherlands has become a Sick Country)* http://nos.nl/artikel/2147381-video-wilders-nederland-is-een-ziek-land-geworden.html

23 Noorloos, M. van, 'The Politicisation of Hate Speech Bans in Twenty-first Century Netherlands: Law in a Changing Context', 40 (2) *Journal of Ethnic and Migration Studies* (2014) 259.

Bibliography

Bacquet, S., *Freedom of Expression v Hate Speech: An Illustration of the Dilemma through and In-depth Analysis of Judicial Approaches in England and France* (VDM Verlag, 2011)

Barendt, E., *Freedom of Speech* (2nd edn, Oxford, Oxford University Press, 2005)

Barendt, E., 'Religious Hatred Laws: Protecting Groups or Belief?', 17 (1) *Res Publica* (2011) 41–53

Belavusau, U., 'A *Dernier Cri* from Strasbourg: An Ever Formidable Challenge of Hate Speech (*Soulas and Others v France, Leroy v France, Balsytė-Lideikienė v Lithuania*)', 16 (3) *European Public Law* (2010) 373–389

Belavusau, U., *Fighting Hate Speech through EU Law*, Amsterdam Law Forum, Winter Issue, 2012, 20–35, http://amsterdamlawforum.org/article/view/253/441

Benesch, S., 'Charlie the Freethinker: Religion, Blasphemy and Decent Controversy', 10 *Religion and Human Rights* (2015) 244–254

Bielefeldt, H., Ghanea, N. and Wiener, M., *Freedom of Religion or Belief: An International Law Commentary* (Oxford, Oxford University Press, 2016)

Boerefijn, I. and Oyediran, J., 'Article 20 of the International Covenant on Civil and Political Rights', in Coliver, S. (ed.) *Striking a Balance: Hate Speech, Freedom of Expression and Discrimination* (London, Article 19, 1992) 29–32

Bonello, G., 'Freedom of Expression and Incitement to Violence', in Casadevall, J., Myjer, E., O'Boyle, M. and Austin, A. (eds) *Freedom of Expression, Essays in Honour of Nicolas Bratza* (Oisterwijk, the Netherlands, Wolf Legal Publishers, 2012) 349–359

Boomsma, K. and Rigter, N., *Process Wilders: Enkel Verliezers* (Trial Wilders: Only Losers), 23 June 2011, www.metronieuws.nl/binnenland/2011/06/proces-wilders-enkel-verliezers

Boyle, K., 'Hate Speech: the United States versus the Rest of the World', 53 (2) *Maine Law Review* (2001) 487–502

Boyle, K., 'The Danish Cartoons', 24 (2) *Netherlands Quarterly of Human Rights* (2006) 185–191

Brems, E., 'Conflicting Human Rights: An Exploration in the Context of the Right to a Fair Trial in the European Convention for the Protection of Human Rights and Fundamental Freedoms', 27 *Human Rights Quarterly* (2005) 294–326

Brink, J. van den, 'Discriminatieverbod vs. Vrijheid van Meningsuiting 1–0? EHRM doet Uitspraak in Féret tegen Beligie', (Prohibition of Discrimination v Freedom of expression 1–0? The European Court of Human Rights brings out its judgment in *Féret v Belgium*), 2732 *Media Report* (2009), www.mediareport.nl/persrecht/29072009/discriminatieverbod-vs-vrijheid-van-meningsuiting-1-0-ehrm-doet-uitspraak-in-feret-tegen-belgie/

Buyse, A., 'Dangerous Expressions: the ECHR, Violence and Free Speech', 63 (2) *International and Comparative Law Quarterly* (2014) 491–503

Callamard, A., 'Religion, Terrorism and Speech in a "Post-Charlie Hebdo" World', 10 (3) *Religion and Human Rights* (2015) 207–228

Cannie, H. and Voorhoof, D., 'The Abuse Clause and Freedom of Expression in the European Human Rights Convention: An Added Value for Democracy and Human Rights Protection?', 29 (1) *Netherlands Quarterly of Human Rights* (2011) 54–83

Chan, S., 'Hate Speech Bans: An Intolerant Response to Intolerance', 14 *Trinity College Law Review* (2011), 77–96

Charter of European Political Parties for a Non-Racist Society, www.coe.int/t/dghl/monitoring/ecri/activities/38-seminar_ankara_2011/Charter.asp

Chopin, I. and Germaine, C., *A Comparative Analysis of Non-discrimination Law in Europe 2016*, European Network of Legal Experts in Gender Equality and Non-Discrimination (Luxembourg, Publications Office of the European Union, 2016)

Committee of Ministers, Council of Europe, Recommendation No R(97)20 on "Hate Speech"

Council Directive 2000/43/EC Implementing the Principle of Equal Treatment between Persons Irrespective of Racial or Ethnic Origin [2000] OJ L 180/22

Council Directive 2000/78/EC Establishing a General Framework for Equal Treatment in Employment and Occupation [2000] OJ L 303/16

Council Directive 2006/54/EC on the Implementation of the Principle of Equal Opportunities and Equal Treatment of Men and Women in Matters of Employment and Occupation (Recast) [2006] OJ L 204/23

Council of Europe, Explanatory Report, Protocol 12 to the Convention for the Protection of Human Rights and Fundamental Freedoms, ETS, 177 https://rm.coe.int/CoERMPublicCommonSearchServices/DisplayDCTMContent?documentId=09000016800cce48

Council of Europe, Information Documents SG/inf (2008) 20 rev, Contribution of the Council of Europe to the Implementation of the Durban Declaration and Programme of Action Council of Europe Action to Combat Racism and Intolerance (2001–2008) Contribution submitted by the Secretary General of the Council of Europe to the Durban Review Conference (20–24 April 2009)

Council of Europe, *Compilation of Council of Europe Standards Relating to the Principles of Freedom of Thought, Conscience and Religion and Links to other Human Rights* (Strasbourg, Council of Europe, 2015)

Cox, N., 'Blasphemy, Holocaust Denial, and the Control of Profoundly Unacceptable Speech', 62 *American Journal of Comparative Law* (2014) 739–774

Cram, I., 'The Danish Cartoons, Offensive Expression and Democratic Legitimacy', in Hare, I. and Weinstein, J. (eds) *Extreme Speech and Democracy* (Oxford, Oxford University Press, 2009) 311–330

Declaration on the Elimination of All Forms of Intolerance and of Discrimination Based on Religion or Belief, A/RES/36/55, 25 November 1981

Dijk, P. van and Hoof, F. van, *Theory and Practice of the European Convention on Human Rights* (London, Kluwer Law International, 1998)

Donald, A. and Howard, E., *The Right to Freedom of Religion or Belief and its Intersection with Other Rights* (A Research Paper for ILGA-Europe, January 2015), www.ilga-europe.org/sites/default/files/Attachments/the_right_to_freedom_of_religion_or_belief_and_its_intersection_with_other_rights__0.pdf

Dutch Politician Wilders Convicted of Discrimination Against Moroccans www.reuters. com/article/us-netherlands-wilders-trial-idUSKBN13Y0OX

Dworkin, R., 'Foreword' in Hare, I. and Weinstein, J. (eds) *Extreme Speech and Democracy* (Oxford, Oxford University Press, 2009) v–ix

Edge, P., 'The European Court of Human Rights and Religious Rights', 47 (3) *International and Comparative Law Quarterly* (1998) 680–687

Equality and Human Rights Commission, *Guidance – Legal Framework: Freedom of Expression*, 2015, www.equalityhumanrights.com/en/publication-download/freedom-expression-legal-framework

European Commission against Racism and Intolerance, *Declaration on the Use of Racist, Anti-Semitic and Xenophobic Elements in Political Discourse* (2005) www. coe.int/t/dghl/monitoring/ecri/activities/14-Public_Presentation_Paris_2005/ Presentation2005_Paris_Declaration_en.asp

European Commission against Racism and Intolerance, General Policy Recommendation No. 15, on *Combating Hate Speech*, CRI (2016) 15, 2015

European Commission for Democracy through Law (Venice Commission), Report on the Relationship between Freedom of Expression and Freedom of Religion: the Issue of Regulation and Prosecution of Blasphemy, Religious Insult and Incitement to Religious Hatred (Strasbourg, Council of Europe, 2008, Study No. 406/ 2006, CDL-AD(2008)026) www.venice.coe.int/webforms/documents/?pdf=CDL-AD%282008%29026-e

European Court of Human Rights Research Division, *Overview of the Court's Case-law on Freedom of Religion* (Strasbourg, Council of Europe, 2013) https://rm.coe. int/CoERMPublicCommonSearchServices/DisplayDCTMContent?documentId= 0900001680666749#search=Overview%20of%20the%20Court%E2%80%99s%20 Case%2Dlaw%20on%20Freedom%20of%20Religion

European Court of Human Rights, *Factsheet – Hate Speech,* June 2016, www.echr.coe.int/ Documents/FS_Hate_speech_ENG.pdf

Evans, M., *Manual on the Wearing of Religious Symbols in Public Areas* (Strasbourg, Council of Europe, 2009)

Evans, M., 'The Freedom of Religion or Belief and the Freedom of Expression', 4 (2–3) *Religion and Human Rights* (2009) 197–235

Feinberg, J., *The Moral Limits of the Criminal Law: Volume 2, Offense to Others* (Oxford, Oxford University Press, 1988)

Fenwick, H. and Phillipson, G., *Media Freedom under the Human Rights Act* (Oxford, Oxford University Press, 2006)

Foster, S., 'Case Comment: Racist Speech and Articles 10 and 17 of the European Convention on Human Rights', 10 (1) *Coventry Law Journal* (2005) 91–95

Gelber, K., 'Reconceptualizing Counterspeech in Hate Speech Policy (with a Focus on Australia)', in Herz, M. and Molnar, P. (eds) *The Content and Context of Hate Speech Rethinking Regulation and Responses* (Cambridge, Cambridge University Press, 2012) 198–216

Goldschmidt, J. and Loenen, M., 'Religious Pluralism and Human Rights in Europe: Reflections for Future Research', in Loenen, M. and Goldschmidt, J. (eds) *Religious Pluralism and Human Rights in Europe: Where to Draw the Line?*, (Antwerp/Oxford, Intersentia, 2007) 311–329

Goodall, K., 'Incitement to Religious Hatred: All Talk and No Substance?' 70 (1) *Modern Law Review* (2007) 89–113

Grimm, D., 'Freedom of Speech in a Globalized World', in Hare, I. and Weinstein, J. (eds) *Extreme Speech and Democracy* (Oxford, Oxford University Press, 2009) 11–23

Hare, I., 'Crosses, Crescents and Sacred Cows: Criminalising Incitement to Religious Hatred', *Public Law* (2006) 521–538

Hare, I., 'Blasphemy and Religious Hatred: Free Speech Dogma and Doctrine', in Hare, I. and Weinstein, J. (eds) *Extreme Speech and Democracy* (Oxford, Oxford University Press, 2009) 289–310

Heck, W., *Drie Argumenten Voor and Drie tegen Vervolging van Wilders* (Three Arguments For and Three Against Prosecuting Wilders) 3 April 2014, www.nrc.nl/nieuws/2014/04/03/drie-argumenten-voor-en-drie-tegen-vervolging-van-wilders-a1426036

Heinze, E., *Hate Speech and Democratic Citizenship* (Oxford, Oxford University Press, 2016)

Hill, M. and Sandberg, R., 'Blasphemy and Human Rights: An English Experience in a European Context', IV *Derecho y Religion* (2009) 145–160

Hitchens, C., 'Cartoon Debate: The Case for Mocking Religion', *Slate*, 4 February 2006, www.slate.com/articles/news_and_politics/fighting_words/2006/02/cartoon_debate.html

Horton, J., 'Self-censorship', 17 (1) *Res Publica* (2011) 91–106

Hotse Smit, P., Stoker, E. and de Vires, J., *Reacties op Wilders Vonnis: Nederland is een Ziek Land Geworden* (Reactions to the Wilders Conviction: The Netherlands has become a Sick Country) 9 December 2016, www.volkskrant.nl/binnenland/reacties-op-wilders-vonnis-nederland-is-een-ziek-land-geworden~a4431076/

House of Lords, Debates, Column 1072–1073 and 1074, 25 October 2005 www.publications.parliament.uk/pa/ld200506/ldhansrd/vo051025/text/51025-04.htm#51025-04_head2

Howard, E., 'Reasonable Accommodation of Religion and Other Discrimination Grounds in EU law', 38 (3) *European Law Review* (2013) 360–375

Howard, E., 'Gratuitously Offensive Speech and the Political Debate', 6 *European Human Rights Law Review* (2016) 636–644

Howard, E., 'Freedom of Speech versus Freedom of Religion? The Case of Dutch Politician Geert Wilders', 17 (2) Human Rights Law Review (2017) 313–337

Howard, E. (2017) 'Freedom of Expression, Blasphemy and Religious Hatred: a View from the UK' in Temperman, J. and Koltay, A. (eds) *Blasphemy and Freedom of Expression* (Cambridge, Cambridge University Press, forthcoming)

Human Rights Committee, General Comment No. 34, *Article 19: Freedoms of Opinion and Expression,* CCPR/C/GC/34, 12 September 2011

'Interview with Kenan Malik', in Herz, M. and Molnar, P. (eds) *The Content and Context of Hate Speech Rethinking Regulation and Responses* (Cambridge, Cambridge University Press, 2012) 81–91

Jeremy, A., 'Practical Implications of the Enactment of the Racial and Religious Hatred Act 2006', 9 (2) *Ecclesiastical Law Journal* (2007) 187–201

Joint Statement by the Special Rapporteurs on Freedom of Expression, Freedom of Religion or Belief and on Racism, Racial Discrimination, Xenophobia and Related Intolerance to the 2011 Expert Workshop on the Prohibition of National, Racial and Religious Hatred, Vienna 9–10 February 2011 www.ohchr.org/Documents/Issues/Religion/CRP3Joint_SRSubmission_for_Vienna.pdf

Kapai, P. and Cheung, A., 'Hanging in the Balance: Freedom of Expression and Religion', 15 *Buffalo Human Rights Law Review* (2009) 41–79

Keane, D., 'Attacking Hate Speech under Article 17 of the European Convention on Human Rights', 25 (4) *Netherlands Quarterly of Human Rights* (2007) 641–663

Kick it Out, www.kickitout.org

Knechtle, J. 'When to Regulate Hate Speech', 110 (3) *Penn State Law Review* (2006) 539–578

Knights, S., *Freedom of Religion, Minorities and the Law* (Oxford, Oxford University Press, 2007)

Lawson, R., 'WILD, WILDER, WILDST Over de Ruimte die het EVRM laat voor de Vervolging van Kwetsende Politici' (WILD, WILDER, WILDEST About the Room given by the ECHR for the Prosecution of Offending Politicians), 33 (4) *NJCM-Bulletin* (2008) 469–484

Lees Hier de Brief van Mark (Read Here the Letter from Mark), https://vvd.nl/nieuws/lees-hier-de-brief-van-mark/

Leigh, I., 'Damned if They Do, Damned if They Don't': the European Court of Human Rights and the Protection of Religion from Attack', 17 (1) *Res Publica* (2011) 55–73

Lester, A., *Free Speech and Religion – The Eternal Conflict in the Age of Selective Modernization,* keynote speech, 2006, www.odysseustrust.org/lectures/274_Hungarytalk.pdf. Also published in Sajo, A. (ed) *Censorial Sensitivities: Free speech and Religion in a Fundamentalist World* (Utrecht, Eleven International, 2007), 151–164

Lester, A., 'The Right to Offend', in Casadevall, J., Myjer, E., O'Boyle, M. and Austin, A., (eds) *Freedom of Expression, Essays in Honour of Nicolas Bratza* (Oisterwijk, the Netherlands, Wolf Legal Publishers, 2012), 297–306

Letsas, G., 'Is there a Right Not to be Offended in One's Religious Beliefs?' in Zucca, L. and Ungureanu, C. (eds) *Law, State and Religion in the New Europe* (Cambridge, Cambridge University Press, 2012) 239–60, available at SSRN, http://ssrn.com/abstract=1500291

Lewis, T., 'What not to Wear: Religious Rights, the European Court, and the Margin of Appreciation', 56 (2) *International and Comparative Law Quarterly* (2007) 395–414

Lisbon Network, Council of Europe, *The Margin of Appreciation* www.coe.int/t/dghl/cooperation/lisbonnetwork/themis/echr/paper2_en.asp

Lopez Guerra, L., 'Blasphemy and Religious Insult: Offenses to Religious Feelings or Attacks on Freedom?' in Casadevall, J., Myjer, E., O'Boyle, M. and Austin, A., (eds) *Freedom of Expression, Essays in Honour of Nicolas Bratza* (Oisterwijk, the Netherlands, Wolf Legal Publishers, 2012), 307–319

Malik, M. 'Extreme Speech and Liberalism', in Hare, I. and Weinstein, J. (eds) *Extreme Speech and Democracy* (Oxford, Oxford University Press, 2009) 96–120.

Malik, M., 'Religious Freedom, Free Speech and Equality: Conflict or Cohesion?', 17 (1) *Res Publica* (2011) 21–40

McKie, R., *Far-right Leader Geert Wilders calls Moroccan Migrants 'Scum'*, 18 February 2017, www.theguardian.com/world/2017/feb/18/geert-wilders-netherlands-describes-immigrants-scum-holland

Memorandum to the Home Affairs Committee, Post-legislative Scrutiny of the Racial and Religious Hatred Act 2006, CM 8164, 2011, www.gov.uk/government/uploads/system/uploads/attachment_data/file/238156/8164.pdf

Molnar, P., 'Interview with Kenan Malik', in Herz, M. and Molnar, P. (eds) *The Content and Context of Hate Speech Rethinking Regulation and Responses* (Cambridge, Cambridge University Press, 2012) 81–91

Murdoch, J., *Freedom of Thought, Conscience and Religion. A guide to the Implementation of Article 9 of the European Convention on Human Rights* (Human Rights Handbooks No. 9, Strasbourg, Council of Europe, 2007)

Nathwani, N., 'Religious Cartoons and Human Rights – a Critical Legal Analysis of the Case Law of the European Court of Human Rights on the Protection of Religious Feelings and its Implications in the Danish Affair Concerning Cartoons of the Prophet Muhammad', 4 *European Human Rights Law Review* (2008) 488–507

Netherlands Institute for Human Rights, *Rechter veroordeelt Geert Wilders voor Discriminatie* (Judge convicts Geert Wilders for Discrimination) 9 December 2016, www.mensenrechten.nl/berichten/rechter-veroordeelt-geert-wilders-voor-discriminatie

Niemandsverdriet, T., *Wilders heeft er Alles aan Gedaan om zijn Process Politiek te Maken* (Wilders has done Everything to make his Process a Political One) www.nrc.nl/nieuws/2016/11/24/pvv-leider-heeft-er-zelf-alles-aan-gedaan-om-zijn-proces-politiek-te-maken-5469305-a1533445

Niessen, J., 'The Charter for Political Parties for a Non-Racist Society', 3 *European Journal of Migration and Law,* (2001) 73–89

Noorloos, M. van, 'The Politicisation of Hate Speech Bans in the Twenty-first Century Netherlands: Law in a Changing Context', 40 (2) *Journal of Ethnic and Migration Studies* (2014) 249–265.

O'Connell, R., 'Cinderella comes to the Ball: Article 14 and the Right to Non-Discrimination in the ECHR', 29 (2) *Legal Studies* (2009) 211–229

OM to Prosecute Geert Wilders on Charges of Discrimination, 18 December 2014, www.om.nl/onderwerpen/zaak-wilders/@90740/to-prosecute-geert/

Ook OM Gaat in Beroep in Zaak–Wilders (Public Prosecutor also Appeals Wilders Case), http://nos.nl/artikel/2149910-ook-om-gaat-in-beroep-in-zaak-wilders.html

O'Reilly, A., 'In Defence of Offence: Freedom of Expression, Offensive Speech, and the Approach of the European Court of Human Rights', 19 *Trinity College Law Review* (2016) 234–260

Parliamentary Assembly, Council of Europe, Resolution 1345 (2003) *Racist, Xenophobic and Intolerant Discourse in Politics* www.assembly.coe.int/nw/xml/XRef/Xref–XML2HTML–en.asp?fileid=17143&lang=en

Parliamentary Assembly, Council of Europe, Resolution 1510 (2006) *Freedom of Expression and Respect for Religious Beliefs,* http://assembly.coe.int/nw/xml/XRef/Xref-XML2HTML-EN.asp?fileid=17457&lang=en

Parliamentary Assembly, Council of Europe, Recommendation 1805 (2007) *Blasphemy, Religious Insults and Hate Speech against Persons on Grounds of their Religion* http://assembly.coe.int/nw/xml/XRef/Xref-XML2HTML-en.asp?fileid=17569&lang=en

Party of European Socialists, *Confronting the Extreme–Right in Europe: our Way,* Resolution adopted by the PES Presidency on 14th of October 2010, www.pes.eu/export/sites/default/Downloads/Policy-Documents/Democracy/adopted_resolution_extreme_right_141010_en.pdf_551059009.pdf

Pieters, J., *Nearly 6,500 People Pressed Hate-Speech Charges against Wilders,* 31 October 2016, http://nltimes.nl/2016/10/31/nearly-6500-people-pressed-hate-speech-charges

Pitt, G., 'Religion and Belief: Aiming at the Right Target?', in Meenan, H. (ed.) *Equality Law in an Enlarged European Union: Understanding the Article 13 Directives* (Cambridge, Cambridge University Press, 2007)

Plant, R., 'Religion, Identity and Freedom of Expression', 17 (1) *Res Publica* (2011) 7–20

Poole, E., 'The Case of Geert Wilders: Multiculturalism, Islam and Identity in the UK', 5 *Journal of Religion in Europe* (2012) 162–191

Programme of Action, World Conference against Racism, Racial Discrimination, Xenophobia and Related Intolerance, 2001, Durban, South Africa www.un.org/WCAR/durban.pdf

Protocol No. 12 of the ECHR, CETS No. 177, Status of Ratifications http://conventions. coe.int/Treaty/Commun/ChercheSig.asp?NT=177&CM=1&DF=19/02/2011&C L=ENG

PVV Leader Geert Wilders will be Prosecuted for Inciting Hatred (update) www. dutchnews.nl/news/archives/2014/12/pvv-leader-geert-wilders-will-be-prosecuted-for-inciting-hatred-and-discrimination/

Rabat Plan of Action on the Prohibition of Advocacy of National, Racial or Religious Hatred that Constitutes Incitement to Discrimination, Hostility or Violence. Conclusions and Recommendations Emanating from the Four Regional Expert Workshops Organised by OHCHR, 2011, and Adopted by Experts in Rabat, Morocco, 5 October 2012, www. ohchr.org/Documents/Issues/Opinion/SeminarRabat/Rabat_draft_outcome.pdf

Rainey, B., Wicks, E. and Ovey, C., *Jacobs, White and Ovey The European Convention on Human Rights* (6th edn, Oxford, Oxford University Press, 2014)

Rorke, B., 'Free to Hate? Anti-Gypsyism in 21-Century Europe', in Molnar, P. (ed.) *Free Speech and Censorship around the Globe* (Budapest-New York, Central European University Press, 2015) 233–252

Rosenfeld, M., 'Hate Speech in Constitutional Jurisprudence A Comparative Analysis' in Herz, M. and Molnar, P. (eds) *The Content and Context of Hate Speech Rethinking Regulation and Responses* (Cambridge, Cambridge University Press, 2012) 242–289

Rutte: Kans dat VVD Gaat Regeren met PVV is Nul (Chances of VVD Governing with PVV is Zero) www.rtlnieuws.nl/nederland/politiek/rutte-kans-dat-vvd-gaat-regeren-met-pvv-is-nul

'Rutte: Ga Weg als je Nederlandse Waarden Afwijst' (Rutte: Leave if you reject Dutch Values) 23 January 2017, http://nos.nl/artikel/2154459-rutte-ga-weg-als-je-nederlandse-waarden-afwijst.html

Sandberg, R., *Law and Religion* (Cambridge, Cambridge University Press, 2011)

Sandberg, R. and Doe, N., 'The Strange Death of Blasphemy', 71 (6) *Modern Law Review* (2008) 971–986

Sottieaux, S., '"Bad Tendencies" in the ECtHR "Hate Speech" Jurisprudence', 7 (1) *European Constitutional Law Review* (2011) 40–63

Stone, G., 'Free Speech in the Twenty-first Century: Ten Lessons from the Twentieth Century', in Koltay, A. (ed.) *Comparative Perspectives on the Fundamental Freedom of Expression* (Budapest, Wolters Kluwer, 2015) 119–139

Temperman, J., 'Blasphemy, Defamation of Religions and Human Rights Law', 26 (4) *Netherlands Quarterly of Human Rights* (2008) 517–545

Temperman, J., 'Protection against Religious Hatred under the United Nations ICCPR and the European Convention System' in Ferrari, S. and Cristofori, R. (eds) *Law and Religion in the 21st Century* (Farnham, Ashgate Publishing, 2010) 215–223

Temperman, J., 'Blasphemy versus Incitement: An International Law Perspective', in Beneke, C., Grenda, C. and Nash, D. (eds) *Profane: Sacrilegious Expression in a Multicultural Age* (Oakland, University of California Press, 2014), 281–313. Available at SSRN: http://ssrn.com/abstract=2712702

Temperman, J., 'A Right to be Free from Religious Hatred? The Wilders Case in the Netherlands and Beyond', in Molnar, P. (ed.) *Free Speech and Censorship around the Globe* (Budapest/New York, Central European University Press, 2015) 509–530

Temperman, J., *Religious Hatred and International Law: The Prohibition of Incitement to Violence or Discrimination* (Cambridge: Cambridge University Press, 2016)

Tulkens, F., 'Conflicts between Fundamental Rights: Contrasting Views on Articles 9 and 10 of the European Convention on Human Rights', in Venice Commission, *Blasphemy,*

Insult and Hatred: Finding Answers in a Democratic Society (Strasbourg, Council of Europe, Science and Technique of Democracy No. 47, 2010) 121–131, www.venice. coe.int/webforms/documents/?pdf=CDL-STD(2010)047-e

Tulkens, F., 'When to Say is to Do: Freedom of Expression and Hate Speech in the Case-law of the European Court of Human Rights', in Casadevall, J., Myjer, E., O'Boyle, M. and Austin, A., (eds) *Freedom of Expression, Essays in Honour of Nicolas Bratza* (Oisterwijk, the Netherlands, Wolf Legal Publishers, 2012) 279–296

Tulkens, F., *The Hate Factor in Political Speech: Where Do Responsibilities Lie?* (2013) https://rm.coe.int/CoERMPublicCommonSearchServices/DisplayDCTMContent?d ocumentId=09000016800c170e

Video: Nederland is een Ziek Land Geworden (Video: the Netherlands has become a Sick Country) http://nos.nl/artikel/2147381-video-wilders-nederland-is-een-ziek-land-geworden.html

Villiger, M., Article 17 ECHR and Freedom of Speech in Strasbourg Practice', in Casadevall, J., Myjer, E., O'Boyle, M. and Austin, A., (eds) *Freedom of Expression, Essays in Honour of Nicolas Bratza* (Oisterwijk, the Netherlands, Wolf Legal Publishers, 2012) 321–329

Voorhoof, D., 'Polticus die Haat Zaait is Strafbaar', Noot onder Féret/Belgie, EHRM 16 juli 2009 (*Appl. No. 15615/07*) (Politician who sows hatred can be punished, Case Comment Féret/*Belgium*, European Court of Human Rights, 16 July 2009) *Media Forum* 2009/11 (in Dutch, translation by author).

Voorhoof, D., *European Court of Human Rights Jean-Marie Le Pen v. France* (2010) http://merlin.obs.coe.int/iris/2010/7/article1.en.html

Vrielink, J., 'Islamophobia and the Law: Belgian Hate Speech Legislation and the Wilful Destruction of the Koran', 14 (1) *International Journal of Discrimination and the Law* (2014) 54–65

Weber, A., *Manual on Hate Speech* (Strasbourg, Council of Europe, 2009)

Weinstein, J., 'Extreme Speech, Public order, and Democracy: Lessons from *The Masses*', in Hare, I. and Weinstein, J. (eds) *Extreme Speech and Democracy* (Oxford, Oxford University Press, 2009) 23–61

Weinstein, J. 'An overview of American Free Speech Doctrine and its Application to Extreme Speech' in Hare, I. and Weinstein, J. (eds) *Extreme Speech and Democracy* (Oxford, Oxford University Press, 2009) 81–91

Wilders won't Attend 'Fewer Moroccans' Trial; says it is a Political Process, www.dutchnews. nl/news/archives/2016/10/wilders-wont-attend-fewer-moroccans-trial-says-it-is-a-political-process/

Wilkinson, M., 'Amber Rudd vows to Stop Migrants "Taking Jobs British People could do" and Force Companies to Reveal the Number of Foreigners they Employ', *The Telegraph*, 4 October 2016 www.telegraph.co.uk/news/2016/10/04/jeremy-hunt-nhs-doctors-theresa-may-conservative-conference-live/

Zijlstra: 'VVD Gaat Niet Samenwerken met PVV' (Zijlstra [party leader of the VVD] VVD Is Not Going to Work Together with PVV) 26 December 2016, https://fd.nl/ economie-politiek/1180964/zijlstra-vvd-gaat-niet-samenwerken-met-pvv

Index